THE PISCATOR EXPERIMENT

THE POLITICAL THEATRE

MARIA LEY-PISCATOR

SOUTHERN ILLINOIS UNIVERSITY PRESS
Carbondale and Edwardsville

FEFFER & SIMONS, INC.
London and Amsterdam

ARCT
URUS
BOOKS ®

Epic Theatre is a phrase which Brecht
borrowed from Piscator in the Twenties
and went on defining until the end of
his life.

—Kenneth Tynan

PREFACE

To walk along, side by side, with someone whose stirring vitality is a daily renascence, is a far greater challenge than one can possibly imagine. In finding yourself in the mirror of the other, you come to like or dislike yourself. I have gone through both of these reactions successively and simultaneously. I have fought naively, dialectically and in opposition. I have reached crises, and played scenes in wild sequences, with and without a cyclorama.

It has been exciting to walk along—and is exciting now to record the facts and events of the New York experience. I have experienced the abundant years with no regrets for the meager ones.

I have been reproached for hiding in the wings, as well as for coming out on stage on my own.

Why did I keep going? I have no answer—except that I borrowed from life the time to do this book.

A human being is born when he becomes aware of his identity.

We awaken with change.

Why?

Discovery of our real nature, sudden stimulation, explosion of some latent idea—to these are the conditions of change. The impact of some reality, of objective existence, whether it be our own or human reality in general.

It happened to me in Berlin on September 3, 1927, when I saw *Hoppla, We Live* staged by Erwin Piscator in the *Theater am Nollendorfplatz.* I did not know Piscator then, but I felt something of importance occurring on that stage, an impact I could not escape, an affirmation of life, in fact the deed and voice of life itself: the merging with one's time. *Hoppla, We Live* opened my eyes not only to the potentials of a modern theatre, but also to its role and function in our society.

Here on a stage, following a story that was not mine, but with which I could identify, I came suddenly to understand the law of cause and effect, the pressure and demands that were driving us on to the impending European crises.

It was theatre, though. I realized that.

It was heightened life, human experience transformed into artistic experience. Technically it was a conscious control of new means and forms; intellectually, a total renascence of ideas; spiritually, an ascent to a higher order.

This was theatre that excited my imagination as much as my intelligence. But it did much more for me. By beholding new vistas—not only those of the physical stage, but vistas in topical, factual, and historical material—I found myself a citizen of my time.

Never before in art had I come face to face with reality. Up to that time, reality had seemed to escape me. I felt much more at home in the Theatre of India, the classical Theatre of Japan and Commedia dell' Arte, or the exoticism of the Paris Theatre of the 'twenties.

Suddenly I found myself comparing art and politics. It dawned on me that the theatre could be an instrument expressing all this and more.

Faced with this sudden awakening, I was forced by my professional career to leave Berlin. As a dancer I had signed for a tour that took me to theatres and concert halls of both Americas. My theatre was again an uncomplicated thing of beauty: a ballerina's theatre.

When I did return to Europe, I saw the folly of precious art. There was no longer any escape for me. I would plunge myself into study, experience, anything that would bring me to a creative reality.

Max Reinhardt asked me to choreograph *A Midsummer Night's Dream*, this time at Salzburg. I joined him at Leopoldskron, his baroque refuge. There I met Erwin Piscator.

The interplay of art and life had reached unity for me.

CONTENTS

THE PISCATOR EXPERIMENT

1) GENESIS
OF AN IDEA

Erwin Piscator's account of his identity begins on August 4, 1914. This is the story, as told by him and retold on many occasions:

"Ypres—Belgium.

"The shells whistle around our heads. The order is DIG IN! I am lying on the ground, my heart beating madly, and like the others I try to use my spade and dig into the earth.

"The sergeant arrives, cursing, 'Dig in, Piscator!'

" 'I can't.'

"Sergeant: 'Why not?'

" 'I can't.'

"Sergeant (howling!): 'What's your profession?'

" 'Actor.'

"I looked at the sergeant helplessly as I pronounced the word.

"What a fraud, what false ecstasy and elusive life of dreams! Suddenly I felt less afraid of the falling shells around me than ashamed of being an actor.

"Something was shattered forever: illusion. The curtain separating life from stage was torn away. Theatre, yes, but a different kind—not a stage, but a platform—theatre as an instrument to probe life and to come to grips with reality— not an audience, but a community—."

• • •

The scene changes and the action moves a quarter of a century beyond the time of the trenches, and a whole ocean away —to January 1, 1939, and the harbor of New York. Erwin Piscator was there, and so was I, both having our first view of Manhattan Island. Three unexpected interviews awaited us.

"Welcome to the Berlin Belasco," said a brash young crew-cut reporter gaily, in the first of these encounters. "How is the theatre in Germany?"

"The theatre is dead in Germany," Piscator answered.

"But you're not a Jew," the reporter smiled.

• • •

While we were waiting in the huge Customs shed, full of flurried passengers and cold-eyed Customs officers, a swarthy, chubby-faced man, nattily tailored, addressed us. He explained that he was a self-appointed official greeter and had been waiting to welcome "the great Piscator."

Shortly after, he was wriggling his uninvited rotund bulk into our taxi, which was taking us to our hotel.

"I can be of great help to you, Mr. Piscator," he purred, adjusting his horn-rimmed glasses, "as I was to Max Reinhardt. You will need an agent."

We both looked at him uncomprehendingly.

"Why an agent?" I asked.

"The most important commodity in the theatre, Madame," he answered, breezing after us as we entered the hotel.

He squeezed into the elevator with us.

"You see, a director cannot direct a play from his hotel room. He needs a theatre and for that he needs money, a producer. And to get a producer you need me."

"But we have a producer—Gilbert Miller."

"Yes, yes, I know. He contracted for your dramatization of War and Peace . . . but . . . someone must look after your interests. After all, you're a stranger in the promised land . . ."

We smiled at this brash advance. But when he had gone, we could not help speculating about why Gilbert Miller had not come to receive us, or sent someone in his place. Perhaps we will need somebody—maybe even a fool. . . .

. . .

The grandeur of the view that spread before us held us spellbound: the icy, sparkling fortresses; the flickering chain of cars passing by on the avenue below; Central Park luminous in the snow, and on the pond the skaters, colored pinpoints, swirling about like characters out of Breughel.

The feeling of enrichment on one hand and impoverishment on the other, of emptiness and of overabundance, of the transparency of the new world and its opaqueness, of being too old for schooling, too mature in experience and yet young enough to be capable of making mistakes.

A curtain was drawn open. The foreboding of a change filled everything, surrounded us, took up the space in the corridor, our rooms, animated every conversation—annihilated the past under its weight; even memory crumbled.

I knew that where confidence had existed we would find skepticism. The most evident truth would be questioned. We had lost roots—this loss would be replaced by a false security.

That which was never doubted would henceforth be a matter of inquiry, or rather the parody of inquiry.

Was this nature's way of recreating life?

I had no answer, except—I thought of the poet, Gerhardt Hauptmann, who in his last hours stubbornly asked the anguished question, *Am I still in my own house?* Would I too one day question in whose house I dwelt—or would I never know if I was still myself or another?

The telephone rang.

"I'm a reporter. I would like an interview."

"Come up."

"Could you come down, sir? They won't let me up except by the service elevator," said the voice.

"Oh! We'll be right down," said Piscator.

We met him in the lobby: a Negro.

The interview lasted into the night. This was the year 1939, and we were oblivious of the embarrassment we were creating among the other guests and the management, and the blot on the prestige of one of the finest hotels in New York City.

. . .

On January 12 a general news item appeared announcing that Gilbert Miller would produce *War and Peace*. "Piscator has planned his production of *War and Peace* as a challenge to our naturalistic stage. He has compressed the titanic Tolstoy novel into a "representation' with a formula—Epic Theatre. To expound the principles of Epic Theatre, in a few catch phrases, is not possible."

These few lines did more than attach Epic Theatre to the great colorful wheel of Broadway theatre. They were a challenge to the mind and afforded an unexpected chance to explain the coming into being of *War and Peace*.

2) WAR AND PEACE— AN EPIC PLAY

War and Peace, as a play, was born in Paris into a restless world. Britain, France, Italy and Germany, in parley in Munich, had agreed to the dismemberment of Czechoslovakia. Prime Minister Neville Chamberlain had returned to London with "peace in our time."

We didn't know how quickly history was going to confirm Tolstoy's theme: peace is at the mercy of chance.

I don't believe that Gilbert Miller was in any way aware of this reality behind Tolstoy's fiction; the hidden reality that plays such a large part in our lives. He became quite enthusiastic when he heard of Piscator's plan to dramatize War and Peace. Something had stirred him deeply. It may have been

Piscator's past unique success, or the fact that the dramatization involved a new concept in directing; or perhaps it was the culmination of a host of new and striking experiences in himself, as he felt the evolution of Paris in the expectancy of war.

He commissioned the dramatization of Tolstoy's novel—an Epic play—for New York production.

On Piscator's suggestion he agreed to engage Alfred Neumann, who had just won great acclaim with his historical novel, *The Patriot,* to collaborate on the project. To seal the bargain he paid a handsome advance—a sum of money, he declared, that was a record for Broadway.

Gilbert Miller's success as a producer depended largely upon foreign plays, which had proved their virtue by long runs in Europe. They presented a wide variety in taste and quality, ranging from the often trivial to the occasionally magnificent. Once presented on Broadway, they typified, strangely enough, American theatre to the average playgoer.

With the forebodings of war the sources of foreign plays had begun to run dry for Gilbert Miller. He had not fostered the American playwright, which made his task of finding new plays difficult.

One can rightly suppose that this situation accelerated Gilbert Miller's readiness to sign contracts in Paris for *War and Peace.* The production was scheduled for 1939, just in time to reassert his name on Broadway.

When the script was finished in German, Gilbert Miller was eager to read it. He perused the first act on his trip from London to New York; the second from New York to Los Angeles and the third on his flight back to Europe. He was a busy man, as anyone could see, and a cautious one, too. He gave the play to one of the finest translators in the profession.

Ashley Dukes was sympathetic with Piscator and Neumann's ideas about Epic Theatre. Unfortunately, he had been rushed into the translation by Gilbert Miller, who wanted to have a script he could circulate for opinions in America. Ashley Dukes had his own theatre in London and was burdened with production plans. While he made a readable translation, he had no time to refine it. While in New York, Miller searched for a new translator.

We, too, joined the search and approached several writers.

Finally, through Kurt Weill and his wife Lotte Lenya, we met with Sidney Howard.

In the American theatre, Sidney Howard was considered a craftsman and a playwright of notable talent. He had written some truly original plays, a touching drama of mother fixation, *The Silver Cord*, and a human comedy of the wine country in California, *They Knew What They Wanted*, which revealed his fine ear for local color and dialect. He had made many adaptations of renown, as of Sinclair Lewis's novel *Dodsworth*, and, for Gilbert Miller, *The Late Christopher Bean*.

We couldn't hope to find a sounder playwright to undertake the adaptation of *War and Peace*.

At first enthusiastic about the project, Sidney Howard regretfully changed his mind. Instead of coming to another meeting, he sent a letter declining the offer.

What was the reason for this decision?

We could only surmise as we questioned around. It appeared that Sidney Howard had deliberately become a commercial writer, very much sought after. He had smilingly said that it would take him at least one year to do a creditable translation of *War and Peace*—one year for which he would be paid a small fraction of the sums he could otherwise earn with standard plays. In a phrase, Sidney Howard could not afford Tolstoy's company.

In the meantime the first translation, in its state of "raw experience," was circulated in New York. Arguments for and against the dramatization grew and became more contradictory as time drew on. It is very difficult today to determine what really happened to the production of War and Peace. It is certain, though, that the translation was not the only source of its troubles.

The particular question for those who read the translation handed around New York was a basic one: can a novel be dramatized?

Of course, every work of art depends on its material. Does War and Peace, as a novel, lend itself to such an adventurous undertaking? Are there any traits in the novel that would qualify it for treatment in Epic style?

Tolstoy's huge, panoramic novel lent itself in more than one sense to modern Epic Theatre.

It was a novel written by a moralist, a novel with a purpose strongly accented by didactic political tendencies. It was an anti-war novel showing the evils of dictatorship and allowing the dramatist to provide a parallel to modern times.

As a historical novel, War and Peace was eminently modern. Begun in 1864 and finished in 1866, it narrates the events prospectively—that is, objectively, except for the idyllic plot treated romantically in the taste of the period. The vast background of Russian-European history, inside its world of characters, remains a piece of life transformed by art.

Probing, as he does, the spiritual and moral virtue of his characters against the background of history, Tolstoy asked two of the most important questions of modern times. First, what is power? Tolstoy answered: "Power is the relation of a given person to other individuals in which the more this person expresses opinions, predictions and justifications of the collective action, the less is his participation in that action." The second question: What force produces the movement of nations? Answer: "The movement of nations is not caused by power, nor by intellectual activity, nor even by the combination of both, as historians have sometimes pretended, but by the activity of all the people who participate in the events, and who always combine in such a way that those taking the largest direct share in the event take on themselves the least responsibility, and vice versa."

War and Peace was also sociological fiction, presenting the peer-and-peasant view of Russian life. Here it touched the aspect that modern Epic Theatre projects best—portraying in a single individual the whole class. Tolstoy builds up a comprehensive picture of an era from many small pictures after the manner of a film, coming from the close-up of individuals to a general view of the whole. History for Tolstoy had never been a matter of individual drama, but always a quest of the laws common to all humanity, discernible beneath strivings toward free will.

As to the style, Tolstoy's novel did not strive for any magic or illusion, not even poetry. But the conflict of passions never lets one forget the clash of ideas. At no moment did Tolstoy bypass what is directly perceptible to the common man. His experimentation in depth, complexity and articulation was always related to man's most arduous achievement, reality.

"I have never understood why the question of adapting a novel to the stage should be a matter of controversy at all. To talk of it as some sort of heresy is to ignore the very origin of theatre itself," said Piscator and he explained:

Was not the narrative, legend, fable, or epic recitation one of the sources of drama, the others being dancing and pantomime?

The Chinese Theatre—the spoken book—is it not more or less the dramatization of an epic subject? Where is the source of the Indian drama to be found, if not in the traditional epic poem? Greek tragedy was inconceivable without Homer. Were not the mystery plays of the Bible acted out? The tragedies of the kings, would they have existed without Shakespeare's dramatizing of history—the civil wars between the Houses of Lancaster and York—or *Romeo and Juliet* without the Italian novel, or *King Lear* but for the Celtic ballad? Tolstoy, Gorki, Dostoievsky, Lessing, Schiller, Goethe, Thomas Hardy, Dickens, Upton Sinclair, Dos Passos, and James Joyce penetrated the closed-up realm of the novel and opened it for the theatre.

To ask whether it is permissible to dramatize a novel is, therefore, an idle question. It is asking de Sade what he would think of having his memoirs dramatized by Sartre. New equations would have to be solved, new creations enter the phase of expansion and balance; new technical mastery would present itself.

Dramatizing a novel has always been done and always will be. The task is to find the new medium to do justice to the novel. The thing read is not "the thing done."

Can a novel be dramatized?

Yes—in Epic Theatre.

· · ·

Epic Theatre seems at first sight a contradiction in terms, but the phrase is full of instruction. The Greek drama was the performance of a rite; that is, the process not only of feeling something but of expressing it in action, receiving an impulse, reacting to it. The Epos, on the contrary, dealt not with action but with speech, song and narrative poetry.

Literature has always kept apart distinctive groups of works with respect to style, form, and purpose. From its religious origin to the entertainment cult of our days, two forms have remained distinct and never combined: epic and dramatic.

· · ·

"Styles are born out of necessity," declared Piscator, "out of the characteristic modes of expression of an era; they are man-made, yes, but made from the mores and customs and social conditions of the moment."

Epic Theatre, too, was born out of necessity. It happened. It was not invented in the quiet study of a playwright polishing theatrical history. It was born in the street . . . in the turmoil of a city impoverished by war and inflation, and in the life of a roving theatrical company, performing in halls and meeting places in the suburbs . . . "Proletarían Theatre."

. . .

The date was Sunday, January 5, 1920, Neukoelln, Kliens Festsaal: primitive stage sets, some black curtains, half a dozen spotlights, a few hastily assembled props which had grown in significance with their use. The name of the play was *The Cripple*; the director and the leading actor, Erwin Piscator, the scenic designer, John Heartfield.

Johnny was eager to do the scenery but, as always, he was not finished in time.

"We waited," Piscator wrote in his book. "and we waited and waited, and still no scenery. Then finally I started to play. We were half way through the first act when I saw Johnny at the entrance door of the hall with the scenery rolled up under his arm. What happened next might have been a director's trick on my part, but was entirely spontaneous. Heartfield exclaimed, 'Stop, Erwin, stop! I'm here!' Surprised, everybody turned around to see the young man, red-faced, just dashing in.

"To continue the performance was not possible. I therefore stood up, disregarding my role as cripple, and called down, 'Where have you been? We waited for you for almost half an hour [affirmative murmurs from the audience] and finally got started without your scenery.'

"Heartfield: You didn't send the car! It's your fault! I ran through the streets; no tram conductor would let me on because the piece was too large. Finally I did get on a tram and had to stand all the way in the back on the platform and almost fell off!' [Increasing amusement in the audience]

"I interrupted him. 'Quiet, Johnny, we must go on!'

"Heartfield [in extreme excitement]: 'No, first my scenery must be put into place!'

" 'Let's go on, Johnny.'

" 'Not without scenery.'

"Since Johnny would not give in, I turned to the audience and asked what I should do—whether we should go on with the performance or first place this piece of scenery.

"The overwhelming majority decided we should first put the scenery into place.

"Thereupon we set Johnny's scenery and, to everyone's satisfaction, began all over again.

"We had no idea that in performing this humble task, we had suddenly and definitely broken with the old canons of theatre. Audience and stage were united in one desire—that of continuity."

That night Piscator's ardent wish to find a way towards a new form of theatre, a theatre to suit the time, mobilized itself into action. It was like unhooking a number of waiting ideas from the wall and putting them into swing. They pursued a perfectly determined aim. They were not only ideas, however. They were the roots from which Piscator could reasonably expect the desired solution for his future. Under the impact of Johnny's failure to return in time, these ideas-at-rest entered into combination: from rebellion against art for art's sake, to art as a means to an end, to starting from the beginning, freedom of action, audience participation and continuity of performance. So ran the course.

Always thereafter, Piscator called Johnny Heartfield "the inventor of Epic Theatre."

. . .

Epic Theatre first became known to audiences outside of Europe through the eye: the visual perception of its technical innovations, such as elevators, treadmills, movable circular stairs, platforms of different heights, film and sound. The professional people—playwright, actor, director—had heard of it as a theatre of social revolt. The intellectuals wrote about it, giving it different names such as Political Theatre, Documentary Theatre, Engaged Theatre, *Zeitstück*, Piscator-stage, *Lehrstück*, in a multitude of complexities.

"If theatre has any meaning at all in our time"—we quote Piscator—"its purpose should be to teach us—of human relation, human behavior, human capacities. It is to this task, consciously, suggestively and descriptively, that Epic Theatre is best suited. It sacrifices atmosphere, emotion, characterization, poetry and, above all, magic for the sake of a mutual exchange of problems and experiences with the audience. In other words: the purpose of Epic Theatre is to learn how to think rather than to feel—moving above the stream rather than losing oneself in it."

Broadly seen, Epic Theatre is marked by the following characteristics:

A theatre of political and social nature. An attempt to reach all people.

A collective ceremony, an invitation to learning, conscious that it must lead to communication.

A rejection of the naturalistic style and the Aristotelian unities.

A theatre with a particular bias for technical innovation, drawing upon other arts and other civilizations.

A theatre for vast audiences, a theatre of action, whose objective is to bring out the stirring questions of our time and to bring about a total re-education of both men of the theatre and the audience.

Epic Theatre has provoked controversy as much as it has aroused enthusiasm. It has often been compounded with Expressionist Theatre, Surrealist and even Constructivist. It was as much a political revolution as it was an aesthetic one; but it is, in both capacities, an evolution.

The Expressionists, as well as the Surrealists, had destroyed the objective world. The destruction of the Aristotelian unities of time, space and action, which consequently came in the theatre, was only slight damage; in fact, it produced a welcome change, a widening of a style or form really expressive of the age, a harmonic expansion such as one can find in painting as well, or in architecture.

Sir Herbert Read, the English poet and art critic, has devoted time to the question of expansion in the arts, expansion "that would fill its space." He sees it quite close to the Chinese concept of K'ai-ho, or "unity of coherence." In the Oriental mind there is nothing that does not have both expanding and winding up. When you expand you should think of gathering up, and then there will be *structure*. When you wind up you should think of expanding; you will have the feeling of *inexhaustible spirit*. There is not one moment when you can depart from K'ai-ho—the unity of coherence!

Structure and spirit—theme and action. But Aristotle's theory of tragedy covers the novel as well. "The biography of a man is not necessarily a plot. Without action there cannot be tragedy; there may be tragedy without characters."

Epic Theatre unites theme and action—the format does not originate from the need for self-expression of a single arbitrary author, but from a universal need. It provides constructive expression for the playwright and the director; not as isolated efforts but as a unit.

The construction is a total one. It does not need to be monumental. In the Epic composition of a play, an idea means more than just an idea, and argument more than just an argument. It involves the whole complex of human relation to life. It reflects a mode of thinking, acting, perceiving and living of a period. War and Peace is the whole of Russia, as it is the whole of France. Hundreds of Natashas could have supplied the romance, but only one Natasha could supply the essence of a spontaneous, nature-wise child in the fight of her maturity.

The arguments for and against dramatizing a novel result in one question for the theatre: how good is the dramatization? What kind of producer able to visualize modern theatre, the synthesis of theatre, will become responsible for the totality of its presentation?

. . .

Piscator had opened up the stage, laid it bare, renounced consciously the artifices of time, place, and action, moved the plot with its sensuous catharsis away from the center, inquired into its necessity and questioned the domination of form over matter. The problems of content were projected in a new light. Ideas went to the front, emotions into the background. Instead of colorful, lyrical, and sentimental illusion, the Epic play went toward reality and analysis of facts. Therefore, the antagonistic voices said, War and Peace, having broken away from the traditional mold, could never be regarded as a play. But perhaps War and Peace would be the long-awaited evidence that one can dramatize a novel.

The fascinating ambiguity with which the term Epic Theatre has been used for years had its equal only in the obtuse and pretentious way its authorship is weighed. Every group claimed finality of judgment and declared itself incapable of making a mistake. It reminded me of the sterile Controversy on the Theatre some two hundred years ago between Voltaire and Rousseau.

Because he did not publish his findings, Piscator had been identified with Epic Theatre mostly because of his inventions of modern stage technology. He had been called an engineer of the theatre, his theories labeled mechanistic and sometimes attacked even as formalistic.

Nothing is further from the truth. Technique was an artistic necessity for Piscator as much as for Picasso, Matisse, Dali, or George Grosz. "The meaning of technique is not very clear to most people," wrote Piscator in one of his articles on technique:

> We have developed with the help of philosophy and the physical sciences new spatial impacts, new visions and a new conception of time and space. This later conception is equal to the transformation of our universe which carries us further than, for example, the contemporaries of Giordano Bruno and Galileo, whose "good sense" would be strongly shaken were they to see our technical progress. We radiograph and televise events. We apply to art the idea of relativity. We have abstract art in painting. We have a twelve-tone scale in music. But whatever one thinks of these new forms, they are scarcely employed in the theatre of today.

But these inventions, stimulating as they well may be to the conception and fantasy of playwright and stage director alike, are not enough to transform technical means into artistic expression.

Form, in the long run, shows itself incomplete. It cannot exist alone. The artistic value of a production does not depend on technique, but it may well depend on modern dramaturgy opening new dimensions which can be best reached through technique.

"I can assure you," Piscator continued in the same article, "that technique is a source of pleasure when it works correctly. One 'takes to it' solely when one does not notice it, and one notices it when it does not function."

Presumably Piscator's stage technique has found its way into all manner of theatre and drama. Egon Vietta, a famous European critic, called Piscator, "the father of the analytical-technical scenery, that has transformed the stage. . . . His aim is to analyze the structure of a play on the stage, to lay things bare, not to create illusion, but to destroy illusion."

. . .

There was more than the eye could see in Piscator's Epic version of *War and Peace*. More than technique, style or form was at stake: the drama.

I refer here to the word drama in its most ancient sense, that of history: *event*. The event is neither the action, nor the conflict. It is the sum and substance contained in the play, the content—the one thing without which the play does not exist.

What is the purpose of the play?

"Is it permitted to have a purpose in art?" asks the Narrator as the play opens. And then he quotes Tolstoy: "Art without a purpose does not exist! On the contrary, art has a definite purpose; to serve the good relationship between human beings, and good relationship between human beings is certainly not served by war."

And he continues:

"In battle and war there are the defeated and the victors. This is certain. But what is not certain is who are the defeated and who are the victors. Some people believe that it is God who determines the result. Frederick the Great held that God was with the stronger battalions. There could come a day when we could all be destroyed. On whose side will God be then? . . .

"But should one question that so openly in the theatre?" pursues the Narrator.

"Of course one should," answers Tolstoy. "Art is a great

matter. . . . Art should cause violence to be set aside." And thus the characters enter.

The Narrator is the recorder of the events but he is not just the storyteller. He is the objective observer, the classic messenger, the one who presents the outside world. He is the "Choregus" of the antique drama who gives the pulse beat of the whole action, and he is also the chorus. He dictates all the rhythms, separates the sequences, speeds the movement or slows it down. He is part of the experience that is essential to the drama: the desire to talk. In Epic Theatre he is the most direct link between the two art forms, the epic and the dramatic; and in War and Peace, the Narrator being the voice of the poet, he is also the teacher of history, the one who knows that theatre is no longer only the abode of cautious esthetics, but the best tribunal of prophecy.

Let the Narrator continue:

"In spite of most men's knowing that war is something horrible, they make new wars all the time. They console themselves with the thought that, although private life is crossed and destroyed through politics, life in its collective unity—the natural life, as Tolstoy said—always continues. But can we console ourselves with this any longer? If we don't become more explicit, militantly, angrily explicit, it can happen that life will not continue any more."

That sounded like a lesson and it was meant to be: war is something unreasonable and against human nature because its results depend entirely upon chance.

Here Tolstoy's idea ties in with the dramatist's purpose, to destroy the audience's dependence on sentimental illusion as well as:

To educate the audience
To warn the audience
To parallel the past with the present

To enlighten the audience through the parallel of the past with the present

To argue for peace.

Should we just take into account the simple fact, which is part of our individual condition, as it is part of the condition of life, that any war is a question of chance?

But though our perception may be dim, it isn't dim enough to obscure one truth: that one must do everything to remain human because it is too simple to be anti-human.

The personal conflict is very strong in Tolstoy. It is doubly important because, with the intuition of genius, Tolstoy has placed all the subjective moments of intimacy within the objective conflict of war and peace.

Such a vision is unquestionably grim, and it could be a grim play were it not that the dramatist makes us understand that not only the characters in the play are condemned if they do not find redemption, but all men who wage war.

. . .

Andrei's conflict with war begins with his youthful marriage. He loves his wife, Lisa, yet he wants to leave her and go to war against Napoleon. "Who am I? What can I do? What am I capable of?" he wonders to Pierre. "Bonaparte, you see, approaches his goal with every step he takes. But I, I am locked up in a bewitched circle. I am chained to a woman and losing every bit of liberty like a prisoner in irons—in salons, gossips, balls, vanities—indeed, a bewitched circle from which I will never escape!"

Pierre sees deeper: his friend's real conflict is between ambition and love. "Ah, that's why you want to go to war. Not *for* freedom and not *against* freedom. Not for Napoleon, or against him. You want to enlist in the war to escape the bewitched circle!"

Andrei denies it. "You are wrong. I want to fight Napoleon

because I admire him. He is the enemy against whom I can show what I am capable of. Napoleon has become great after his victory at Toulon. This war against him is the turning point in my life. I too shall have my Toulon!"

But it happens differently. Andrei is wounded on the battlefield. He returns from the war with longing for peace, to find his wife dead in childbirth. He elaborately thinks out and plans his future. A joyless future, because he no longer believes in the new ideas of Napoleon. His idol has fallen from its pedestal. Napoleon has forgotten the revolution and has become the conqueror. The tragedy is heightened to an almost Grecian level because, despite his doubts, Andrei continues to do his duty, working at reforms on his estate. It becomes still more dramatic when Andrei's reforms are successful while Pierre—who is dedicated to reform—fails.

Yet Andrei's destiny is not determined by his reforms. Again it is the war. He has met Natasha Rostova and fallen in love with her. He wants to marry her, but his father, Prince Bolkonski, decides that the young couple should wait a year, a year which Andrei should spend abroad. Natasha is desperate about the decision. Why a year? What if there should be another war? Before he leaves, Andrei, who considers himself engaged, releases Natasha from any pledge. "We are engaged, Natasha, but I want you to feel yourself free. If, during this year, you realize that you don't love me any more— that you love someone else . . ." And while Natasha protests, he leaves.

What if there should be another war? There was. Czar Alexander, certain that Napoleon would attack him, prepared his armies. Napoleon, equally certain of Alexander's warlike intentions, also made ready for war. The monstrous challenge of war reaches the most private of lives, that of the young girl Andrei has left. Anatole Kuragin, the worthless young aristocrat, on his way to the front, seduces Natasha in a moment when she is in despair. Too honest to hide anything from Andrei, she cancels their engagement. The story now expands tragically. Andrei has come home in despair. He lives with the idea of punishing Kuragin. But it is not Kuragin who is at the bottom of his misery, nor is it Natasha. It is doubt in himself at all levels which devours him. He even stops his reforms and confides to Maria, his sister, his complete conflict: "Should I throw myself at Napoleon and become traitor to my own conscience? Shall I go over to Napoleon and betray my fatherland? Should I give help to the reactionaries whom I detest? Or should I fight freedom, which I love? What am I to do, Maria? Please help me. Tell me what I am supposed to do! I am a soldier on the way to the front, but I can't see any goal at the end of the road."

In the meantime, Pierre has also come to the end of his mission. His religion, his blind love for peace, has stopped on the battlefield of Borodino. He realizes that there can be no peace with any Napoleon. He becomes chief of the partisans and meets with Napoleon before Moscow. Napoleon's soldiers arrest Pierre, whose partisans have set Moscow afire, but Napoleon issues an order to let him go free. The whole tangled design culminates in their meeting: the former revolutionary and present dictator and the present rebel and former pacifist. The wheel has turned full circle.

The battlefield of Borodino, as staged by Piscator, has been recognized as one of the truly great gems of genuine theatre. As theme, world perception, the nonsensicality of war, which one finds in the play, is pushed to its utmost plasticity. Pierre, who has succeeded in going to the front as an observer, is guided by the Narrator toward a slanting dais—the stage of destiny—scattered with models of tin soldiers, cannon on hills and pieces of forests and fields, and the relief of a village, Schwardino. These models are stylized and so small that Pierre in this landscape looks like Gulliver among the Lilliputians. And now the Narrator gives Pierre the chance not only to watch the battle, but also to play the game himself.

There is the opening shot. Napoleon attacks. Both armies advance against each other. Pierre moves the Lilliput French army forward. Then, as he bends down, he sees between his outspread legs a Russian battalion. The soldiers are still joking. The genius of Napoleon has miscalculated. Pierre looks over the battlefield to see the consequences. Little has happened. There are orders that have not been executed on the other side. The bridge of Borodino has been taken by the Russians? No, wrong. The French have retaken it. In the midst of it all, one shell bursts after the other and Pierre bends down again very tenderly and carefully brings up an isolated little tin figure. "Andrei? What do you say, Andrei?" He holds the little figure to his ear. "You can't die. You do not want to die, and all of a sudden you love life and light, grass and earth and the air." He picks up a small stretcher from the battlefield and places Andrei's tin figure on it, then puts the stretcher back. Next he addresses himself to another corner of the battlefield. "How, Sire? How is the battle going? Your cold is bothering you? The Russians haven't given up? They prefer to die fighting?" And, turning away from Napoleon, he picks up Kutusov, the Russian General. But Kutusov keeps silent. Pierre takes another reproachful look at Napoleon. "You see, Sire, your antagonist knows better than you—that he doesn't know anything! Chance decides."

And while speculating on the outcome, Pierre for one moment enters the character of Napoleon and for another moment that of Kutusov, as in a fascinating tonal montage of point and counterpoint he asks the question: "Why had these men to die, and for whom? Why has war to happen?" Chance or fate? "It is fate," says Napoleon. "It becomes fate," he says, "when I direct it. It is a matter of luck, if it glides out of my hands. It is pure chance that I am giving you back your life. To you—it is fate."

"Is this true?" asks the Narrator. And he answers himself, "Not for us—not for our time."

Tolstoy's belief in "genius" was a mark of his generation. Napoleon's "genius," was his luck. Modern history rejects the belief that man is nothing more than the victim of fate. Would it not be a little odd for a soldier whose "idea of theatre" began well back in the trenches of Ypres, to present the intervention of any deity in human affairs on stage; be it called fate, destiny or whatsoever.

The wheel turns full circle once more, this time the dramatist's communion with the novelist becomes a total one. The dying Andrei finds himself in the field hospital next to the mortally wounded Kuragin. Anatole recognizes Andrei fearfully, but Bolkonski stretches out his hand toward his enemy. Both hands clasp while the Narrator states: "This is the true victory of Borodino—perhaps the only one!"

By the end of spring the arguments for and against the production of War and Peace had entered a trivial stage.

Gilbert Miller, too, had grown restless but not because of the war. He had given the Piscator-Neumann dramatization to more people to read. In fact, it was no less than a poll, from theatre people to errand boys. The vote was obvious at this particular time.

Characteristically never at a loss for a way out, Gilbert Miller fell back on another adaptation he had commissioned shortly before our arrival: Ladies and Gentlemen, adapted by Ben Hecht and Charles MacArthur from a play by the Hungarian playwright Busz-Fekete.

With this production under way, starring Helen Hayes, the decision reached us that Gilbert Miller had decided to abandon all plans for War and Peace. The dubious reason given to Piscator and Neumann was that Helen Hayes, to whom Miller had proposed the role of the young Natasha, had refused the part of a sixteen-year-old girl.

Plays have strange destinies. This was not the end of War and Peace, only the beginning of its fabulous career.

3) THE EXPERIMENTAL 'THIRTIES

Piscator's Epic Theatre was born not in the poet's mind but in the reality of the street fighting of Berlin in the 'twenties. It was not Socrates, Diderot, Schiller, nor even Marx, that created Epic Theatre; it was the whole generation of the 'twenties—artists astride history—who created it, as a team, a great one that included Piscator, the director; Brecht, the poet; George Grosz, Berlin's Daumier; Walter Mehring, the pamphleteer; Ernst Toller, the playwright; and Walter Gropius, the architect. The war had shocked them all into rebellion, but at the same time into cool objectivity about art. The rebellion was not only political, but ethical, social and esthetic. Neither Dadaism nor Expressionism nor Surrealism dominated it. The latter were notions—something to think about but not to draw off one's energies.

The team kept the different avant-gardes (cubists, futurists, constructivists) as spiritual kinsmen and allies who stimulated discussion about formal questions but did not influence the subject matter.

There in Berlin, in Piscator's back-street-theatre studio, a curious collaboration started. A collective method of working was invented, a kind of spiritual partnership which shared the values of the dramaturgical, technological and even programmatical innovations. Property rights didn't matter. Everyone was needed to build because they knew they had to build from scratch, not innovate but invent.

Epic Theatre had many theatrically effective faces. It remained Epic because it envisaged a larger concept than just theatre. Epic Theatre entered, of course, the philosophical realm as well—the team was German.

This team invented something else, which in consequence became a startling contradiction. It invented "America." Everything that was useful, effective, expedient, operative, performing properly and instrumental for production, was called American. Even time had an American tempo and was valued as such. None of them had seen America, any more than had the Romantic writers a hundred years before. But these twentieth century rebels did not just admire America, the beauty of it, its landscape, its exoticism, its virginal purity. They admired what seemed real to them: the objective existence of the land of plenty, its material genius, with its prosperity, its slogans, and the great god—the machine. It is impossible to understand the complexity of Epic Theatre without taking into account this capture of the imagination by America, while, at the same time, the period was idealistically entangled with the new Russia.

• • •

Good theater is never separated from real life. And life in America in the 'thirties had been burning the candle at both ends. The great need of social change became an issue after the crash of 1929. It set fire to the theatre, but the blaze soon faded out and little more remained than occasional pyrotechnics. The year 1939 was the end of the committed decade. Compared to the theatrical rebellion during inflation time in Germany, the committed theatre in America seemed only a gauntlet flung down. A gauntlet that had never really been picked up.

The reason for this failure was not, as has so often been said, that the militant theater in America was not militant at all but middle class.

The reason was rather that most of the leftist plays were neither political dramas nor good plays. The playwrights were people of thriving vitality but not major talents. They were opportunists rather than knowledgeable writers. Nor did they have the passionate integrity that commanded respect.

The militant theatre started in loud, brash, demonstrative and marvelous call to action but, with few exceptions, did not advance the cause of social theatre of the period nor the cause of world theatre.

The range of plays presented by leftist theatres fell into three categories: plays from European playwrights, mostly Expressionists and Activists; Living Newspaper and "agitational-propaganda" plays (called Agit-Prop plays), also under European and Russian influence; and new plays by American authors treating problems of social significance, mostly anti-Fascist.

The earliest efforts belonged to the workers' theatre. The ProletBuehne, founded in 1930, went in the direction of radicalism in the eyes of the conservative critics and was most effective. It imported the agitational-and-propaganda concept from Germany and Russia. Half-improvised plays of action confronted the audience less with a work of art than a political act or demand for social justice. While they sometimes missed the political point, they never missed a solid amount of emotionalism. One could see fists held high at the elegant Chanin Theatre, hear anti-philanthropic discussions at the richly sponsored Heckscher Theatre, strong indictments of private enterprise at the prosperous Sutton Theatre, and advanced polemics at the New School for Social Research. For four years the ProletBuehne presented such drama with amateurs, dealing with the Depression, the New Deal and the New York political scene.

Being not too successful, the ProletBuehne was transformed by Elia Kazan and Al Saxe into a professional theatre. They continued to present plays of political propaganda under the name of Theatre of Action.

One year earlier, in 1933, another workers' theatre was created, which, in spite of conflicting opinions, made a valuable contribution to the drama of the committed decade. It was the Theatre Union.

The Theatre Union was the first overtly engaged professional theatre in New York City. Its credo was the Marxist slogan, "Theatre as a weapon." Its purpose was to produce plays of the working class written from the point of view of the working class. There were not many such plays on the market but the advisory board of the Theatre Union included such first-rate writers as Sherwood Anderson, Countee Cullen, John Dos Passos, John Howard Lawson, Lewis Mumford, Sidney Howard, and Elmer Rice. The group had taken over Eva Le Gallienne's Civic Repertory Theatre, and presented Maltz-Sklar's anti-war play, *Peace on Earth*, on November 29, 1933. On April 18, 1934, the Theatre Union followed its first success with *Stevedore* by Paul Peters and George Sklar, and on December 10, 1934 it attracted general attention with a play from the pen of a European writer, Friederich Wolf's

Sailors of Cattaro. Wolf's play is based on an actual revolt by the sailors of the Austrian Navy in the Bay of Cattaro, an inlet of the Adriatic Sea. The action is laid in the last year of World War I, when the Viennese Socialists demanded overtures for world peace and reform. The revolt was crushed, the leaders executed.

Sailors of Cattaro attracted large crowds and received favorable attention from the leftist press. The reason for this unusual success may have lain in the fact that the playwright was effective and less concerned with slogans and the heroics of the revolt than with the causes of its failure.

The Theatre Union also offered in 1935 a presentation of Brecht's play *The Mother.* Its style baffled many admirers of Brecht. It seemed much more grounded in Expressionism that in an attempt to show any aspect of Brechtian alienation, which the left wing considered new theatre, and already discussed in various and confusing ways. The Theatre Union's last two productions were Victor Wolfson's *Bitter Stream,* an adaption of Silone's novel *Fontamara,* and John Howard Lawson's impressive *Marching Song.*

Even rightist theatres, such as the Theatre Guild, scored successes with leftist plays, with little awareness of what they were doing. They produced Soviet and American Marxist writers in such plays as Tretyakov's *Roar China* in 1930, and John Wexley's *They Shall Not Die.* The Group Theatre produced the rather disturbing Clifford Odets and The Federal Theatre Project gave special attention to the *Living Newspaper* while the Mercury Theatre climbed on the bandwagon of social drama. The non-leftist playwright—more aware of the responsibility of commitment as the decade wore on—entertained the possibility of plays of social revolt. Maxwell Anderson with *Both Our Houses,* an attack on politics; S. N. Behrman with *Rain from Heaven,* actively combating Fascism, and Elmer Rice with *The Adding Machine, We the*

People, Flight to the West, and *Two for Passion,* continued the political avant-garde.

The concept of commitment in the theatre was even accepted by capitalist theatre lovers, such as the late Otto H. Kahn, head of Kuhn-Loeb, one of the Wall Street eagles and a promoter of the Metropolitan Opera. Since all art must have seemed to Otto H. Kahn by definition *committed,* as he paid generously for it, sponsored a group of young devotees rising to the defense of the underprivileged under the name of New Playwrights Theatre. It had a short triumph in spite of presences such as John Dos Passos and John Howard Lawson.

Parallel was Theatre Collective stimulated by Mordecai Gorelik, formed of members of The Group Theatre. They presented plays by Clifford Odets and Albert Maltz. They also established a program of technical training for actors taught by Lee Strasberg, Morris Carnovsky and Cheryl Crawford.

In June, 1934, The League of Workers' Theatres presented *Dimitroff,* an agit-prop by Art Smith and Elia Kazan. Not in itself a good play, it prepared the way for Odets' *Waiting for Lefty.*

In 1935, The League of Workers' Theatres became The New Theatre League, taking several concrete stands: mass appeal; struggle against war, Fascism and censorship; and theatre at its highest artistic and social level.

The League had the good fortune to present at the Civic Repertory Theatre on January 6, 1935, on New Theatre Night, a one-act play which had won a contest, *Waiting for Lefty* by Odets. It was later presented by The Group Theatre on Broadway, in March of 1935. By June this play had been performed by groups in fifty American cities. The New Theatre Players of Boston were arrested for acting in an "obscene" drama. New Haven police prohibited further performances in that city.

In January, 1936 the League presented *Private Hicks* by Albert Maltz, Paul Green's *Hymn to the Rising Sun*, and *Bury the Dead* by Irwin Shaw.

In the middle of the decade, the American government stepped into theatre history by signing its name to the Federal Theatre Project. It was not only the most ambitious theatrical project ever undertaken by the federal government, but truly one of the largest co-ordinated theatrical experiments in the history of the world.

In a certain way, the Federal Theatre came the nearest to a *théâtre de peuple* as Romain Rolland had conceived it in his famous book. It also approached, in spite of different aims and ambitions, Jean Vilar's *théâtre du peuple* and the Volksbuehne of Berlin created just after the first World War. (This still exists today, with 140,000 members all over Germany, too many for one theatre; therefore tickets for the Volksbuehne are also honored at other theatres.)

The source of the Federal Theatre's strength, however, was the source of its weakness. The Federal Theatre was an agency to alleviate the unemployment of American theatre artists during the Depression. It was designed for the relief and conservation of theatrical skills.

It was Hallie Flanagan, formerly production assistant in Professor Baker's 47 Workshop, then appointed in 1925 Professor of Drama at Vassar and director of its Experimental Theatre, who was chosen as National Director of the Project. In this capacity she was responsible for the functioning of theatrical programs in some forty cities and towns and had the supervision of more than a thousand productions in four years, 1935 to 1939.

We learned from her personally that at its peak the Federal Theatre employed some ten thousand people, published a nationally distributed theatre magazine, and conducted a Planning and Research Bureau, which served not only the Federal Theatre projects but thousands of schools, churches, and community theatres throughout America. In the year before our arrival they had played to audiences totaling many millions.

Emphatically a people's theatre, the Federal Theatre drew on various kinds of entertainment, serious and light: classical and modern plays, musical comedies, children's plays, marionette shows, and cycles of Shakespeare as well as other famous authors.

It is difficult to define the values of a people's theatre or its common ideals and techniques. What could be the kind of theatre for these people? In the Age of Enlightenment, Diderot himself, who drew the blueprints for the first modern people's theatre, recognized no opposition between entertainment and instruction. Romain Rolland formulated on a more pragmatic scale ideas that could be and were turned into reality.

By definition, the people's theatre must cater to the people. But who are they? What kind of audience did the Federal Theatre attract? *Federal Theatre Magazine* defined this audience in an imaginative way:

> We are a hundred thousand kids who never saw a play before. We are students in colleges, housewives in the Bronx, lumberjacks in Oregon, sharecroppers in Georgia. We are rich and poor, old and young, sick and well. We are America and this is our theatre.

Even the classical repertory organized itself with the help of the audience. Shakespeare was played in parks and religious shows blossomed on the hillside. The inimitable *Federal Theatre Magazine* again reported:

> We are the theatre for the children of the steel mills of
> Gary, Indiana; we're the theatre for the blind in Oklahoma.
> We're dramatic companies and vaudeville companies and
> marionette companies touring the CCC camps, touring the
> flood areas, playing in schools, playgrounds, prisons,
> reformatories, hospitals. We're the Living Theatre, the
> Yiddish Theatre and throughout America playing not only
> in English but in French, German, Italian and Spanish;
> we're the file, we're the record, we're theatre history.

It was Hallie Flanagan's great distinction to develop the first nationwide federally sponsored theatre in the United States. It was her merit to establish an American international repertory as well as a regional one; a Negro theatre; an Epic Theatre with new techniques from abroad such as the Living Newspaper technique which favored a narrative editorial manner. Contrary to some authorities, the Living Newspaper technique was used in the early Piscator theatrical productions of the 'twenties. We can trace it further back, to the montage technique of Eisenstein and Meyerhold. Patterned after film documentaries, showing problems of modern social life in short, swift-moving scenes, the Living Newspaper, successfully developed by Piscator, was used as well in England for adult education and propaganda in the armed forces during World War II and, of course, has been adopted since by radio and television.

The Federal Theatre production of the Living Newspaper dealt with burning social and economic subjects, such as housing in One-Third of a Nation, flood control in Power, and agricultural problems in Triple-A Plowed Under.

Criticism arose nevertheless. Elmer Rice, who had directed the New York wing of the Federal Theatre for one year, left when censorship of the Living Newspaper was imposed by Washington in January, 1936. Although the Living Newspaper editorialized as well as reported on politics and economics, it had never engaged itself beyond the New Deal position.

The resignation of Elmer Rice was more than just a regrettable event. It was a picture of the confusion of the times.

• • •

Continuing in the experimental vein, the Federal Theatre offered a musical fantasy by Edward Crankshaw and W. H. Auden as well as a dance-drama version of Euripides' *The Trojan Women* by Phillip H. Davis.

Among the socially significant plays was a comedy of liberty in George Bernard Shaw's *On the Rocks*, and a musical revue, *Sing For Your Supper* by Harold Hecht, in the tradition of *Pins and Needles*. The Federal Theatre's history reached its climax with Valentin Katayev's *Squaring the Circle*, Lantz's *The Revolt of the Beavers*, and Annie Nathan Meyer's *Black Souls*, and it ended with the production of George Sklar's experimental play, *Life and Death of an American*.

The Federal Theatre Arts Project, as Hallie Flanagan expressed it pertinently, was an experiment "to deal with physical hunger." But there was another deeper craving which was the basic cleavage in the theatre of the 'thirties: theatre as part of the social community versus after-dinner theatre.

This schism between the subjective and objective, the dramatic and epic, led to investigation and criticism before the House Committee on Un-American Activities. During the hearings in 1938, Congressman Starnes asked Hallie Flanagan a question that troubled many minds during that period.

"Do you believe the theatre is a weapon?"

To this Hallie Flanagan answered candidly, "I believe that the theatre is a great educational force. I think it is entertainment. I think it might be all things to all men."

There was a struggle in Congress.

The House voted to liquidate the project but the Senate voted to salvage it. On June 30, 1939, the Federal Theatre was closed down by Congressional action.

. . .

The most striking, original talents of the first two years of the Federal Theatre were Orson Welles and John Houseman. In the summer of 1937, the two men broke away from the Federal Theatre and established the Mercury Theatre with a repertory of such plays as Thomas Dekker's *The Shoemaker's Holiday* with a score by Marc Blitzstein and incidental music by Lehman Engel; a *Julius Caesar* with Caesar in the guise of Mussolini, an all Negro *Macbeth*, and the German masterpiece by Georg Buechner, *Danton's Death*. Orson Welles introduced many Epic features, such as the stage without sets, the bringing up-to-date of remote classics, and the participation of the audience.

Meanwhile, theatres of importance were being created in different universities. Drama departments, theatre arts departments, laboratory theatres, playwrights' as well as actors' workshops, appeared around the country. For the first time the movement was not concentrated on a single phase of the theatre arts but on the totality of all the arts and crafts of the theatre.

The major activity was continuous productions, sometimes housed in million-dollar structures like those at the University of Wisconsin, Yale University, the University of Iowa, and some others surpassing by far even Broadway theatres in size and equipment. There were the Carnegie Institute, Cornell University, the University of North Dakota, Princeton University, and the University of Michigan, which enabled students to experience broad theatrical activity as well as to innovate experimental plays.

Some of these university theatres flourished rather as the result of the participation of highly ingenious theatrical personalities than because of their embarrassing riches. Outstanding among those experimenting with new productions and plays was Hallie Flanagan Davis.

Another experiment which came out of the University movement, quite different from activities mentioned, was the University Players Guild. It started in the summer of 1928 when a cooperative group of college students who wanted to act established themselves as a stock company at Falmouth, Massachusetts. This group represented in its growth an important credit to the American theatre.

The University Players (they later dropped the Guild) not only changed the idea of a summer stock company—the straw-hat circuit—but attracted Broadway stars such as Ethel Barrymore, Jane Cowl, Helen Hayes, Ina Claire, Nazimova, Laurette Taylor, Katharine Hepburn and many others. As it became big business, it established the talents of its own people, mostly actors. Unlike the Provincetown Theatre, the University Players did not become a playwrights' theatre but an actor's theatre, turning out a notable generation of theatre talents from their own company. Among these were Joshua Logan, Laura Houghton, Bretaigne Windust, Myron McCormick, Barbara O'Neill, Margaret Sullivan, Henry Fonda, and James Stewart.

. . .

Discovering a new ground to build upon is a dialectical process, an inevitable developing of tensions and contradictions. One way to ease these tensions is by accepting existing conventions, in order perhaps to create a new convention, more in accordance with the contemporary consciousness.

The famous commercial success image of the 'thirties—the Theatre Guild—was one of those conventions.

With the 'thirties, the Guild succeeded in balancing such opposites as idealism and materialism, individuality and universality, reason and unreason, Right- and Left-wing plays. Its honor roll pays homage to an array of professional idols who, on our arrival, had already been set up in their niches, such as Bernard Shaw, Eugene O'Neill, Maxwell Anderson, Robert E. Sherwood, Elmer Rice, Thornton Wilder, Philip Barry, John Steinbeck, Pirandello, Karel Capek, Franz Werfel and Ferenc Molnar.

We were, of course, searching for plays related to experiences in Epic Theatre.

Among the outstanding productions that had Epic dimensions was Dostoievsky *Brothers Karamazov*, the novel dramatized, adapted, and directed by Jacques Copeau and presented at the new Guild Theatre on January 3, 1927. It was regrettable that we had not seen it. Also during 1928, the Theatre Guild presented three O'Neill plays. (Of course O'Neill was the nearest to an Epic playwright we had come to admire.) *Marco's Millions* was followed by *Ah! Wilderness* and *Strange Interlude*, which had a record of four hundred performances in New York; and finally, in 1931, *Mourning Becomes Electra*, with the great Russian actress Nazimova.

Of course the great moralizer and critic of society, Bernard Shaw, was offered in several plays which in subject matter were Epic, such as *St. Joan* (1923), *Arms and the Man* (1925), and *Back to Methuselah*.

Parallel to the Shaw plays, a number of expressionistic plays were presented by the Guild, touching on important social themes: notably Georg Kaiser's *From Morn to Midnight* (1922); Ernst Toller's *Men and the Masses* (1924); Elmer Rice's *The Adding Machine*; and the beautiful *Goat Song* by Franz Werfel. Maxwell Anderson's *Elizabeth the Queen* (1930) was a most interesting attempt to update history and bring documentary evidence into the theatre. Robert Sherwood's Pulitzer Prize play, *Idiot's Delight*, offered by the Guild in 1936, was a reminder of our own task because it was the first successful anti-war play.

Using new poetic impulses as well as taking up moral issues in the spirit of further experimentation, the Guild produced in its first ten years such plays as Marc Connelly's sensitive treatment of Negro religion, *Green Pastures* (1930), and a folk drama, *The Lost Colony*, by Paul Green.

There had been several forerunners of Epic Theatre in the Theatre Guild's early history. One of them was Paul Claudel's *The Tidings Brought to Mary* at the Garrick Theatre in December, 1922. It was Paul Claudel, together with Darius Milhaud, influenced by the Japanese Noh play, who developed a new operatic style which tended toward Epic Theatre in *Christophe Colomb* (1929). I should also like to mention here Luigi Pirandello's *Right You Are if You Think You Are* because of the critical analysis of the characters, which is Epic in essence.

• • •

Although repertory theatre had never found roots in America, the magnificent effort of Eva LeGallienne, London-born daughter of the poet Richard LeGallienne, to establish a repertory theatre in New York City was well known here and abroad.

Beautiful, courageous, and educated in the severe routine of the Academy of Dramatic Arts, she had come to New York to join the legitimate theatre. She won high praise for her outstanding interpretations of Ibsen and Strindberg and finally decided to create a repertory theatre in New York. In 1926 she opened the Civic Repertory Theatre and during the next six years offered a most distinguished program of foreign and American plays, acting in most of them herself. The Civic Repertory awakened in its audience a critical awareness of the classics. The most admirable of Miss LeGallienne's achievements was that in spite of her concentration on Repertory Theatre, she succeeded in cultivating and introducing new writers and actors such as Egon Brecher, Josephine

Hutchinson, Harold Moulton, Sayre Crawley, Robert Ross, Alma Kruger, Paul Leyssac, Donald Cameron, J. Edward Bromberg and Jacob Ben-Ami.

. . .

Of all the adventuresome experiments we had heard of, the Group Theatre's fame and fortune seemed most vital to us.

For some months the Theatre Guild had been faced with the fact that a revolt was growing among playwrights, actors, and its own directors, until one day *Variety* headlined their formation as a unit under the name of Group Theatre. The Group's intention was not to forment revolt but rather to affirm the needs of the theatre as they thought it should be: a collective, in the service of art, and a communion of the artists and audience. They had envisioned the creation of an independent studio in the manner of the various studios in Russia, which still remained under the aegis of the parent organization. In short, they wished to create a Guild studio, whose ventures would be subsidized by the Guild but which would function independently. It was Copeau's *Manifesto of the Theatre* and not Marx's *Das Kapital*, that was the Holy Book of the new Group Theatre.

In 1931, the Guild consented to present the Group's first play, *Red Rust*, about the early days of the Russian Revolution. The outcome was quite characteristic of the era. Although the play was directed without an ideological bias, it oddly enough attracted many more leftist sympathizers, along with the militant intelligentsia, than were desired, and innocently became an unexpected antagonist of the bourgeois deities, especially when an enthusiastic audience began to sing the *Internationale*.

I myself have never thought of the Group Theatre as being radical but, rather, full of spirit, experimental, reflecting life—heir of the various studies in Russia, the Freie Bühne in Germany, the independent theatres in England, the Théâtre

Libre in France, and Copeau—of course, Copeau. It was an example of the collective approach in the theatre, which gave unity to its theatrical productions.

Nevertheless, after the short but turbulent performances of *Red Rust*, the Theatre Guild decided to drop the Group. To soften the overstrained relationship, the Theatre Guild consented to release to the new Group Theatre the rights to a play it had been holding on its tentative list for several seasons. How much this generous gesture should be appreciated in retrospect is hard to say. The fact was that Paul Green's *The House of Connelly* became a luminous triumph for the Group.

The audience seemed to be confronted with a new kind of theatre, which, abstractly speaking, was a drive toward an artistic totality as well as a social unit. The Group was a school and a theatre. The schooling took place in rehearsals and was well planned by its three directors, Cheryl Crawford, Harold Clurman, and Lee Strasberg. The result was a permanent company and a functioning organization. It was a great pity that it had to rest on a makeshift foundation—that is, to work from production to production. The organization ran according to rules under which behavior and manner were regulated by the general interest of the Group as a whole, a commonly shared philosophy and a social code. This was further than any other theatre had developed.

One of the disappointments of the Group had been Erwin Piscator's dramatization of Dreiser's novel *An American Tragedy* under the title of *The Case of Clyde Griffiths* (1936), the first Epic play New York had seen, directed by Lee Strasberg. The play had scored a success in the tiny Jasper Deeter Hedgerow Theatre in Pennsylvania, but it did not survive its didactic interpretation in New York. Strasberg suggested to Harold Clurman he write a letter to the press making clear that "the Group was not to be held accountable for the playwright's ideas or tastes."

After the great success of Sidney Kingsley's Pulitzer Prize winner in 1934, *Men in White*, the Group Theatre became an integral part of the Broadway scene. Performances were kept at a high level and served as an example of collective enterprise. Some of the more notable Group members were Stella and Luther Adler, Margaret Barker, Dorothy Patton, Frances Farmer, John Garfield, Elia Kazan, Franchot Tone, J. Edward Bromberg, and Morris Carnovsky. Mordecai Gorelik joined the Group as a designer and created some superb sets, as did Cleon Throckmorton.

However, one of the most important strokes of good fortune was the Group's discovery of a playwright in its own midst. With the introduction of Clifford Odets to the American theatre, a new era was born. *Waiting for Lefty* opened on January 5, 1935. Harold Clurman called it "the birth cry of the 'thirties." He asserted that "youth had found its voice." The fact was that audience and players became one. The play got rave reviews. It was a blazing start and seemed the true debut of an explosive avant-garde. *Awake and Sing,* directed by Harold Clurman, followed a month later, but the new play did not live up to the earlier spirit and was deficient in theatrical emotion.

Clifford Odets had absorbed much of the committed drama and some of the meager evidence of Epic Theatre which had reached America.

. . .

It was the second summer here and, with Piscator deeply involved in the school's program, my desire to work grew.

The Group had established its summer quarters at Smithtown, Long Island, not far from our own home. We had rented George Grosz's house in Douglaston.

Harold Clurman, who had remained with the Group that summer, realizing my predicament, invited me to come to Smithtown to teach there.

One day the car sent by the Group to take me to Smithtown was delayed. While I was waiting, I wondered whether Stella Adler, whom I had met in Paris, had not been right to deplore the fact that we had not come earlier, at the time when the great American drama had come to life with the Provincetown Playhouse and Eugene O'Neill.

Piscator had directed O'Neill's *The Hairy Ape* in Berlin. Nothing could be more exciting now than to see more O'Neill plays.

Why was O'Neill silent in 1939?

Could it be possible that he had withdrawn from the theatre after his greatest success, the trilogy *Mourning Becomes Electra*, based on the Orestes cycle? Why had he refused to allow any of his new works to be staged?

What was his position in these times when it had become clear that it was no longer enough for the writer to explain, but that he had to find a solution? Not enough to record life, but to change it—or withdraw.

The car arrived.

A rather pleasant young man, with close-cropped hair, and dark, soft eyes over a hard mouth came toward me. He addressed me—"Mrs. Piscator?"—apologized hastily and without introducing himself escorted me to the car.

On our way to Smithtown the driver didn't speak, but I sensed him restless.

To break the awkward silence I told him that the Group Theatre was really to be congratulated for having discovered Clifford Odets, a playwright who had inaugurated a new era in the American theatre.

"What do you mean, a new era?" the driver asked.

I suddenly felt warm and communicative. "Didn't *Awake*

and Sing make for a new era? Communicate a coherent world view instead of drama floundering in a sea of hysteria? These plays did not only influence Odets' good fortune but the good fortune of the theatre."

He looked up, surprised. "Did you see any of these plays?"

"Yes. We both did. Piscator and I. They were wonderful."

"You mean that . . . literally?"

"Of course. I think Odets is an exciting writer."

The young man leaned back slightly in his seat. His aggressiveness seemed to have withdrawn under cover. He looked like someone suddenly wanting to make friends.

"America is not going in Piscator's direction."

I looked at him, surprised. "In what direction do you think Piscator is going?"

"Political theatre . . . throwing up the banner."

His attitude struck me as odd. How seriously he took himself! What was he afraid of?

Epic Theatre or political theatre? Hasn't the theatre always been political—an expression of its time? Time itself has never been a metaphysical unmeasurable destiny-designed pattern, but a product of class wars within the presiding society. The feudal theatre of the courts, the bourgeois theatre of liberal individualism—were they unpolitical? Or perhaps the theatre of the Greeks—for the masses—the abode of the gods and hero worship? Were they also unpolitical, like the festivals for the saints, or honoring the monarchs chosen by God? The theatre has never been unpolitical. But there have been epochs where the interest of the dominating classes demanded that politics be more or less hidden. In other epochs when the ruling classes were disintegrated, they escaped into an apolitical attitude, *above the mêlée,* as if into some kind of dull amusement. The unpolitical theatre was the political claim of a period in which all the positions of power withdraw from the dangerous realm of social controversy.

"Epic Theatre has a hard life, like every avant-garde, if that is what you mean," I answered finally.

He smiled at me somewhat ironically.

"If it is what you want me to mean, then I have to disappoint you again. America has never sustained an avant-garde, has never been able to create a movement as France, Germany, and Russia."

He drove on silently for a while and presently said: "Well, it is a vast country. Anything can happen."

He didn't speak again until we arrived at the Smithtown Playhouse.

I got out of the car a little shaken after this somewhat jostled conversation, and the young man remarked casually, "I wish Piscator good luck for his Epic Theatre and"—he hesitated for a second—"I am sorry not to have introduced myself properly, but you startled me when you spoke so nicely about my plays. I am Clifford Odets."

4) THE NEW SCHOOL

Alvin Johnson, Danish-born and raised in the resourceful boldness of the Viking spirit, had become in America an explorer of a special kind, a pioneer in education.

Director of the New School for Social Research, the leading institution for adult education in the United States, which he had created—he was the man we were facing across the desk.

While still teaching the social sciences at Cornell, Dr. Johnson had conceived the idea of a school that was not an extension or an adaptation of collegiate instruction but designed to inform the adult mind. This idea led him restlessly from one university to another until he finally succeeded in financing his own school.

But what made him a glamorous figure was the fact that since 1933 he had been a sort of Scarlet Pimpernel, snatching anti-Fascist and Jewish scholars from the grip of the Hitlerites, just as the fictional gentleman rescued French aristocrats from the guillotine. The result was the establishment of a University in Exile, acclaimed by President Roosevelt as a demonstration of "American adherence to the principle of intellectual freedom."

This was one of the reasons why we wished to visit him. Another was the more and more pressing question of immigration. There was great danger in any return to Europe, with Hitler's war pressing on. A teacher's visa—the only quota open—would allow us to stay.

The room was silent as we entered. Then, from behind an ordinary desk overflowing with an abundance of papers, a man rose, silhouetted against the window.

A great man does not reveal himself in terms of a material figure. One feels him not as a body but as a presence. I could not remember afterwards any specific features of Dr. Johnson, but I can never forget the impact of his person.

Facing him across the desk, we soon had the unsettling sensation that we were sharing his attention with someone else. We looked around the room. The circular walls were a striking Byzantine red. At the center of the ceiling was an overhead light, and under the light an antique statue of white marble.

Realizing our surprise, Dr. Johnson explained that he had received the statue as a gift from a friend, Joseph Urban, the architect who had designed his school. He had received it on condition that he would never let it go out of his possession.

"It is the Aphrodite of Cyrene," he continued. "It was found in 1914 by Italian soldiers digging a ditch on the site of ancient Crete. It was kept underground during the first World War and was set up after the war in a special alcove of the Museo delle Terme in Naples. I think she is the most beautiful of all the Aphrodites."

She was more than that. She had a living quality, as if she were some kind of medium that could activate the mutual understanding of this important hour, fill that spaceless space which has no body, that empty space of unsaid things. The validity of these feelings and its importance for us became apparent later.

Johnson seemed to be stretching himself inwardly.

"Americans have been pioneering in the theatre for several centuries. Nowhere has man's instinctive craving for drama, whether as self-expression or as diversion, been more strikingly demonstrated than in the United States."

He talked and we listened. He talked in a slow, halting manner, with a mischievous smile.

We learned that with the withdrawal of the Spanish from the new territory, the drama had disappeared from the states of Texas and New Mexico, and that it had only gained new impetus with the American expansion over the Alleghenies down into the Mississippi Valley. The geographical scene became more familiar when he mentioned the thespian societies and the histronic experiments, in which the Kentuckians won over those of Fort Pitt. Episodes shaped themselves and characters came forth because theatre is the same everywhere.

"Of course, we could still learn a little," he said, enjoying himself hugely. "Why not teach your theatre here?"

"I am not a teacher," replied Piscator. "I am a theatre man —an artist."

"An artist who becomes a teacher usually does so at the sacrifice of his rightful creative claims, but not you. You are an inventor—you will explore ideas, animate the spirit of the future. Besides, you are going to continue a great tradition. You belong to a long line of men who 'engaged' themselves."

"We were all churchmen, Dr. Johnson."

"Precisely."

Unobtrusively and humorously he shed light on the opportunity of teaching. Here was a chance for Piscator to become more than just another foreign director. And all the while he was treating his subject with lightness and grace, we felt him aware of the complexity of the situation.

Dr. Johnson was not a young man who would make hasty decisions. It had not taken him long to realize that Piscator's presence in this country was a propitious circumstance for him. A school of liberal education should give the theatre a prominent place in its arts program.

As the conversation continued, it became clear that it would be a waste to limit Piscator to lectures instead of engaging him in active and appropriate work. Finally, Piscator suggested a dramatic workshop. The students would be enabled to translate ideas into practice.

What were the potentials that Piscator had to offer to the American theatre through the services of the New School? And what could Piscator—who had come to this country an already famous man—expect from the New School if he were to give up his prerogative as a creative artist and become a teacher?

It seemed to me that while both men were weighing their resolution, decisive for their destinies, they could not have been more sympathetically aware of each other's problems.

Dr. Johnson leaned back in his armchair and closed his eyes for a moment.

Silence. The afternoon sun broke through the window behind Dr. Johnson's chair and lighted up the life-sized statue of Aphrodite. Johnson's head nodded to her smilingly as he continued:

"See how perfect she is; the prow of my ship. Pure simplicity. Contented in herself. The trouble with most people is that in all they do, think or feel, they begin at the end. The trick is the right beginning."

"I have always started from scratch, Dr. Johnson," said Piscator. "In fact, it is a dream of mine always to start at the beginning. But dreams have a reality in art. Part of my dream is to bring the theatre back to its real function as being the best educator in the world. Theatre owes its origin and character not to some exclusive qualities of the Greek spirit, but to the human spirit in general. It has been said about me that I view theatre as a tribunal and the public as a legislative assembly. I have played with ideas like that. The fact is that theatre interests me only when it is a matter of interest to society—when it expresses a meaningful universe."

"But the social aspect is only one aspect of theatre, isn't it, Piscator?" asked Dr. Johnson.

"Yes of course. I feel that our present age, which teems with so many ideas and problems, needs clarification of expression. Naturalism confines us to purely individual experiences, reactions and thoughts. Realism may reveal something affecting and true in a more general manner, but there are times when we find it necessary to relate experiences to even larger realities—those of the Epic life."

Dr. Johnson confessed that he was tempted. He wished he had more time to reflect on the various aspects of a dramatic workshop, especially one point: what would happen to his school for adults if youth entered through the doors of the theatre department?

Alvin Johnson was born of a generation which believed that education was not just something that happened. It had to be nurtured, cherished, even fought for.

After a moment's consideration, Dr. Johnson continued:

"Don't misunderstand me, Piscator. I am not questioning

you, nor deriding the theatre. To me education and art are one. They both make our planet livable. One is concerned with our discipline, the other with our freedom. Art and education can be one if people would only try harder—the old and the young together. The theatre can become extremely helpful," he concluded, "in the battle for human decency and social reform."

In his keen gaze one could read other things: that living is drama; the innumerable shadings, the all-moving unrest of contradictions; man's wooden-headed simplicity; the dialectical solutions of the laws of social existence; the disinclination for learning and the contempt for what is great—a problem which will never be solved if art does not involve itself with reality.

The afternoon sun broke through the window and lit his face. He sat there now, sturdy and straight-backed; his eyes were still twinkling.

"I have been told that your last productions were of a political nature. Some people have misinterpreted that," Dr. Johnson remarked, shuffling through some memoranda placed on his desk.

"I was completely unpolitical," Piscator responded, "when I was young. It was one of my dreams to become a tenor, or at least a classical actor. But the trenches at Ypres happened. Berlin happened. When I saw the death dance in the streets, with inflation and hunger, I took to politics as a kitten to milk. And then I started to scream. And I screamed it out. I made Political Theatre."

There was silence.

"I never quarrel with a man about his past." Dr. Johnson was covering a long yellow pad with surrealist hieroglyphs. "You wrote a book about it, didn't you?"

"Yes. Hitler burned it. The first chapter was titled 'From Art to Politics.'"

Another half-mile of silence.

"Perhaps one day you will add another chapter, 'From Politics to Art,' " said Dr. Johnson.

A third silence.

"You are a successful man, Piscator," he continued, rising. "Every successful rebellion becomes at long last a tradition. In the chain of history, each link of tradition has been forged by a rebel of the previous period. When would you like to start?"

"As soon as possible," replied Piscator with a smile.

"I've often been called a 'modern scholar gypsy.' I can foresee a great future for your Dramatic Workshop, Piscator, impossible as it may sound now."

"It is precisely in the counterplay of the possible with the impossible that we progress, Dr. Johnson."

"That's the theatre man talking."

He relaxed in his chair, quite satisfied, and smiled at Aphrodite.

In the dimension of symbolic experience, the spaceless space was filled.

When he took us jovially to the door, I realized that I was still clutching the letters of introduction from Sinclair Lewis, Albert Einstein, and Reinhardt, which I had brought to Dr. Johnson.

5) A BLUEPRINT

The blueprint for the catalogue of the Dramatic Workshop with the brilliant personalities involved, was a constant source of stimulation for us. To complete it we were to check with the assistant Dean.

Clara Woollie Mayer was the youngest member of a large and powerful family. According to Dr. Johnson, she had won three-fold support for the New School: first, from her father, a solid and significant businessman in whose memory the auditorium of the New School was later dedicated; second, from her mother, who had been an educator in her early life and remained so to the end, and third, from the strong brothers and brave sisters, who had also enrolled themselves in the battle for the New School.

"Did you bring the introduction for the catalogue?" she asked. "All it needs to finish it is the foreword."

"I cannot write such a foreword in a hurry, Miss Mayer. You must understand that."

"I do understand. But we need it. You have to explain the aims of the Workshop and what you intend to do. Your plans."

"I have no plans. How can anyone have plans now?"

"You mean with Hitler's invasion of Poland and Danzig annexed by the Germans? My dear Mr. Piscator, after the sinking of the Maine by the Spaniards everyone went about his business here. Art grows out of necessity too."

"I have grave doubts that Theatre is art or, rather, that at this moment it should be," answered Piscator. "What we need at this hour is mass communication to learn the news and to be relieved of our anxiety."

"The war is not here yet. Our life still goes on."

Piscator seemed tired.

After a pause he said: "It is not enough, Miss Mayer, not any more."

"What do you mean?" she asked, her superior air fading.

"Something has been overlooked by everyone, public, press, the artist himself."

"What?"

"The cognition of the significance of life is not an end in itself any more. It is not enough. How to protect this life, how to preserve it, is the question. Peace—what to do to preserve peace. Can art teach us how? To teach us to respect life and serve it more abundantly and sanely, seems to me the only role for the theatre of today."

She smiled and started writing. After a moment she handed him a note.

"Well here it is, your introduction. It is written down, you have only to sign it."

She had taken off her glasses and now one could appreciate her sensitive face. It bore a slightly satisfied and perhaps cunning smile. I realized the enormous ability of this apparently unsophisticated woman to guide events.

Piscator signed and I sat back amazed.

"Before you go," she said, "I want to show you something."

We had heard of the genius of Orozco rising in Mexico. We had not seen the murals, but knew they were Dr. Johnson's special pride.

The spirit never believes that it is selling itself wholesale as an observer-onlooker in the arts; that it is playing against opponents, stronger and subtler than itself; that the contemplation of a painting, for instance, involves study for its comprehension. But the most dramatic part of this puzzle is the imagination which we call the surprise moment and which takes us unaware.

The Orozco murals were part of such a surprise moment.

I had seen wall paintings in Italy and France—the classic frescoes, but it seemed to us that Orozco had imbued this very form of expression with a deeper passion. Color assumes an unusual force when you are exposed to it long enough. It enters the brain with a conquering intensity. Soon the coherence of the ideas underlying those colors spoke a definite and clear language in which I could read all the agitations, maniacal folly and evils which besieged our lives.

My admiration was redoubled.

It was clear that Dr. Johnson had given Orozco all freedom to express his ideas, and that Orozco had used this freedom.

"It's like a montage of a film," said Piscator, walking away from the wall, "a magnificent, colorful film. Montage of action, of thought, of conflict—a montage of drama. It is a blending of things, people and events. What a succession of images, to illustrate the association of ideas, clear as headlines! What a release from petrified painting! It is not accidental that the spiritual metamorphosis in the arts comes at the same time as the technical transformation of its tools. It is the same in the theatre."

"You have just explained Epic Theatre to me," said Miss Mayer.

Piscator laughed. "Not altogether, Miss Mayer. My Epic Theatre has many faces. Of course, I, too, am calling for montage in direction and production. Naturally, I speak for the principle of reporting, for an epic succession of tableaux and stations and the gathering of documentation as we see it here. But this mural would not be alive were it not for the dynamic succession in which the painter has arranged his images. He has created a *moving path*, expanding the material in space and time. In the same way, we have to remove the boundary between the observer and observed in the theatre. We, too, have a create a *moving path*—first of all, in ideas."

"I'll try to help you to find that path," she remarked as we returned to her office.

On our way down, we stopped at Mrs. Urban's office.

It was Charles Mayer, the brother of Clara, who had suggested that Urban should design the New School building. His fees were far beyond anything the New School could pay at that time. What had tempted Urban to accept the proposal is hard to say. Perhaps he felt that the sand in his life-glass was running out, perhaps he liked the freedom Johnson had offered him to do his work in the way he saw fit.

Mary Urban had become Director of Public Relations for the New School after her husband's death. Mary could do that, but she could do more. She could handle people. She had learned that great old art from her husband and he in turn had inherited it from that bejeweled old capital of the Hapsburg Empire, Vienna.

"I wish you had come here in the 'twenties, Piscator," she said.

"Lee Shubert made me an offer then."

"Why didn't you accept it?"

"Because I had already made a commitment for a film in Russia."

"Why did you prefer to go to Russia instead of coming here?" she asked.

Why? We stayed silent instinctively.

How could she understand it? Russia, at the time when Piscator shot his film, represented the great longing of every real artist. It was the country of the future, of peace, of progress, of truth. All the lies of World War I would be buried, silenced and forgotten, as Europe would be, confused and treacherous Europe.

"Many artists went to Russia at that time, Mrs. Urban."

"I know, I spoke to André Gide in Paris. No man could have been more disappointed. And Meyerhold? What about Meyerhold? What was the name of your film?"

"*The Revolt of the Fishermen of Santa Barbara,* adapted from Anna Seghers' famous novel."

I had seen Piscator's film in Paris in one of the foreign movie houses on the Champs-Elysées, before I met him. I had a strange impression, almost a painful feeling, similar to what I had experienced at the Paris Opera listening to Toscanini conducting Ravel's *Bolero.* Then, if ever, I believed in a demon which battled, not with words like Sartre, with sicknesses like Genet, or with visions of the void like Beckett, but with an undercurrent of violence, of convulsive beauty, erotic and explosive. It was a brilliant bravura exercise in classical style by a 20th century Romanticist.

Somehow, as it goes with isolated works if they prove of

artistic value, the film came to America, but too late and badly damaged. Later it was shown at the President Theatre, which was part of the Dramatic Workshop. Benoit-Lévy, the great French producer-director of *La Maternelle*, saw it at that time and qualified it as the only film he had seen which retained so much of genuine invention that it could still serve our generation as an example.

. . .

A few more days passed. Our preparations went ahead.

"Why *universal* theatre?" asked Dr. Johnson, while we were looking over proofs of the catalogue.

"Modern man *is* universal," replied Piscator. "War or no war. In the morning when he opens his newspaper, the whole world jumps in his face. He is everywhere at once in the midst of life. How can we expect this man, who embraces the whole world at a glance, to be satisfied with anything less than universal? Why should an evening in the theatre offer him less?

"Art is in its essence universal. I have not missed anything in America that I have not missed nearly everywhere. It is a dream of mine, I fear, and one generally feels embarrassed about one's dreams. But dreams have a reality in art and the will to realize them is indispensable to the artist, even if his work is dependent upon material realities.

"Part of my dream is that there is room in the theatre for every style that expresses the meaning of a play. I have merely felt that our present age, which teems with so many ideas and problems, needs an intensification of expression. Naturalism or realism confines our approach to purely private experiences, reactions and thoughts. Realism may reveal something affecting and true about the group, but there are times when we find it necessary to relate experiences to the larger realities of the day. Both styles have much to offer, and they can be broadened and supplemented, or basically intensified.

"There is another part of my dream of the universality of the theater. Representing the stream of the living theatre, it should be sensitive to all viewpoints and committed to none, except in terms of what the individual play requires. However, I don't believe that dreams are realized by wishful thinking. That is my reason for hoping that an institution like the Dramatic Workshop, especially when it receives the cooperation of the American theatre experts, can serve as a focal point. Stanislavsky's rehearsals lasted for years. Gordon Craig requires years of preparation. Our experiment may last forever." *

Dr. Johnson laughed in his very non-commital way. "We Americans are peculiar people. Big words frighten us. I know what you want but let them discover it."

The final edited catalogue contained a note from him: "The student will wish to gain light on the problems of social change, or the relations of classes, races, and nations. He will need history for perspective, psychology for insight, philosophy for point of view. He will wish to take account of the universe in science, literature and art."

Now we were sure. Dr. Johnson no longer had a quarrel with the word "universal."

On the administrative side we had Mrs. Urban, director of public relations; Agnes de Lima, a charming, gifted director of publicity; and Issai Hosiosky, the treasurer.

I don't want to forget, and I could not ever, one of the unique figures in this blaze of names and abilities we met with now, Miss Eleanor Fitzgerald. She was the new executive secretary of the Studio Theatre.

"She was the incarnation of a mystery," e.e. cummings wrote about her, "the mystery of individuality; of a mightily sorrowing and rejoicing, a prodigious, generous, a fearlessly unique and passionately human being."

* "The American Theatre," New York *Times* (Jan. 21, 1940), IX2:5.

We really came to know and cherish Fitzi. Her courage and enthusiasm, her sensitiveness and her hard-headedness, were as invaluable to us as they had been to the older group of the Provincetown Players, from whom she came.

For the moment, however, Fitzi managed a million and one details for the school. Tall, with short-bobbed white hair, a colorful beret perched uneasily on it, a strong face with eyes that looked directly at you and never wavered, Fitzi always gave me the impression of a candle burning at both ends. She was already in her sixties when she came to us, but her youthful spirit never left her until the day we buried her—nor did her courage. Fitzi could resist oceans of nervous, irritating students; she could face first performances that looked disastrous; she could face members who hadn't paid their subscriptions, but clamored for seats; she could face the Board of Trustees and ask them for money; she could face the Board of Education and ask them for help; she could even face Mr. Hosiosky, zealous guardian of the Treasury of the New School!

Fitzi knew what makes or breaks an artist. At the original Provincetown Playhouse she had spent her life with great ones: O'Neill, Bette Davis, James Light and many more actors as well as directors and playwrights.

"Every creative man is a riddle," Fitzi used to say. "We may try to solve that riddle in various ways, but it is rare to find the right answer." It was clear that she saw in Piscator such a riddle.

"You need a theatre, Piscator," Fitzi said one morning out of a clear sky. She had been following him around for several days, from the classrooms on the fifth floor down to the auditorium.

"We must first concentrate on the school, Fitzi—make a go of it."

"But you need a theatre—a real one," she persisted.

"We must wait."

"Wait! What for?" Fitzi burst out. "You must not. . . ." She stopped suddenly.

"What is it, Fitzi?"

"I just thought . . ." Fitzi answered, "Don't put your whole soul in the school. Those who sow, reap, says the Bible. Teaching is sowing. Not you, but future generations will reap what you're sowing now. The theatre is different from the Biblical plants."

Piscator knew his Bible well. He had been called a "rebel with tradition."

. . .

Three German towns, on the road taken by the Spanish invaders to the Netherlands, were the scenes of Erwin Piscator's youthful influences: Herborn, Dillenburg, and Marburg.

Already in the year 914 Herborn had been known as a Christian community under the patronage of St. Peter. Given as a gift in 1231 by the Counts of Nassau to the Knights of the Cross, Herborn served as a haven for a spiritual as well as a worldly brotherhood.

During the Reformation, Herborn became the cell of Protestantism for Germany. The Lutheran Credo of the Augsburg Confession of Melanchton is still the Credo of the Evangelical Church of Nassau-Hesse today.

It was in the second half of the 16th Century that Herborn won international importance, when in 1584 William of Orange created a Hohe Schule, patterned after the Geneva example, as a spiritual defense against the Counter-Reformation. The most important teachers were Kaspar Olievian whose name is linked to the Heidelberger Catechism, Johannes Althusius, the famous jurist, and above all Johannes Piscator, whose forty years of indefatigable activity brought the Hohe Schule to full bloom.

Born on the day that Luther died, Johannes Piscator from his early youth dedicated himself to theology and later became professor of the Holy Word at Strassburg. It was said that Latin, Hebrew and Greek, the languages "in which the apostles and the prophets have written," came more easily to him than his native German.

Tyndale's elegant, smooth translation of the Bible made Piscator "uncomfortable." Piscator's wish was to translate the Bible from the original sources. When his efforts at translating were discovered, he lost his professorship. In order to hide himself from the wrath of Rome he latinized his name. Fischer became Piscator. Unbowed, he worked patiently shaping his text day after day, supporting the Zwinglian controversy in his translation.

It is said that one day, having found a blank in the original text: Mark 8:12, and being unable to supply the missing words, he inserted a personal reminder to himself, "May God punish me . . ." and went on with his translation.

There was considerable confusion over this pious ejaculation when the Piscator text was printed, and his Bible was subsequently christened by some Lutherans "The May God Punish Me Bible."

Erwin Piscator could claim as heritage from his famous ancestor not only his uprootedness, his religious and moral concern, but also his pedagogical genius.

When William of Orange called on Johannes Piscator to teach theology at the Hohe Schule of Herborn, the new professor surprised the students with an extraordinary point of view: the idea of developing political concepts within religious boundaries, and an interpretation of the Bible concerned with the social and political problems of the day. He explored the economic conditions of the age and created what was later known as "Federal Theology," which did away with the concept of "the divine right of kings." It was due to

Piscator's vision and his teaching that Herborn became one of the cradles of modern democracy, one hundred years before Rousseau wrote his *Le Contrat Social*.

• • •

If Herborn had given the young Piscator a sense of democracy, another town drew him deep into politics: Dillenburg.

Nestled between two hills, the fertile Taunus valley and the barren Westernwald, Dillenburg traced its origin back to the time of Charlemagne.

Dillenburg was the seat of the Princes of Orange. Tourists can still see the old elm tree where the famous meeting of William, Count of Nassau-Dillenburg, Prince of Orange, with the ambassadors of The Netherlands took place. William became famous in history as the silent Prince, the head of the first democratic government in Holland, and although of royal blood the founder of the Dutch Republic.

There was a fascinating contradiction in this nobleman. Brought up at the court of Charles V in the Hapsburg practices of imperial conquest, he became a dedicated fighter against despotism. The records speak of him as a superior statesman, savior of Protestantism, protector of religious freedom, a shrewd politician and a harsh enemy. He was also patient and understanding with his friends, always ready to mediate and to reconcile opinions. In his fight to liberate The Netherlands from the tyranny and inquisition of Philip II of Spain, he sacrificed his possessions and his life. He was shot by a traitor at the age of fifty-one at Delft, but the freedom of The Netherlands was secured.

• • •

Then there was Marburg—the third town.

Marburg, lying high on a hill, its castle with its defenses, untouched by World War II still gazes down at the river. It was here that Luther and Zwingli met, where the doctrine of the Lord's Supper was argued. The Elisabeth Church, one of the masterpieces of early Gothic, is much more than religious monument. Its masters guided and directed the life of the city for years.

But it was Marburg's university, founded in 1527, that showed the young Piscator the image of the future: the two faces of power: war and peace.

Next to Wittenberg, Marburg's university was the nation's first seat of learning. It has acquired a great reputation throughout the Protestant world and had become the meeting ground of the reformed Renaissance leaders, particularly Philip Melanchthon. Many of his friends and foes visited him there. Many famed scholars throughout the centuries have studied or lectured at Marburg.

In spite of such masters of wisdom, Marburg was also heir to the unrest and folly of Europe. Here the pattern was shaped to become the new Gloria Teutonica.

Here leaders, graduates, undergraduates, fellows, alumni groups and associations, the whole confederacy of students laid claim to the Kantian philosophy of the categorical imperative, forgetting that the supreme cause is a moral one not a racial one. This error of judgment showed its full colors at the beginning of World War I.

Erwin Piscator hated the categorical imperative. He didn't know that he was going to run up against dictatorship, but his intuition had disclosed an intimation of what was to come. His peace poems in the trenches of Ypres became poems of action.

6) SOUNDING BOARD—
BERLIN

At the Workshop we wondered how we could best inform young minds unfamiliar with Piscator concepts. We had to find a sounding board which would be attuned to *Epic Theatre*.

We had Piscator's Berlin experience to rely on.

Berlin's geographical position being the axis between the East and West made the Weimar Republic the last stronghold of freedom in the arts.

Germany lived on borrowed time and on borrowed money. Large sums were spent by the Socialists and also by Big Business people on artistic enterprises.

The war had brought significant changes in German theatre organization. The old court theatres had disappeared with their Maecenases, and their tradition was transferred to government theatres, namely theatres directly under the control of the state. Nevertheless, economic difficulties made large cooperative undertakings necessary. This led in part to the establishment of *Volksbuehnen*, whose financial resources were supplied by small annual subscriptions which entitled the playgoer to an extraordinary variety of theatre fare. Although these Volksbeuhnen also received money from Socialist organizations, they offered by no means Socialist theatre. On the contrary the enormous range of repertory was addressed mostly to the middle class.

Berlin was the center of all theatrical activity in Germany. All playwrights, directors and actors sought recogniton on the Berlin stage. Every celebrity passed through the city, every worthwhile artist presented his works there. Dorothy Thompson, the American journalist, wife of Sinclair Lewis, called those Berlin years "golden years of theatre."

What kind of theatre was this? Any kind that was different, any kind that was new. One avant-garde movement followed the other without producing any enduring satisfaction until Dadaism did away with all of them.

Originally a *l'art pour l'art* movement, Dadaism became, after the war, a political movement under the guidance of the painter Huelsenbeck, George Grosz, the satirist; John Heartfield, stage designer; Walter Mehring, poet; Bertolt Brecht; and Erwin Piscator. Its goal was to destroy one of the traditional German concepts which for the past 100 years had sustained the Teutonic pride, the idealisms of Prussia.

Anything to break with idealisms, to attack pseudonobility, prerogatives of any kind to fight with every means, even violent means, to work with satire, bluff, irony, castrate the hero, defeat posterity, tear down the idols—these were the conscious aims of Dadaism.

Although Dadaism prepared the way, it was Expressionism that actually cradled the Epic Theatre.

Expressionism made itself known through a radical change in playwriting which attracted writers of stature. It is hard to believe how few of them are known to the average theatre person, with the possible exception of Karel Capek, Ernst Toller and Franz Werfel. The fabulously prolific dramatist Georg Kaiser, the great satiric writer Karl Sternheim and the poet Fritz von Unruh, a convert from militarism to pacificism are practically unproduced and unpublished.

Within the Expressionist movement another group appeared, the Activists. While Expressionism gave postwar drama a new form, Activism gave it a new philosophy: change through the spirit and not through violence. Violence was the cherished maxim of the past—the survival of the fittest—which had reached its peak in the most insane of all manifestations of violence—war.

Activism in the theatre became closely connected with pacifism—pacificism in the old sense of the word of the great founders of religion, of prophets, philosophers, pilgrims, creators, heretics, rebels and guardians. And what else were they but Activists too, the new men of the modern theatre? Epic Theatre!

The battle around Epic Theatre started in 1918 when Max Reinhardt created a dramatic society, Young Germany.

It may seem strange to speak of Max Reinhardt as a revolutionary. To the majority of people, Reinhardt is best remembered for his illusionary theatre; a baroque synthesis of various theatrical arts: acting, dancing, music, mime, etc.

Max Reinhardt had begun his directing career by dusting off the youthful plays of Goethe and Schiller. He became the sorcerer, the dispenser of joy to the *nouveaux riches* of the Wilhelmnian era, whom he astounded and amused. But if

Reinhardt was the last word of the enchanted theatre, he was also among the first to question it. His sensitivity made him quite aware that the war had brought an era to its close and that therefore new experiments were needed if the theatre was to progress.

He broke down the four-wall interior, spilled the action over into the audience. He removed footlights as well a curtains, and brought the actor close to the spectator. While Stanislavsky sought a theatre of intimate experience, Reinhardt reached out for vast audiences. He performed in broad arenas, in front of the Baroque Cathedral of Salzburg, before Notre Dame in Paris; in the gigantic square of the Rathaus in Vienna; in Venetian palazzos, and above all, in his great colosseum, the Theatre of the Five Thousand in Berlin.

But for all his efforts to reach for the future, Max Reinhardt could not cross the bridge. Like Stanislavsky, he was outrun by time.

Although Reinhardt had surrounded himself with a circle of young playwrights and sanctioned the production of their plays—radical, pacifistic, even socialistic—he maintained a position of reserve. Except for the plays of Fritz von Unruh, Reinhardt did not take on any Expressionist work.

Yet the German avant-garde is as unthinkable without Reinhardt as is the Russian avant-garde without Stanislavsky.

The second decisive step in the direction of new theatre was taken by Leopold Jessner, Director of the Staatstheater in Berlin.

Jessner was a newcomer to the Berlin theatrical scene. He was a practical artist and an imaginative director who thought of the theatre as a medium to awaken the audience at large to the new reality. While Reinhardt's revolution was a theatrical one—a revolution of stage effects—Jessner probed the inner conflicts and made them manifest symbolically through architectural forms. He discarded the illusionist settings and created in their place an articulated space with platforms, cones, and pillars. The "Jessner Stairs" became famous.

With the appearance of Karlheinz Martin, a writer-director, the theatre became a realm of ideas and a battle-ground for the intelligentsia. The stage emerged as a tribunal. Not only was the audience included in the action, but it was also the jury.

The most important of the plays Karlheinz Martin produced was *Transfiguration (Die Wandlung)*, Ernst Toller's first play, at once his own biography and that of the era. Its theme is antiwar; its goal, redemption through understanding and love.

Friedrich, the hero, is clearly Toller himself. He is an abstract symbol of defeat who appears at the same time as a soldier, professor, judge, priest, and artist. As a sculptor, his last futile effort is to create a monumental statue to the Fatherland. However, with the visit of a crippled war veteran, Friedrich, the sculptor-hero, realizes the grotesquerie of war. The long awaited transformation within himself takes place. He destroys the statue and enrolls himself in the Socialist revolution.

Karlheinz Martin sought new ways for the collective regeneration of the theatre. He organized at the Tribunal an actors' democracy. All of the actors had their say in the production of a play. In order to shun the traditional "star" system, no credit was given to any actor, director, or stage designer— no names were mentioned.

During the strike of the metal workers in Berlin, the actors of the Tribunal went every morning to read to the strikers poems and short novels pertinent to the time. One morning after a reading, a young working girl rose from the back of the hall and asked: "May I know the name of the actress?" All at once they knew that their theory of remaining anonymous was nonsense.

Berlin was a battlefield. The front went through the heart of the city, through the heart of every man. Day after day Germany grew more Janus-headed, especially after the meeting of Briand and Stresemann at Thoiry. The Left fully adhered to Locarno, while the Right pressed forward ruthlessly to get concessions from the Allies.

Politics was no longer solely the toy of the Reichstag. Street-corner politics brought a new class to the foreground: the proletariat. But Germany was moving farther and farther from democracy. One could see the day when the Weimar Republic would break up. The Germans were ripe for dictatorship.

Aware of such danger, Karlheinz Martin left the Tribunal and threw himself into creating the first Proletarian Theatre. "In spite of my efforts the Proletarian Theatre would have died an early death had it not been for a young man," according to Karlheinz Martin, "who had come to see me. This young man was Erwin Piscator. He told me he had come to Berlin from Koenigsberg where he had been running a theatre also called the Tribunal. It had gone under in a most honorable bankruptcy. His ideas of theatre were exciting, grotesque, beautiful, with the purity of first enthusiasm."

Under the direction of the young Piscator, the Proletarian Theatre performed in places never before the scene of theatrical events, halls and meeting places in the suburbs. His intention was to reach the workers right where they lived. He hoped to create a true "People's Theatre," intelligible to the broad masses, that could serve to enlighten and, by the nature of the plays produced, sound a warning against the imminent Fascism. No similar theatre existed in Berlin.

In his autobiographical *Political Theatre*, Piscator describes the sort of problems his enterprise faced; stage settings were bound to be very primitive. But these simple, hastily painted linen screens grew strangely in significance. They served as the background of the play and explained events. As a result, a new dramaturgical element was born into the performance: the teaching, pedagogical aspect. The theatre no longer aimed at touching the audience merely through feelings.

At first the Proletarian Theatre excluded professional actors and presented plays mostly with members of the different workers' unions. Slowly, however, this changed, and professional actors, writers, and directors were asked to contribute their services without salary. There was not even the aspiration to glory, as the theatre was not rich enough to have so much as a printed program. Yet six big productions, among them the works of Upton Sinclair and Gorki, were presented with resourcefulness and artistic integrity.

Anyone who knows halls such as those that served Piscator as a theatre realizes the problems. They smelled of stale beer and men's latrines and were covered with the faded flags and bunting from the last Bockbier festival. The man in his shirt sleeves and the woman holding her baby in her arms were not interested in seeing their own image in the mirror held out to them from the stage, nor in any lesson they could learn from history. They came to be amused, relieved. They felt like trapped animals, who, having hoped to escape their daily despair, did not want to experience this same hopeless situation in the evening, nor to feel they were being pursued from the stage by well-meaning teachers or moralists. They were not ready to be educated by or through the theatre. The dry, anti-romantic approach, the primitive décors, the underplaying actors, the dialectics they could not grasp, failed to create the success that Piscator had hoped for. The proletarians did not care for the Proletarian Theatre.

When the Berlin police department did not renew the license, the Proletarian Theatre died without mourning in April, 1921.

Nevertheless Piscator had gained the reputation of being the most vital of the young directors. But what was a director without a theatre?

Searching for a new theatre, Piscator met Hans Jose Rehfisch who wanted to dispose of the Central Theatre in 1923. If the Piscator Proletarian Theatre had proved to be a crusade, the Central Theatre was a forward step in Piscator's career.

The new Central Theatre and its director planned to accomplish what the Proletarian Theatre had failed to do: to become the real Volksbuehne of Berlin, a theatre by the people and for the people.

The lease of the Central Theatre cost three million marks, one million to be paid immediately and the rest three months later. In spite of their supreme confidence, both Piscator and Rehfisch realized this would take some doing. Then inflation came to their aid. One million was paid off by the membership, while the other two million was paid by tearing out the heating pipes in the theatre and selling them to a junk dealer.

The only asset that Piscator had was the four or five thousand members of the Proletarian Theatre. If he wanted to keep the membership, he had to activate it and enlarge it by drawing upon the middle class.

The economic chaos of Berlin grew from day to day and had strange effects on Piscator's production plans. Sometimes he was forced to drop actors for lack of money, then half an hour later found himself able to re-engage them, thanks to the spiraling inflation.

In order to attract new members, Piscator had, in a measure, to abandon his avant-garde position. The playbill at the Central Theatre was more or less conservative (Gorki, Rolland, Tolstoy, some Expressionists).

An actors' general strike, supported only by the Piscator theatre, precipitated a conflict. In the fall of 1924, Piscator lost his theatre, but he had gained something that proved more important to him: knowledge of his capability as a director.

Oddly enough it was the plush Volksbuehne that was going to have the advantage of this. It was at the Volksbuehne that Piscator developed the kind of staging that formed the final concept of his Epic Theatre and laid the foundation of his future productions. There his great innovations began. For the first time he had a superb theatre, adequate financial backing and the opportunity to work with important actors and designers.

The Volksbuehne was still considered the most modern theatre of Berlin. It possessed an auditorium lined with mahogany of rich and somber color and a seating capacity of 2,000. The stage was equipped with what was considered the newest and most complete machinery of the day—an assemblage of mechanical contrivances. But what was more important was another progressive milestone: the Volksbuehne's membership mounted to about 30,000 people.

Siegfried Nestriepke, the Director of the Volksbuehne, had been a courageous fighter for the practical realization of the Volksbuehne idea. He was also an effective organizer who understood the necessity to democratize the theatre and was not averse to propaganda, which he considered not necessarily inartistic. Besides, he understood that Piscator's kind of propaganda theatre, in this time of trouble, presented a healthy reaction against the ponderous pathos of the traditional German theatre and could readily be accepted by the wealthy ticket buyers who were the backbone of the Volksbuehne.

Piscator's sensational experiments at the Proletarian Theatre and Central Theatre seemed to be a realization of Siegfried Nestriepke's ambitions for the Volksbuehne. He made the daring step of asking Piscator to direct the forthcoming play at the Volksbuehne: *The Flags*, by Alphonse Pacquet.

This invitation was more than a surprise to Piscator. It launched a crisis of conscience: could he work in a theatre that he had serverely condemned for failing to live up to the noble purpose for which it had been created?

It was only later, in the years when Piscator was his own producer in his theatre at Nollendorfplatz, that he realized the pressure of the economic battle which was the true reason for Siegfried Nestriepke's sometimes crafty administrative measures.

Piscator's acceptance of the offer was rooted in his own feeling that he might be able to turn the tide; that the inscription over the theatre door, "Art for the People," would not remain an empty phrase any longer; that the obligation would be assumed. "The origin of the theatre is social in nature," wrote Oshilevsky, a close associate of Nestriepke, in defense of Piscator's ideas. "From the days of antiquity, theatre has tried to influence, change and determine public feelings. . . . The public is the theatre's most living substance. One must proceed from the public if the theatre is to have a really solid base."

The program of the Volksbuehne was still tied to Naturalism. Ibsen, Strindberg, and Gerhardt Hauptmann had not stopped gratifying the audience. This was not a style which corresponded to Piscator's own development nor to Nestriepke's new ideas.

But what was to be his style?

He did not know yet. His notebook is full of contradictory and confusing remarks. He felt that he had to de-romanticize the theatre, depart from the sterility of art for art's sake, to arrive at a believable reality. Construct instead of interpret. Go from intellectualism to truth, from fiction to report from sentimentality to sentiments, from plot to event, from psychological mystery to the facts of life. To this end new means, new shapes and forms had to be created. They had to prove themselves and communicate not only the material, but also the mental and spiritual world.

For that, one would have to start at the beginning—start from scratch—with the author: "In the beginning was the Word."

Concerning *The Flags,* a new play about anarchism in Chicago, Piscator wrote:

> I have to ask for better texts from that poor creature, the author. I have to be honest with the facts, truthful to the people who come to see these plays and want to find an answer to their own problems. I have to bring history up to date, even at the danger of presenting something unfinished or eliminating what could be effective.

His notebook continues:

> How horrible to destroy first, before you can rebuild. But everything has to be subordinate to the truth, to the overall goal. To create ART? No, let us consciously create unfinished products. We don't have time to build formally. So many new thoughts push on to the light. Time is so precious, we cannot wait for the last refined purification. We take the means of expression wherever we can find them—scold us if you like—that way we create in spite of you—what is most needed, the interim achievement.

It was said later that most of the plays Piscator directed at the Volksbuehne were related to the Expressionistic trend of Jessner or the biomechanics of Meyerhold or to the theatrical theatre of Alexander Tairoff. His productions were even compared to the work of Eisenstein, whose film *Potemkin* had become one of the milestones of the European film industry.

Piscator had never seen a production of either Meyerhold

or Tairoff. He would not have appreciated either at that time.

With the production of *The Flags*, Piscator found his style, a theatre between narration and drama. For the first time in theatrical history these two words were linked—Epic Drama.

The next production was Ehm Welk's *Storm Over Gothland* (1927), a drama of the Russian Revolution.

This production precipitated a crisis. Some members of the Board of the Volksbuehne considered its political impact to be too powerful. A great battle raged with the Board. The dissension that followed grew to the point of public controversy in the Berlin Senate. Could the theatre be accepted as a political instrument and still be art? In spite of the different attacks on Piscator's production, public opinion turned out to be in favor of the Political Theatre. The Volksbuehne was embarrassed to find that not only the artists, writers, actors, and politicians but even the conservative newspapers defended Piscator. The young subscribers took the same position as the newspapers.

Nevertheless, the Volksbuehne and its chief guest director soon parted company. Piscator was once more left on his own, but this time he could see his way more clearly. Not only had he achieved a sensational success, but his craft had been enriched by the fact that he had, in his production, also revolutionized the technical means of the theatre.

It must also have been pleasant for him to know that he could count on a potential audience of the young Volksbuehne for his future ventures.

It was not until 1962 in West Berlin that Nestriepke and Piscator met again. The occasion was Piscator's re-engagement at the newly-built Volksbuehne thirty-five years later.

"There is no doubt that Nestriepke esteemed that great man of the stage from the very beginning," wrote Oshilevsky for the opening program. "It was an unforgettable experience when these two proud men found each other again in the spirit of brotherliness, to work anew on a common cause."

Later, at the new Volksbuehne, Piscator produced among other plays, Rolf Hochhuth's *The Deputy*, *The Case of J. Robert Oppenheimer* by Heinar Kiepphardt, and *The Investigation* by Peter Weiss with music by Nono; three successes which made theatrical headlines around the world.

Plays of rebellion? Yes, and for good reason. It would seem to us, in reviewing our sounding board, that since the 'twenties the theatre has not rebelled enough.

7) THE
BREAK
WITH
TRADITION

Piscator's break with tradition became a fact with the earlier historical productions. For the 1927-1928 season, Piscator set up his own independent company in the Theater am Nollendorfplatz. It was a distinguished theatre, which had housed classic revivals. But its Italian Baroque auditorium did not seem to be in step with the time nor with the new productions planned. However, Piscator made the most of it: he changed the atmosphere, as he changed the name. In 1927, the Theater am Nollendorfplatz became the Piscatorbuehne.

"Like many pioneers," wrote George Grosz in his *Marginal Observations on the Subject: Theater am Nollendorfplatz*, "Erwin did not stop at something once tried—a piece of that old Wagner yearning in him . . . too. I frequently saw him on the thorny search after the great overall work of art, encompassing *all* forms of art."

He tells us that Erwin, intrepid and tough like his forebear, the old hard-hitting Bible translator Piscator, kept his sharp nose to the wind and was looking out for new possibilities.

"I know," said George Grosz, "that at that time Piscator carried the plan for his stage complete and finished in his head."

The plays he proposed to do were not just obliging symbols like Picasso's *Dove,* but plays of active protest, a deliberate *J'accuse;* a reportage and montage; a warning, history marching on; political satire, morality plays and court trials, purposefully shocking.

Piscator's opening production of *Hoppla, We Live,* by Ernst Toller, must have been such a shock to the audiences.

Ernst Toller was the great new playwright of the German revolution. However, before we speak of the dramatist Toller, we must speak of the man, who was equally great.

The news of the outbreak of war reached the young Bavarian student in July 1914, in Grenoble. After many adventurous experiences at the closing borders, he enlisted in Munich and rushed to the defense of the Fatherland.

At the front the frail and sensitive young patriot suffered a heart attack and was invalided out of the army. Forlorn and shaken by the horrors of war, he became a leader of the revolutionary students at Heidelberg, organized to bring about world peace by uniting the youth of all countries. The organization was firmly crushed. Toller escaped to Berlin, and thus began his long, punishing battle with the authorities supporting the war. But he went forward with his plans for peace. With the Social Democrat Kurt Eisner, Toller organized the strike of the munitions workers in Munich as a protest against the war. The strike failed; Toller was arrested and condemned to prison.

After he was released, he immediately plunged into the social fermentation that followed the Armistice and was one of the leaders in the formation of the Bavarian Free State, headed by Kurt Eisner.

When Eisner, of whom he had become a close friend, was murdered, Toller was asked to become chairman of the Munich Social Democratic Party. He felt he was too young for such a responsibility and, more important, he did not want to engage in a political career. It was precisely this refusal that endeared him to the masses. Finally, during the great chaos in Munich, he accepted the chairmanship of the Zentralrat, which was the only orderly power in Munich. In the Munich revolution of 1919 he played a prominent part. But once again he came to grips with the official demagogues. He had torn up orders for arrest and death warrants, had freed hostages from other political parties and even refused to have the officers of the White Guard shot. For this he was arrested and again accused of high treason. This time he was condemned to five years' imprisonment in a fortress.

While in prison, Toller wrote the *Schwalbenbuch* (*Book of the Swallows*). In this most beautiful poetry he described a pair of nesting swallows. They consoled a prisoner for a whole summer, singing at his window and bringing him greetings from life; in gratitude he transposed them into poetry.

Toller came to America too late. His theatrical influence had already gone down considerably. His last years—George Freedley tells us—were spent in aiding the Dramatists' Guild of the Authors' League of America to work out its copyright problems, and in working for the victims of Fascist terror in Spain.

A few years later, in 1939, Toller hanged himself in his hotel room in New York City.

Anyone who has seen *Hoppla, We Live*, will remember the story of a man who, after spending ten years in a lunatic asylum, having been convicted of a political crime, is released. He finds it impossible to make any sense of the outside world and events. He believes the world is itself insane and longs to return to the safety of the asylum. But before he can go back, he is enmeshed in the violent political affairs of this outside world—the world of the 'twenties—and is thrown into prison. Desperate to escape insanity, the hero hangs himself.

In Piscator's production, a newsreel reviewed the ten years of world events that had taken place while Toller's hero was in the asylum. There flashed before the eyes of the audience the following reminders of a desperate decade:

1917—March 8, Russian Revolution begins.

April 6, U.S. enters World War I.

1918—January 8, Wilson's 14-point address to Congress calls for self-determination, removal of economic barriers, and the League of Nations.

July 16, Czar Nicholas II and family shot.

November 11, World War I ends.

1919—June 28, Versailles Treaty signed.

1920—January 10, League of Nations officially inaugurated as Versailles Treaty goes into effect.

January 16, Prohibition in U.S.

March 19, U.S. Senate rejects Treaty of Versailles because of League of Nations proviso.

1922—October 27, Mussolini marches on Rome.

1923—November 8-9, Munich Beer Hall *putsch* led by Hitler put down; Hitler sentenced to five years, serves less than one; writes *Mein Kampf* in jail.

1925—July 20-21, Scopes evolution trial held in Dayton, Tenn.

1927—May 20-21, Lindbergh flies solo across Atlantic.
August 23, Sacco and Vanzetti executed.
November, Trotsky expelled from Communist Party.

However, it was not only the playwright's genius, but also the director's innovations, that made the performance sensational. Never before had two theatrical media been used together: the structural and dramaturgical elements of the speaking stage and the dynamic and visual elements of film.

With *Hoppla, We Live*, the social mission of modern theatre was beginning to come clear to Piscator. He became conscious of the real influence of the artist in society, an influence to be fully realized only within an equally powerful sense of responsibility to that society. This duality determined his every decision. It made him impatient with naturalism, since he considered it an evasion of the actual problem. His aim was to achieve a heightened realism: the poetry of the stage could be surpassed by the poetry of the film. The test was the unity of the two media for which he fought in his next productions.

Physicians, lawyers, writers, teachers, economists, bankers, became enthusiastic members of the Piscatorbuehne. The bejeweled *nouveaux riches* paid unheard-of fees to ticket agents to assure them first-night seats.

The liberal democratic press became the theatre's chief support.

"The opening of a theatre in Berlin, under Piscator's directions, is of greater significance than any German theatre of the past. It is a chapter of the struggle in which the whole German theatre is presently engaged," wrote *Die Action* in April 1927.

Piscator's struggle became something more than a one-man

revolution, or an esthetic problem. It reflected the whole contemporary situation. With the bourgeoisie dying on its feet, the Theatre of Illusion was on the way out, and with the Political Theatre coming in, an avant-garde of indubitable power had entered the theatre.

It was clear that the young man who had returned from World War I with the conviction that modern theatre had to be related to real life, had made the step which neither Reinhardt nor Jessner nor Fehling nor even Karlheinz Martin had dared to risk. He had broken with the tradition.

Unless he is a fool, a man does not accidentally engage himself in a moral cause. Beaumarchais did not write his *Figaro* until he had involved himself in the American Revolution; nor did Sartre become political until he had lived through the occupation of Paris; nor Brecht before he had come into contact with the Nazis.

As concerns Piscator's career, *Hoppla, We Live* was the turning point. Overnight he became a famous and controversial figure.

He was denounced as a charlatan, a rabble-rouser, and he was acclaimed the leader of the progressive theatre movement and a genius.

. . .

On November 12, 1927, the Piscatorbuehne presented its second play *Rasputin*, by Alexei Tolstoy, with Tilla Durieux as the Czarina.

Tilla Durieux, Germany's Sarah Bernhardt, had retired from the stage when one evening she saw Piscator's sensational production of Schiller's *The Robbers* at the Staatstheater in Berlin.

She was enthusiastic, and expressed the wish to see the young director. This was not the death of the classics as everyone seemed to predict. This was the revitalization of the classic drama, inseparable from and necessary to the development of the day.

It was through Durieux's good offices that Piscator received enough financial security to assure the first season at the Theater am Nollendorfplatz. The budget was approximately half a million marks. It seems a bit startling to find in Piscator's Political Theatre a statement that he was not at all happy about such an arrangement.

"To everyone else it would have seemed an extraordinary piece of luck. To me it seemed a terrible risk," he said.

This statement is not as incongruous as it first appears. What Piscator wanted at this time was not the financing of a play, but a financing of the theatre. A specific kind of theatre —his Total Theatre which he had planned and designed with Walter Gropius, who had made the blueprints, and for which negotiations for property near the Halleschen Tor were under way. Total Theatre was to be a complete break with the feudal forms, including the Court Theatre.

"The Total Theatre provides a stage in arena form, a proscenium and a back stage, with two thousand seats disposed in amphitheatre form. There are no boxes, but by turning the big stage platform which is part of the orchestra, the small proscenium stage is placed in the center of the theatre and the usual set replaced by projecting scenery on twelve screens placed between the twelve main columns supporting the structure," explains Gropius.

What was most important to Piscator was that the structural elements of the theatre were so flexible that he could present any play, any style of drama.

It was obvious that half a million marks would never build such a theatre and so Piscator had to confine himself to his present productions. Nevertheless, he offered the role of the Czarina in *Rasputin* to Tilla Durieux.

It was tactically a brilliant maneuver to add to his group of excellent actors a star of the magnitude of Tilla Durieux, a strategy that proved equally successful when he engaged Max Pallenberg for the role of Schweik in his next production.

Rasputin, the Romanoffs, the War and the People Who Rose Against Them by Alexei Tolstoy, was, according to Piscator, a "bloody melodrama." What interested him was the material: the beginning of the Russian revolution, this time seen from *above*.

It was indeed material bound to make interesting theatre, with sharp and believable characters. It had one basic fault, which turned it into a melodrama—it limited itself to the personal and private destiny of Rasputin. "As interesting as the adventurous figure of Rasputin was, we were not concerned with him, nor with the conspiracy around the Czarina, nor with the tragedy of the Romanoffs. Our concern was world history: the destiny of Europe 1914 to 1917."

"Where does history end and where do politics begin?" asked Leo Lania in the program for *Rasputin*. "What can history mean to a world which is exploding with problems, destinies much more bitter and more gigantic than any before? Historic drama, to interest us today, cannot be the tragedy of some hero, but must be the political document of the age."

· · ·

For his production of *Rasputin*, Piscator designed a stage set shaped like a globe, a globe which would open up in segments and turn on a revolving platform. The globe, covered with white cloth, was to serve as a projection screen. Everyone was convinced that the pictures would be completely distorted and much time was spent in experimenting from the most outlandish angles. But the doubts were completely unjustified because the curving plane showed the pictures particularly effectively, with unusual plasticity and aliveness. Another screen was hung above the globe, while a narrow film-strip, a kind of "calendar," on one side of the stage kept a multitude of events rolling, giving dates and marginal footnotes. Three film projectors and six thousand feet of film were used to show contemporary history. A crew of artists, photographers, historians, writers, and cameramen was sent out to probe the libraries and film societies for all material concerning Russia.

The film in *Rasputin* played a much more important part than in *Hoppla, We Live*. A new dramaturgy had started.

"As in Greek drama, realistic and idealistic principles alternated. The dramatic interchanged with the epic . . . In Piscator plays the film replaced the chorus. This 'chorus filmicus' took over the realistic part of the play while the dramatic scenes provided the idealistic sequences," wrote Bernard Diebold, Editor-in-Chief of *Querschnitt*, Berlin.*

In this way the film accompanied the action, clarified it, and sometimes even anticipated it.

Tilla Durieux recalled a scene:

> I was in my boudoir with my lady-in-waiting. We were not yet fully aware of the danger, and conversed gaily. Suddenly, on the film next to the segment of the open stage on which I stood, I saw the Red Army troops on the march. I was so shaken up that I forgot my lines and couldn't go on. It is hard to understand, and then I wondered how terrifying the impression must have been to the audience at that moment.

Of all the productions at the Theater am Nollendorfplatz, *Rasputin* had the greatest echo. From then on Piscator was identified with great theatre, for better or for worse. An amusing historical proof was that two personalities—characters in the play—sued the Piscatorbuehne for having portrayed them on stage. They did not consider themselves his-

* Article on *Das Piscator Drama*, January, 1928.

torical figures since they were both still alive: Rubinstein II and Wilhelm II. Dmitri Rubinstein was the secret financial advisor of the Czar, director of a bank in Paris, and general counsel; Wilhelm II, the Kaiser of all the Germans, exiled in Doorn, Holland.

Needless to say (although Piscator lost his case with the Kaiser), from then on there was standing room only at the Theater am Nollendorfplatz.

. . .

One day during rehearsal of *The Good Soldier Schweik*, by Jaroslav Hasek, Piscator set up a gigantic drawing board in the auditorium. He placed it in front of George Grosz, who was watching the rehearsal, then walked away.

After a while George Grosz's master strokes began to appear on sheet after sheet, film-like, clear, simple, not too thin, somewhat woodcuts out of Gothic books. Finally, Grosz had sketched the finest satrical images of Hasek's masterpiece.

I have been told that by the opening night performance there existed some seven to eight hundred sketches, of which only a few were used.

What was it that attracted Piscator to Schweik?

Hasek was relatively unknown at the time and the literary publishers did not take him seriously. Max Brod created a commotion when he translated one of the episodes of the book and declared that the book belonged to world literature. In the small Adria Theater in Prague, the painter-actor Longen and the comic Burian staged scenes from *Schweik*, fragments that filled the evening gaily. The idea of dramatizing the episodes was Hans Reinmann's. Reinmann was known for his pseudo-comic farces about life in the army. Brod and he settled down in Prague and drank for weeks and discussed Schweik. At that time *The Good Soldier* existed only in the form of separate installments.

One evening, Brod went to a book store and asked for the

last installment to discuss it with Reinmann. The bookseller gave him a sour look. Then he said, "I haven't any."

"Can't you order it for me?" asked Brod.

"I don't know what good that will do. Yesterday, Mr. Hasek was here and brought me only a few copies. God knows when he'll be back. Perhaps next week. That is, if he doesn't get drunk on the way."

Indeed, as Brod found out, Hasek was not very regular about delivering installments, but he always delivered them in person in exchange for a meal or a glass of wine.

After *Hoppla, We Live*, which showed a decade of German history, or *Rasputin*, in which one could see the roots and the drives of the Russian revolution, what could Piscator see in *Schweik*?

The triumph of common sense over the intellect? It was much more than that. While other poets took a stand against the war, Hasek succeeded in putting the war out of business—bankrupting it forever. He created a figure that was simultaneously an individual and a mass man. No artist could aim at more: the figure rising from the profoundest depths of the popular spirit, immediately recognized as genuine by the people, reflecting all that is unspeakable and crazy and wonderful, just as did the Knight of La Mancha, Don Quixote, who was originally meant only as a caricature of the Spanish, but became the tender symbol of all fantastic behavior in the good as well as the bad sense.

On the 23rd of January, 1927, the curtain rose on *The Good Soldier Schweik*, who accepts anything, anything at all, and walks through this wicked world invulnerable, while right and left the cautious come crashing down and the foresighted fare the worst.

It was not Max Brod's and Hans Reinmann's dramatization that the audience saw this first night. It was the combined effort of Piscator's playwrights' collective, which in-

cluded himself, Leo Lania, Felix Gasbarra, and Bertolt
Brecht. It was satire, true enough, but on a different level—
satire like *The Inspector General, Dead Souls, Candide, Tartuffe.*

It recounted the adventures of *The Good Soldier Schweik,*
with his unshakable zealousness, primitive reasoning—always
hitting on the wrong solutions—from the day he was drafted
until he had assimilated all the lessons the army had to offer.
But Schweik, in this new dramatization, did more than that.
While he took sides against himself at all times, siding instead with his superiors, he showed the insanity of the impe-
rialistic war of 1914-18.

The opening performance revealed Schweik—Max Pallenberg, the great comic of the German theatre—starting toward
his new life in the army, his first march to Budweis.

Schweik is of the kind who obeys orders. He makes one
step. Then another. Then more. He marches in a straight
line, looking neither right nor left.

There was a long moment's silence in the audience. Then
Homeric laughter. The Good Soldier Schweik has not advanced a step. Why? He is walking on a treadmill that pulls
him back with every step. However he strives, whatever effort
he expends, the treadmill keeps him always in the same place.

A backdrop springs into line, turning into a large film
screen. An army building appears, a pub, a physician, a general, a German field marshal, even his landlady. Cutout car-
toon soldiers march alongside him and pass him by. So do all
the other characters. Also the signal lamps, railroad tracks,
gates at the crossing, and even the highway. The night sky
seems to move as well, against the hilly landscape. Finally, a
map of Budweis appears.

But even Budweis seems bound for somewhere else and
also passes him by. Only he, the truly good soldier, obedient
subject of the Kaiser, fails to advance.

From the moment the audience understood the meaning of the horrendous spoof of the soldier who never reaches the front, in spite of his good will, the buffoonery became serious.

Schweik's instinct of the *picaro* tells him that it is not his fault that he doesn't arrive in Budweis. He likes to march. He loves the army. He wants to obey. He uses every means, from persuasion to moodiness and stubbornness, in order to reach his destination. But there is strange and dangerous company which he encounters on his way. This, too, he has in common with the *picaro*. But his encounters are not with garrulous jailbirds or medieval highwaymen. He meets with lovable shady characters like Lieutenant Lukach, who is more of a pimp than an officer, with railway mercenaries, police of all grades, bellicose lawyers, heavy-sworded Austrian generals, spies and deserters, and even howling skulls hidden in *Pickelhaube* helmets.

At the end of the momentous march to Budweis, Schweik himself is suspected of being a deserter. He is pushed into an army train which rambles along the treadmill in the same way as he did—without ever getting anywhere.

After the declaration of peace at the end, Schweik is bound for home, disgusted that he was unable to do his duty for the Emperor. He is finally killed by an even more patriotic Hungarian patrol who is unaware that they are both on the same side.

At the end of the premiere performance, it seemed to the majority of the audience, as well as to the reviewers, that Piscator's *The Good Soldier Schweik* had beyond doubt made history in the theatre.

8) A NEW
VISION IN
THEATRICAL
EDUCATION

For many Americans, Epic theatre was as startling an innovation as Picasso's abstract painting. Both called for a new way of viewing, a new receptivity. Epic theatre had never been clearly defined except in literary magazines and reviews of foreign productions that were not easy to understand. The characteristic elements of Epic theatre—the short scenes, narrations, sequences of events never reaching a catharsis—proved most troublesome for playwrights and directors, not to mention the actor.

· · ·

The confusion that arose in the Dramatic Workshop had nothing to do with the quality of the students, among whom were some fine talents. They soon realized that we were moving in a new direction. They knew that they had to start from scratch.

The faculty of the Dramatic Workshop took a different position. They were all professionals, possessing a great deal of experience. In spite of their perceptive minds they were, at times, captives of old theories. How could we ask them to start from scratch; their experiences had been isolated ones, personal ventures in the theatre. One could distinguish a "blue period" or "rose period" of theatre in the acting, directing, and playwriting department. These periods, as valuable as they were, could never have created the kind of theatre to which we aspired. This situation with the faculty would have been a challenge if we had had more time to create our own tradition in which various methods could have gone along concurrently until all had reached a point of convergence in a full-scale production.

There is a theory if a melody of six tones is played and six new tones added to it, a third pattern establishes itself without losing the original melody. It gives the whole a new impetus—a new form quality—which takes over.

Piscator's plan for the school was to create a new totality of theatre. The very name of workshop implies such totality. Not an academy of theatre, not a department of a university, but a training ground in which each member would be an exponent of the whole. Then everything would easily fall in place—the experience and talent of the teachers, the freshness and curiosity of his students, Piscator's pioneering spirit, and the vigorous life of the America around us.

This totality of theatre was not a new idea for Piscator. In his short-lived studio in Berlin (in conjunction with his Nollendorfplatz theatre) just before Hitler's advent to power he had assembled some of the best young talents. For the first time he put his practical knowledge of the theatre into a theoretical framework from which a whole new acting style was born, called *objective acting*.

The Third Reich scattered these actors all over the world. Oscar Homolka, Alexander Granach and Peter Lorre went to London, then to America, then to Hollywood; Carola Neher to Moscow where she died. Lotte Lenya went to New York. Helene Weigel Brecht went to Copenhagen. She is now the head of the Berliner Ensemble.

Objective acting was probably the greatest gift Piscator could bring to his American students. The American theatre had never been sympathetic to the over-emphasized European style of acting. Objective acting was realistic in its foundation and therefore easier to accept.

There were other working aspects of the Berlin Studio which enriched the curriculum of the Dramatic Workshop:

The training and shaping of the total body of the Workshop, faculty and students—as one professional unit

The acting experiment: actor-dancer, actor-architect

The literary experiment: analysis, dramaturgy

The audience experiment: a people's theatre

The social experiment: the learning play (*Lehrstück*)

The political experiment: dialectical theatre, dramatized history, universal theatre.

Total Theatre needed universality of spirit. If one was willing to grant this to the Dramatic Workshop, even if only by way of temporary experiment, a conclusion followed, which at first sight was surprising. No more ideal background to establish understanding, insight and stimulation for this project could be found than the New School for Social Research itself.

There are admittedly two varieties of universal; the practical and the moral universe. The Dramatic Workshop could not hope to create either one alone; but in collaboration with the New School and its faculties it could be done.

. . .

The New School was not just another university. It had cultivated three outstanding institutions under its own roof.

The Graduate Faculty of Political and Social Science, set up in America to maintain and further the traditions of European culture and to contribute new elements to American life, had received immediate and enthusiastic acceptance from leading American intellectuals. The late Oliver Wendell Holmes, on retiring from the Supreme Court, accepted only one appointment in his last years—his membership on the Graduate Faculty Advisory Committee. On the Committee were also Charles C. Burlingham, former head of the New York Bar Association, and John Dewey, Professor Emeritus, Columbia University, among other luminaries. The first Dean of the Graduate Faculty was a world-famous economist, Dr. Emmanuel Lederer. Alvin Johnson himself was on the faculty; so were Horace Kallen, the philosopher; Max Wertheimer, the psychologist; Frieda Wunderlich, Hans Staudinger, Max Ascoli; lecturers, tutors, research scholars of the richest experience.

The University in Exile, established October 2, 1933, was created to provide refuge for ranking European scholars while the forces of darkness in Germany were preparing for war. It included an Institute of World Affairs and was granted an Absolute Charter for teaching and research in international affairs. The faculty included teachers and research workers from virtually every major nation in the western world. The single criterion applied was intellectual competence.

The Ecole Libre, youngest of the units at the New School for Social Research, represented the foremost free Franco-Belgian institute in the world. It was made up of distinguished scholars from French-speaking lands and was established in February 1942 shortly after the Nazi invaders closed the University of Brussels. Its faculty was a veritable Who's Who of Franco-Belgian culture including such men as Jacques Maritain, the distinguished philosopher, Paul van Zeeland, former Prime Minister of Belgium, the cinéaste, Benoit-Levy, who directed *La Maternelle*, and the actor Charles Boyer.

We, at the Dramatic Workshop, represented another development in the New School, a special activity in the arts. Although we were training people towards professional theatre, the goal was a theatre for life: to better life.

This totality of life and art is not a new vision but an ancient one. Twenty-four centuries ago Plato made it the basis of his ideal educational system.

Practically all great artists in their field: Michelangelo, Leonardo da Vinci, Dante, have struggled to acquire such total scope. Balzac favored law, Hugo—politics, Shakespeare—history.

Some perception of the relevance of this totality has filtered down to our world but not through the educators. Psychologists such as William James, John Dewey, Theodor Reik and Otto Rank; artists such as Tolstoy, Schiller; philosophers such as Diderot and Buber, have written masterful defenses for the union of art and science and the guidelines for a theory of art as a basis of education.

Although Stanislavsky had recognized the need of a wide education for the artist, it was Dalcroze who provided the first link between science and art. He encouraged the sense of rhythm and harmony inherent in music and man, and made it a key to the "relationship" which opens the door to truth.

But neither Plato's ideals nor Dalcroze's work have developed into a modern educational system. The majority of people see only a schizophrenic connection between art and science. The very principle of coherence in the universe; the knowledge that our life rhythm is nothing but a succession of units striving towards a totality, has never become the basis of teaching, but remains still a modern paradox.*

Out of these thoughts came another idea: why should the Workship not create such a modern educational system by making a much stronger link with the other departments of the New School? Since Epic Theatre declares itself to be total theatre it combines Art and Science, and requires total education.

Although endowed with a protean diversity of ability, Piscator could not carry such a project into reality at the New School without the help of the New School itself. The reasons were obvious.

Piscator would be dealing with people who had not experienced World War I, or the death struggle of a postwar republic, or the chaotic state brought about by the rise of Hitler.

True, many of our students had been born in and had experienced the Depression, and they had heard about America's part in World War I, but they had never sensed the tortured conflict of the artist under the stress of a totalitarian power like the Fascists. The burning of books, the smashing of human rights, the preparation for a new war, the destruction of the greatness of Europe.

The Dramatic Workshop could easily broaden its curriculum, embracing new forms of intellectual activity without endangering the specialized training. The courses in the other faculties would include philosophy, history, anthropology, law, psychology, and above all, sociology. This was, after all, the New School for Social Research.

Staffed with teachers of intellectual magnitude covering the social sciences, philosophy and the liberal arts, drawing from the European background as well as from American thought,

* Read, Herbert, *Education Through Art*, Pantheon Books, New York.

the New School had the most universal outlook to be found. If a solidarity between the scholars and the teachers of the Dramatic Workship could be created, education in the theatre would lose its identity as a narrow province of its own and could become universal education.

The experiment for the student would be that of total vision, which the "Swiss music master" Dalcroze had apprehended as the power to perceive. It would take the student out of the confines of the trained specialist and encourage him to participate in the overall advance of culture. For the teachers, it would change the basis of learning. Education in the theatre would be theatre as well as an education.

Prospective students would be interviewed by the department heads of the different institutions without consideration of race, creed, or political views. They would be chosen according to their maturity and also their formal education. They would be encouraged to formulate, document, and cross-index history; use it as a *persona-dramatica* of the collective thought of centuries, and liquidate the old drama as naught but a Daguerreotype.

A Studio Theatre would aid in this activity. The productive use of creative material is bound to lead to scientific discovery no less than it is bound to lead to a work of art. The two opposites would then come together in a performing union with reason and feeling merging into one, creating free activity and universal spirit, forming and formative in expression, objective and subjective, dramatic and epic—a new vision of theatre to drive us on. In that way, and only in that way, the Dramatic Workshop would become the link between education and theatre—a link Dr. Johnson had instinctively foreseen the first day we met.

The Studio Theatre would stress a repertory of important themes rather than important plays. These themes would have preference over classics and modern plays, even works of distinction. The New School would, in that way, be the first institution to become a sounding board for world events, openly on stage to assume responsibility not only to preserve and foster a universal culture but also to produce stimuli for the great themes of native American expression.

. . .

Our vision of education in the theatre was considered a great one by everyone we talked to. But theories concerned with understanding and insight look different in practice.

Reality, itself a total organic expression, provided the basis of the undoing of our plan. From practice we went down to mere theory again, back to the ideals of our earliest education —I suppose by the Muses and Apollo, as Plato had so beautifully argued. Nor did Dalcroze win in the wider aspect of preparation of activity. We were left alone on a bare field of abstraction which could have been converted into fruitful activity—but it was lost.

The explanation of this partial defeat was simple and it became clearer and clearer and most distinguishable as time went on. Was it practical to start with such an ideal vision at the moment when war news clouded every horizon? Was it practical to think of theatre as a moral institution when survival alone counted? Were we to add to and complicate the imaginary invalid's fanciful tragi-comedy and pretend to a paper virtue, in a dog-eat-dog world where theatre had to ally itself with exploitation and became undistinguishable from it?

No, theatre would have to be valid for the years just to come, as it was an adventure governed by economic and commercial considerations. It had to pattern itself as much on entertainment as on serious thought.

Above all, would it be wise to involve the young, who had to strive to make a living and therefore had to work sometimes on the lowest platform of imaginative life—would it be wise to involve them in a battle which has to be fought on the highest platform, that of fundamental truth and the law of growth, the laws of the universe?

The time had not yet come.

We felt that this vision would have to grow organically— perhaps grow out of the achievements of the Dramatic Workshop itself, become alive through the personalities who in turn we would have exposed (besides their training) to a mental activity that could be regarded as coherent, intelligent, systematic, and sound. Perhaps, it was for these, these coming artists, to unify the opposites, to integrate consciousness in art, dissipate the lack of communication, and destroy the fundamental inhibitions of our society, which today affected the realization of our idea.

I now know, in retrospect, that this vision was too formidable; but it was prompted by a great wish to use the theatre in the service of life; use it not as a conqueror or despoiler, but as an inquirer, as it will be used in the future—to understand man and his universe.

9) DRAMATIC WORKSHOP

Actors: Marlon Brando, Anthony Franciosa, Harry Bela-
fonte, Tony Curtis, Rod Steiger, Nehemiah Persoff, Walter
Matthau, Eli Wallach, Martin Brooks, Woodrow Parfrey,
Mike Conrad, Gerald Price, John McLiam, Harry Guardino,
Robert Carricart, Ben Gazzara, Gene Saks, Arthur Storch,
Steve Gravers, Robert Osterloh, Walter Mullen, Gerald
Prosk, Scott Hale, Dan Matthews. Actresses: Judith Malina,
Elaine Stritch, Shelley Winters, Virginia Baker, Bea Arthur,
Madeline Sherwood, Dorothy Dill, Carol Gustafson, Avra
Petrides, Toni Hollingsworth, Betty Miller, Sylvia Miles,
Vinette Carroll, Maia Abelea, Sylvia Myers, Eva Stern,
Lillian Storch. Playwrights: Tennessee Williams, Frank

Gabrielson, Dan James, Elaine Dundee, Oliver Pitcher, Philip Yordan, Mae Cooper, Ted Pollack, Michael Gazzo. Directors: Irving Stiber, Jean Dow, Anna Berger, Jack Garfein, Marvin Silbersher, Louis Criss, Eugene Van Grona, Ted Post. Designers: Robert Ramsey. Producers: Chandler Cowles, David Ross, Claude Traverse. Companies: Dramatic Workshop Theatre, Sothold Playhouse, Deal Conservatory Theatre, Center Stage '48, Norwich Summer Theatre, Rockaway Summer Theatre, Civic Light Opera Guild, The New York Repertory Group, Inc., Interplayers, On-Stage, Off-Broadway, Inc., We Present, The People's Drama, Studio 7, Dramatic Workshop Players.

It is, of course, impossible for any school to claim directly or indirectly the credit for such a glorious list of names.

But names are people.

These people came to us of their own volition and worked with us at their own risk. They searched with us and they pursued the elusive new, the thing that was not formulated but grew each day. It grew at times beyond what they could recognize, although they were living through it.

What makes one actor different from any other actor? What makes an Olivier, a Laughton, a Spencer Tracy, a Burton or an O'Toole? What makes for the anonymous thousands, who struggle year after year for one role, then another, without ever reaching distinction?

The answer is almost too obvious to be true.

The same difference that makes for a great man in the theatre makes for a great man in life.

"I was just thinking."

"About what?"

"I was thinking about how a great man is put together."

"How is he put together?"

"How? Well, sensibility—extreme mobility in certain

threads of the network—that is, the dominant attribute of mediocre people."

"Doctor, what a terrible thing to say."

The above comes out of the writings of Diderot, the eighteenth-century moralist and encyclopedist, well known for his serious work on the theatre, but also for his paradoxes.

Simone de Beauvoir in her book, *The Mandarins*, describes a priceless scene: two great writers meet in the streets of Paris. They don't take time to greet each other but they eagerly ask, "How is your book?"

I overheard a young actor talking to his partner during rehearsals. "Wasn't I magnificent? Of course, my analysis this morning was excellent."

There is a simple story of a famous actor sitting in a commuter's train and being stared at by a little man opposite him. Finally, amused at the stare of the stranger, he asks: "Do you want me to give you an autograph?" "No," says the little man. "But if you can spare the flower from your buttonhole . . ." The actor pulls the flower from his buttonhole and hands it to the little man; it has lost its luster.

Does celebrity look like that?

I have seen in Ypres an arch of triumph, with thousands of names inscribed on it. Names of American and Canadian soldiers. They seemed infinitesimally small, yet they were famous. The names of the glorious dead of Ypres. They were to remain famous for generations to come, but they had been forgotten by the time the Second World War came around.

These were uncomfortable thoughts and even as they vanished—as if a thought could ever vanish!—and we saw nothing but that wonderful new world of America opening up before us, spelling success with a capital S, we were weary of the future of all that had happened, and wearier of what was going to come.

The Dramatic Workshop had opened its doors. Twenty students had been registered. What more could we expect? I remember most of them, but there were two who have become part of my life. Yet, I know that there was also a time when twelve hundred students registered in a single year. One thousand two hundred students, who had to be kept occupied in two theatres running every day. A $500,000 budget was hardly enough to take care of them.

But on that January day in 1940, twenty keen young people, just as keen and hopeful as we were, had come to take the lead in the inauguration of the Dramatic Workshop.

It was more than an inauguration, it was a coming into existence, not of a contemporary possibility, but of the perennial idea of the theatre as human life and action.

"Remember Schweik?" I mentioned casually that evening to Piscator.

"Why?" he responded.

"He said man is indestructible."

The first thing in the theatre to make sure of is to be indestructible. This was something we kept on remembering specifically during the fabulous years of expansion.

On the surface it may appear that the Dramatic Workshop was no different from any other theatre school, but this was not so. It was quite different.

The point has often been overlooked that the Dramatic Workshop did not start as a coherent whole of ideas, and methods system, of theatre, some kind of final concept of the Piscator method or something that sprang from his head ready-made. On the contrary, there was endless working and reworking of ideas, experimenting and experimenting again, difficult problems, initial failures, improvements of techniques, of a more flexible heart; a rejecting and accepting, formulating and improving and then still making further amendments to these improvements—there were also many afterthoughts, of which I am going to speak later.

I shall try to give an image of the Workshop from some central idea or ideas underlying its activities, without consideration of chronology, but an image which will enable us, I hope, to encompass the objective values of this institution over a span of years.

The first concept of the Dramatic Workshop, which was at once the motivation for its existence and the form of its realization, lay in its duality, described later in a phrase that became popular: *A school that is a theatre.*

Our next concern was to stimulate an avant-garde movement from which playwrights, directors, designers, and actors would emerge.

The third aim was to start a tradition, the creation of a possible ensemble, which would eventually lead to a repertory theatre.

These were basic ideas, general ideas, not too different from what had been expressed by other theatrical schools in New York or other cities. But there was something different, which soon manifested itself in imponderables. Call it atmosphere or mood—a purpose, a passion or suffering, a kind of *actus secondus* above all aims, which asserted itself beyond the Workshop's substantive existence. To pin it down (though who can pin down essences?) one could say it had to do with the longing for a meaningful theatre.

As a school, the Dramatic Workshop provided training for the actor, director, playwright, designer, and technician of the theatre, and later added classes and seminars on film, television, and radio. It offered intensive studies under the leadership of outstanding men and women. There were daytime and evening classes, beginning and advanced; seminars, laboratories; an abundance of courses, slowly and organically created out of the need of the students and the expansion of the institution.

Its learning objectives detailed in the catalogue looked like this:

> *To educate students to make a living in the theatre of today.*
> *To lift the student's vision to the full possibilities of the living theatre, with its social and cultural potentialities.*
> *To stimulate the development of the repertory theatre as a non-commercial institution of artistic expression with the same position in our society that the symphony or the art museum enjoys.*

The professional emphasis was on "learning by doing," made possible by the intensive production program.

Piscator was a theatre man and a theatre man knows that the human being is a very complicated contraption, and that there is no good or bad, but good and bad, and that good comes out of bad and the other way around. And students are the more demanding the younger they are. They want to be given everything on a silver platter. Could the Dramatic Workshop afford a silver platter?

How is a great actor put together? This was the question.

What is the stuff of which he is made? What tricks, what chicanery, what craftiness were his? What kind of influence had made him rise, made him more daring and stronger than others, made him the superb freak—or what made him the open-hearted, above-board, untutored, unaffected, unassuming darling of the nation? What made his performance unique for an audience that had seen everything?

What were the energies that set in motion his first meaningful gesture, that made him utter the precise word, the right word for the right situation, for the right agent, the right producer? How did he learn to belong?

Then there were other students, asking other questions.

How is great theatre put together?

Can it be brought into being, or is it a pipe-dream?

What are the incomprehensible moral urges in the theatre, which will never die?

Why have people been hungry for it with the hunger of intelligence?

What kinds of influence have helped to renew the theatre again and again and make it correspond to the radical transformation of mentality of our time?

What is the basis of it all? Art or life?

"Not art," said Piscator. "Life. From its very beginning here at the Workshop, let it be life. The Here and the Now. Art is man's ambition to create beyond reality. What is needed now is reality. Reality—the sphinx of all sphinxes. The riddle of all riddles. But every new beginning—is it not a riddle?"

The nightmare of Europe had left us with a desire for stability. It made Piscator particularly aware of the practical needs of the School. No student should ever leave the Workshop without being equipped in one way or another to make a living in the theatre. If he had majored in a particular field, he should be able to function as well in another field. He should be competent to work as a stage manager or a lighting assistant or a speech teacher or something else in the theatre. Without planning, simply by completing the curriculum, the student would acquire one of the rarest things of all in the theatre—a total education in its crafts and skills.

To this end—considering that the theatre is more than a "long patience"—the student, before receiving permission to matriculate, would have to sign up for a testing period. This would allow us, the student as well as the faculty, to know each other. The groundwork would start with an invitation to the student to take perspective of his profession.

Day after day the incoming student was encouraged to visit

the Workshop as a critic. Not actively engaged in any studies, he was allowed to observe courses in playwriting, directing, technology, scenic design, acting, dancing, speech, voice, etc. —After several weeks of this silent apprenticeship—when the first cockiness had rubbed off and the visitor was no longer sure that he could do so much better than any other actively engaged student—the time had come for another step; he was allowed to engage himself in some practical activity.

Now that he had a general perspective and a more objective outlook, the student was to familiarize himself with the *common substance* of theatre. He became an apprentice to the different technical departments, gained some elementary knowledge of handling properties, lights, costumes and even scenery. He learned how to prepare a stage for performance, and to work as well behind the scenes; to turn a turntable by hand if necessary. He knew how to pull a curtain as well as he knew what a curtain-call is. The thrilling and precise knowledge of a whole performance became his.

The next step led to the varied substance of theatre. The student was permitted to attend formal classwork in his specialized field of action.

There is, of course, nothing so inadequate as the classroom system of teaching. Nevertheless, the accepted conventions demand that the theatrical skills be taught by separate specialists in seperate classrooms.

There were classes for speech dealing with articulation, intonation, the analysis of standard speech required by the American theatre, and the correction of regional deviations. And, of course, the phonetic system for those who were ambitious.

Speech courses were elementary and advanced, as was voice work. The development of the quality, range and volume of the voice, the establishment of individual pitch, the improvement of breath control were basic demands. America has a habit of neglecting speech, and the voice problems of the students were sometimes staggering. They were so serious that we had a teacher-physician attached to the school to treat individual cases.

Then came dance and stage movement, fundamentals of classic technique and modern dance, corrective exercises, group work and improvisation—improvement of body control leading to mind control.

Then came acting, elementary and advanced. Of course, elementary acting dealt with the simplest exercises. Nothing is as difficult for the actor to acquire as the sense of real life. Like a child, he has to learn to talk, walk and listen, behave like a normal human being, simply, naturally, organically correct and without constraint. The basic problem remained always the same—to teach the actor how to get rid of the theatre; and he could only get rid of the theatre if he forgot about being an actor.

The advanced acting work dealt with the actor's more special abilities and qualities and gifts, such as imagination, concentration, the feeling for truth; and above all with the art of controlling all these elements and carrying out whatever objective he set for himself.

Realizing that he is his own instrument, the actor has to go through a process of initiation. The human machine is not easily called to obedience. One cannot relax on command, nor can we easily set about play as children do; but it is precisely this kind of innocent play, with its exploration of feelings and imagination, that starts the small physical actions, small physical truths and the moments of belief. Lord Dunsany says about art "that it goes far deeper than study; it passes beyond reasoning and, lighting up the chambers of the imagination, quickens the body of thought and proves all things in action." Let us replace the word art with play, and we shall have exactly the kind of experience that stimulates and directs nature and allows the subconscious creative work to pull through. This free improvisation of play is the beginning of the creative interaction of thought and feeling.

The counterpoint to this attitude of play is discipline, which the actor must acquire. Whoever has watched a child playing can not help but become aware of the complete merging of playfulness with seriousness. This seriousness is the beginning of professionalism. This is the moment when the subconscious work of nature ends and conscious work asserts itself in action; that is, logically, consistently, and in accordance with the laws of nature.

We are back to Plato; the three-fold division of the soul. Plato defined three approaches to life; the sensuous and acquisitive; the spiritual faculty which would act even at the expense of the personal existence; and the rational faculty, the dominating law.

While the Dramatic Workshop's aim was to prepare in two years its graduates to compete with professional life of the theatre, it also held out the ideal of a wider field of theatre activity and emphasized community theatre, university theatre and other forms of theatre around the country.

. . .

Interrelation of the different departments became the keynote of the Dramatic Workshop. It was not only an exchange of knowledge and techniques, but it was a sharing of the longing for the world of the marvelous in the theatre: the pleasure of learning, and growing together.

This poignant fabric of dreams, this pseudo-Dionysian network, found its expression in the "March of Drama."

. . .

The March of Drama was a survey of drama as a comprehensive art inalienable from civilization. It was summarized in a lecture series starting with the classical masters, the drama of East and West throughout the ages to the development of theatre in the western world; the European and American galaxies. These lectures were documented by John Gassner's book, *Masters of Drama*, and were required for all students.

Piscator amplified these lectures by John Gassner, illustrating them with staged readings by advanced students and invited guest artists. These weekly streamlined presentations of representative plays of every prominent period and style were not only a center of learning for our own students, but became enormously desirable for outside students and even the general public.

The simple lecture course of the March of Drama became in this way a *living history of the theatre*, offering weekly in chronological order masterpieces seldom, if ever, seen, in a contemporary approach to production.

This made the course not only a necessary supplement to the study of drama for our own students, but a valuable innovation for theatre students of other schools and colleges, as well as an instrument of learning for English teachers of high school and college level. I should like to think that even for our audience the March of Drama proved itself an enormously interesting and amusing way of seeing the theatre as a potent organ for the expression of human experience and thought. These different masters of the drama, were they not in a sense masters of life?

John Gassner must have thought of that when he organized his lectures. He had not only the cardinal task of teaching history of the theatre in chronological order. Each March of Drama was a composite portrait of each period; the synthesis of thought became a synthesis of the theatre. If the March of Drama dealt with Sophocles and the development of dramatic technique through a presentation of *Antigone*, it was not just the basic conflict of *Antigone*, the rival claims of the state and their individual conscience. It was the beginning of modern social drama as well. *Antigone* is still an excellent lesson to the modern dramatist. Antigone, instead of quailing before the new ruler of the city, defies him and so takes herself out of her paper existence of a theatre convention and becomes significant for our day.

This approach opened to the students new vistas, not only of the theatre, but of its human sources and its origins at the crossroads of history. Staging these plays, even in an improvised way, kindled the imagination of everyone taking part in the March of Drama. Gassner's course was not merely a survey of plays by a brilliant scholar, but a continuing demonstration that the destiny of the theatre is linked with the political and cultural history of every period.

If after Sophocles, Euripides continued in the making of democracy and brought the audience a new kind of "philosophical enlightenment," together with the deepening of psychological values and humanitarian desires. *The Trojan Women* sounded a warning of the military evils of aggression and imperialism.

Political satire had its say, too. Another pacifist theme, this time scintillating and filled with laughter, enhanced the variety and resourcefulness of the actors as well. Aristophanes' *The Wasps* and *Lysistrata* were in the early programs of the Dramatic Workshop.

The medieval drama was presented, and brought the students nearer to the idea of communion with the audience; also, the role of morality first bound to the church and then coming together in wordliness, with the Tudor propaganda plays.

Early Commedia dell' Arte, which originated in marketplaces teeming with humanity, were represented on the Workshop stage by scenes from *Mandragola*. Lope de Vega, and Calderon followed. With *Sheep Well*, we staged the first

communal drama of the Spanish theatre. Marlowe was represented by scenes from *Dr. Faustus*, and, Shakespeare with
Richard II and *King Lear*.

Corneille and Racine were not an easy experience for the
American student, nor was Molière's "humor of the mind"
easily understood by those never before exposed to French
drama.

On the other hand the gallant fools, scandalmongers and
flirtatious women of Congreve and the Restoration comedy,
parading in *The Way of the World* found great acclaim.

German drama and its prompting followed; Lessing and
the religion of reason, and Goethe's Faustian romanticism.

The second section of the *March of Drama* started with
Ibsen's *Peer Gynt*; then came Strindberg and the naturalists;
Hauptmann, the German exemplar of naturalism, with *The
Weavers* and *The Rats*.

Neoromanticism, Maeterlinck and Rostand, continued
the French drama of the twentieth century. Pirandello's *Six
Characters* and *Tonight We Improvise* provided provocative
fare. The Russian drama was not missing. *The Inspector
General* was a delightful addition to an already rich program.
From Gogol to Tolstoy, to Chekhov to Gorky, every week
brought a new aspect of Russian realism.

Then came Expressionism with Kaiser, Toller, Capek—the
German battlefield of dramatic distortion and stylization and
the rise of Epic theatre with Brecht and adaptations by Piscator.

That wasn't all. There was a week of Irish theatre; Synge to
O'Casey, scenes from their representative plays, then Bernard
Shaw.

The twentieth century English theatre was exemplified by
Galsworthy, Eliot, Barker, Barrie, Masefield, with an effective
reading of *Journey's End* to follow.

Finally, O'Neill and the awakening of the American theatre: Anderson, Sidney Howard, Rice, Paul Green, Behrman, Hellman, Odets—American theatre in our time.

For the American March of Drama, guest speakers were invited— a forum created; speakers such as Harold Clurman, Aline Bernstein, Orson Welles, Maxwell Anderson, Sam Jaffe, George Kaufman and many others. By the end of the year, the March of Drama had become a glowing production and discussion forum. It was "not a lesson anymore but a filter," to paraphrase John Gassner.

Gassner treated the March of Drama much in the same way as Alexander treated his troops. After having sent them out in search of conquest, Alexander brought them together again in a great wedge to drive home his victory. This was, of course, history; but, if a lesson existed, it was the lesson of generalship.

A fever of excitement had taken hold of the school—rehearsals became more and more frequent and more and more impetuous. No exorcism of any kind could relieve the possessed now.

Even plays of stark realism became the object of tender theatrical devotion. It was the kind of fascination which answered the audience's question "Why?" with "Why not?" and the next, "Where does this play lead to?" with "We'll show you."

Two years after its opening, the Dramatic Workshop could pride itself in announcing a Drama Festival: three full-length plays which had emerged from the March of Drama: *Hannele's Way to Heaven* by Gerhardt Hauptmann; *Dr. Sganarelle* by Milton Levene; and Shakespeare's *Twelfth Night*.

George Freedley, the eminent critic, honored us with three glowing reviews in *The Stage Today*. What made these reviews so impressive was not the fact that they heightened the image of the Dramatic Workshop, but that George Freedley, by virtue of theatrical intuition showed himself a prophet.

He was the first critic to single out Marlon Brando as an actor:

> Easily the best acting of the evening was contributed by
> Marlon Brando, a personable young man and a fine actor,
> as the school teacher, and as the angel in the dream
> sequence. He has authority, smoothness, careful diction and
> an easy command of the stage to commend him.

The second play during the festival was a special triumph. One could call it an accident of chance. Milton Levene, a playwright-student, had the rather shocking idea to any classicist of combining two of Molière's plays, *The Doctor In Spite of Himself,* and *The Imaginary Invalid* into one. This was all the more incredible as the first one was written by Molière at the beginning of his career—a broad farce, while the second, touched upon tragedy, was written near the end of his life.

This "new Molière" was called *Dr. Sganarelle.* It was delightful, and for the audience, which had not been exposed to comedy of manners, the play had a touch of madness which tickled.

Under John Gassner's loving care, another reading from the March of Drama, culminated in another full-stage production: Shakespeare's *Twelfth Night.*

"Foolery, Sir, does walk about the orb like the sun: it shines everywhere." Nothing could be more true. Whoever entered the New School during these months could see Sir Toby Belch riding up and down the elevator searching for Sir Andrew Aguecheek to rehearse with him. The "triste" Malvolio prompted himself aloud in the silence of the library. Feste and Maria made most unwelcome entrances and exits through the Graduate Faculty rooms.

We laughed it off together with the audience.

. . .

The critics raved.

George Freedley wrote he had not seen any staging more imaginative then Chouteau Dyer's since the Second Art Theatre's performance in Moscow a decade or so before. He referred once more to *Hannele* and *Dr. Sganarelle* and recommended the Dramatic Workshop as "a school that was really fulfilling its function and deserving public support."

He congratulated the students, especially Marlon Brando, who this time handled only a bit part: Sebastian. "It would be interesting to see what he might do one day with Feste or Orsino."

Since then Brando has seen himself in the mirror. Who was Marlon Brando? The answer may have been simple for anyone else. It was not for Marlon. He was not a seer.

Brando reasoned himself out of his natural tensions and timidity. He became "the great invalid" himself, as much as "the great lover" and even more flattering, "the great accursed one"! For he had reached the unknown—himself.

We were happy for him then. It all seemed such a marvelous beginning.

Every department had a chairman or several chairmen. Among the faculty were personalities known for their courage and boldness in experimentation.

Names denote not only identity but qualities. I shall try here to cover the qualities and values of some of these outstanding people, without going into a personal biography.

I recall first of all New York's finest critic, Brooks Atkinson. Atkinson was drama critic for *The New York Times* and had earned a wide reputation among people in theatre for his enlightening criticism. Piscator had convinced him that it is most important for students to understand the task and the responsibility of the critic and reviewer.

The next personality of significance to the School, was John Gassner.

He became associated with us at the time he was named head of the Theatre Guild's Playwriting Department. He had dramatized some novels: Herman Melville's *Moby Dick*, under the title *The White Whale*, which received an award; and Emil Ludwig's novel *Versailles*, which was produced for the Theatre Guild in 1931 under the name of *Peace Palace*. He made another adaptation of a novel, Stefan Zweig's *Jeremiah*, which was also produced by the Theatre Guild in 1938.

But he had already published several books: The anthologies, *Twenty Best Plays of Modern American Theatre* and *A Treasury of Theatre*, and his own books, *Producing the Play* and *Masters of Drama*, had just come out. This was the foundation which later brought him wide and well-deserved fame as a scholar of international reputation, a distinguished drama critic, theatre historian and anthologist, who has developed some of our leading dramatists of the present day. Some of these leading dramatists John met first at the Dramatic Workshop. It is his great merit to have realized the poetry and power of Tennessee Williams' plays, in spite of the failure of *The Battle of the Angels* which the Theatre Guild had tried out in Boston. *The Battle of the Angels* later became the successful *Orpheus Descending*.

John was, and still is, a distinguished guardian of the theatre who believes in the great tradition; but he is also a rebel, ambitious for change and with an unfailing vision for recognizing the new.

Outside of his achievements, John had a further attraction of a specific kind: his wife, Mollie Gassner. Mollie's simultaneous representation of John's work and of himself remains an uncontested triumph. She succeeded in advancing her husband's reputation without ever boring or antagonizing anyone.

I do not remember if Mordecai Gorelik came to us in the first year of the Dramatic Workshop, but in memory he has always been there—he simply belonged. An early friendship with Brecht had inspired him to believe in the "renewal" of the theatre. He was in Berlin when the Piscatorbuehne opened, and became an early advocate of Epic Theatre. When we met him, he was gathering his experiences abroad for a book, which since has become a "must" for theatre students: New Theatres for Old.

Barrett Clark was a prince of literature, a democratic prince with a sharp eye and some Broadway argot, but with a worldwide vision of theatre. An actor, a director, editor of America's Lost Plays, writer of volumes on the American and European drama, he became invaluable to the students.

Theresa Helburn, beautiful and vital, co-director of the Theatre Guild, returned through the Workshop to her first love, playwriting. Together with John Gassner she conducted Play Analysis, a seminar in which one could witness the progress of works of students such as Arthur Miller, Tennessee Williams, Arthur Pollack, Philip Yordan, Robert Anderson, and others.

Representing opera and the musical stage were Erich Leinsdorf, who had been assistant to Toscanini and Bruno Walter, and had conducted the NBC Symphony Orchestra and the Philadelphia Orchestra. There was also Jascha Horenstein, well-known guest conductor of leading orchestras in Europe.

Felix Brentano, associated in the past with Max Reinhardt, came to us in the capacity of stage director, and proved to be a notable influence on the faculty.

Ladislas Czettel, came from the Metropolitan Opera to us; he was a wonderful theatrical personality who brought perhaps one of the rarest of all things to the Workshop: exquisite taste.

One of the most extraordinary teachers was Ernst Ferrand, whose appreciation of music explored the ordinarily hidden world of sound for the actor; the dormant and vibrant notion of rhythm. Ferrand had been professor at the Conservatory of Music in Budapest, stage director for the Classic Festival of the *Antique Greek Theatre* in Sicily and a close associate of Dalcroze.

Ferrand was one of the mentors of my youth. With the change of politics in Germany, he decided on my invitation to leave Hellerau where the Dalcroze school was located and came to Laxemburg, near Vienna, former country estate of Emperor Franz Joseph.

Paul Zucker, another foreign scholar of renown, was in charge of History and Sociology of the Theatre. He was also the author of many books, and he was formerly a practicing architect and professor at the University of Berlin and the Institute of Technology. Zucker was a glowing admirer of Walter Gropius and never stopped talking in his heavy German accent, lightened by the quickness of his intelligence, about the Bauhaus experiments in Total Theatre.

Kurt Pinthus, a scholar and advisor of Max Reinhardt, a drama and film critic, had emigrated to America with his impressive theatrical library. This alone insured him a post at Columbia University and we saw him only from time to time, as a guest lecturer. Pinthus had a strange twist in his appreciation of Piscator. If someone praised Piscator's theatre, Pinthus violently criticized Piscator as a man. If someone spoke up for Piscator, the man, Pinthus attacked his theatre.

A Latin accent was brought into the school by an Italian scholar, Paolo Milano, Ph.D. from the University of Rome, and former stage director of the Teatro de Villa Ferrari. He became an associate of John Gassner and delighted the students with excerpts from his book, *The Stanislavski Method and the Myth of the Italian Actor.*

The general survey of the history of the drama had other lecturers of importance such as Barnard Hewitt, a Ph.D. from Cornell University, assistant professor at Brooklyn College, associate editor of the *Quarterly Journal of Speech*, and author of *Art and Craft of Play Production* and of several one-act plays and adaptations; also Thomas G. Ratcliffe, Jr., formerly a Harvard student and member of England's Old Vic Company, assistant play editor to Metro-Goldwyn-Mayer and Columbia Pictures, who directed plays as passionately as he played tennis.

. . .

According to British authorities, acting had been falling between "two schools" since the turn of the century: the rhetorically conventional, "a technique outworn and discarded," and the naturalistic, "an attempt to do without technique."

This did not dictate Acting classes.

There was a definite air of relaxation, for example, about those that had studied with Raiken Ben-Ari, who had reinforced his memories of the Stanislavsky system by using elements of *Commedia Dell'Arte*. Ben-Ari was a former member of the Moscow Habima Theatre, He had worked with Vakhtangov, Stanislavsky, Meyerhold and Reinhardt. Ben-Ari served as one of the directors of ARTEF, and he was Director and founder of the first American Hebrew Theatre, Paragod. He was also the author of *Habima* which was awarded first prize as the best book of the year (1941) on theatre.

There was Dr. Illya Motileff, also associated with Stanislavsky, who was also a playwright and taught his students how, as actors, they could serve the author's idea, to make it clear and intelligible in form and content.

Margaret Wyler, an exciting Viennese actress, had played over two hundred roles in leading theatres in Europe. She brought to the students a challenge which cannot be overestimated, the métier. Every actor, as in repertory, should be able to play any role. She knew style and styles and inspired her students.

There were also personalities who had never taught before and with whom we gambled successfully. One was Herbert Berghof, a Viennese actor, who was trying to overcome the language barrier. Berghof brought a personal quality to his teaching—a tight relationship to his students, a kind of umbilical cord which manifested itself sometimes as much in hate as in love, but which he used well as a director.

With Stella Adler, something entered the Dramatic Workshop which is rare in the theatre any day: theatricality. In fact, she was Theatre—dazzling, beautiful, erratic, hopelessly involved in every zigzag of theatre but with an unfailing sense of reality and the skill to please friends, admirers, and students alike; a mixture of wit and sentiment, gaiety and melancholy, realism and fantasy, delicacy and hardness. To Stella, play-acting was hereditary, a natural outlet in her youth and in later years a symbolic rite.

I know that the play instinct resists all analysis, all logical interpretation. It cannot be defined nor can it be denied. It is the eternal manifestation of the play instinct. It is curious that Stella, in spite of her play instinct, is so little aware of her talent that she holds on tightly to Stanislavsky's Naturalism. This reminds me in a way of Isadora Duncan, who believed that the Grecian world was a natural world. The highly sophistcated culture of the ancient Greeks was as removed from nature as the theatricality of Stella is removed from the Moscow Art Theatre.

Among the remarkable young personalities who had joined the Workshop at that time first as a student, then becoming one of the directing staff, was Chouteau Dyer. She came from St. Louis and was a graduate of Bryn Mawr and the Royal Academy of Dramatic Art in London. She had appeared in some Broadway productions and had been associated with the Henry Street Settlement House as a director. Chouteau was indefatigable, forging ahead, even against inevitable odds—even against herself. I still think of her endeavors as something as brave and mad as a solo transatlantic flight of the 'twenties.

· · ·

We knew that there were also actors who, even after attaining a high degree of professionalism, often spent many months without an opportunity to set foot on a stage. To satisfy their need for constant exercise, theoretical and practical, the Dramatic Workshop offered a special curriculum for these more advanced theatre artists, the Rehearsal Group.

This so-called Rehearsal Group was also to take specially designed courses in scene acting, coaching, interpretation, directing, scenic design and costume, and the history and philosophy of the theatre, plus a seminar in dramaturgy.

To be a professional is often defined merely as the possession of an Equity card. However precious this possession, the card does not turn the student into a professional. Amateur performances, off-Broadway productions, and college performances are sometimes of a higher professional quality than performances on Broadway.

The word "amateur" was respected in other days. It comes from amare—to love. Those who loved the theatre were honored with the word "amateur." Today it is the opposite—we deny its true definition.

Love for the theatre is shown by the great enjoyment which one has in it. Most professionals have forgotten that the theatre is not only a means to make a living, but also a means to enjoy life in free creativity.

· · ·

It was only a few months after Dr. Johnson had given the green light for the opening of the Dramatic Workshop that

Piscator offered two new departments to the students: a Play-writing Laboratory and Theatre Research.

The Laboratory grew out of the Playwright Seminar. It was the experimental ground for actual work projects. Here the students analyzed, prepared, and staged short dramatic sketches, scenes of different styles and periods. The other students came and criticized in a constructive way. Scenes were rewritten and restaged so as to improve the play.

With this collective activity the old triangle unit of Meyerhold was broken; the director was no longer sole head of the undertaking, but playwright, director, and actor together assumed responsibility for the performance.

Did this put the playwright at a disadvantage? No. Through the Laboratory the playwright found everything he needed: a real stage instead of the mysterious platform of his imagination; daring collaborators; trained actors, and even an improvised audience. If he were any playwright at all, he discovered a great deal about himself and his writing, especially after having gone through the mill of criticism. He even had a second chance. He could bring his play back rewritten and in better shape.

Outside of the School activities was a play-reading bureau, the link between the Laboratory and the outside world. If an outstanding script were discovered, then professional critics and commercial producers were invited for an official showing. This was a procedure later adopted by the Actors Studio.

It also happened that new writers, not enrolled in the school, sent in scripts for reading and criticism. If a script were exceptional, then the author was invited to become a member of the Laboratory, where his play would be prepared for production with the group's assistance.

Theatre Research became the center for the whole Dramatic Workshop. Here, all students could come together, exchange opinions, meet with Piscator and other members of the faculty, bring their problems up in open discussions, ask questions and, most of the time, find answers.

• • •

What had the Dramatic Workshop achieved in its first year?

Piscator reported to the governing body at the end of the first year his belief in the growing potential of the Workshop. It was significant that the largest number of students were in the playwriting classes—for in the search for a new theatre one would have to start with the playwrights.

10) DEFINING
AVANT-GARDE
THEATRE

It has been suggested that there is no true avant-garde in the theatre, as theatre is basically traditional. It can renew itself but not create itself anew.

The doubt comes from the ambiguousness of the term itself.

Avant-garde is a revolt and a liberation. It is a movement and not an isolated experience. The term is applied often to the first works of talented painters, poets, and writers, while in truth it should be applied only to the work of the mature artist, who has found a new way to express himself.

In the theatre we refer to it mostly—and erroneously—as experimental theatre.

Avant-garde is the synthesis of many experiments, sometimes even of several generations. Preoccupied with meaning of life, and not only with the observance of human law, it restores true meaning to the word "religion."

On the other hand, avant-garde is often declared a manifestation of poseurs, charlatans, hypocrites, shockers, and the like. Yet for all its battles, real or sham, the avant-garde is never a result; it goes back to the roots, the roots of a culture, a country, or a generation.

Avant-garde doesn't live by interpretation. It is essentially creative; it communicates a new way of thinking, and therefore it demands a new way of doing. Picasso did not design his ballets for Diaghilev. He created his own *Parade*. Cocteau did not interpret the house of Atreus in *The Infernal Machine*, he invented Greece anew.

Therefore, we could say that every avant-garde is an invasion into society, a spearhead; in a literal sense it is backed up by many formal forces and machinery which have been refined by years of experimentation. The experimenters remain aside and apart from the spearhead body. They are part of the revolt, not of the liberation.

That may be the reason—considering the overwhelming urge to conformity—that the avant-garde had never entered the arts in America except in the painting of the most recent years. The theatre remained content with experiment.

An experiment confirms or disproves something. It demonstrates some known truth; it conducts some tests which range from fashion to embellishment, from research to speculation. Experimentation always communicates an intimate experience, a personal formula, never the secret of an era.

Avant-garde movements such as Europe had seen were formal processionals in the arts. They flourished and developed towards utmost expression, even if it took an effort of years.

The First World War had proved a fabulous catalyst for

new art forms and social expression. It produced a ferment and arrived at an outburst of avant-garde movements which extended to all the arts. It enrolled the most daring experiments and innovators and produced the most startling contradictions—pursuit of newness, desire to shock, eccentric behavior, scandal and charlantanism, as well as courageous attempts to plough one's way through the thick haze of decaying values and to inaugurate, on a higher level of sincerity, discipline and organization, a self-sufficient reality.

It has been said that the avant-garde of all countries and all nationalities is essentially French. All movements, great or small, originated in Paris. Like a central fire, sending sparks to the rest of the world, which come to burn in different forms and character, France seemed to be the home of imaginative daring before any other country.

I have no quarrel with this statement, except for the fact that the twentieth century has shown my generation three totally different expressions of avant-garde, which have modified or changed the direction of the theatre.

Germany's avant-garde, Expressionism, interests us mostly in its second phase: the post-war movement of World War I—its social revolt.

France's Surrealism inherited from the Dadaists a certain scorn of intellectualization and turned, in its rebellion against Realism, to the abstract.

Constructivism, Russia's rebellion in the arts and of the theatre, was openly political.

. . .

German Expressionism had two faces: one, turned backwards to Romanticism; the other, looking forward bravely towards a new world and what was significant in it. The horrors of war were not likely to be forgotten, and the seething spirit of the time demanded more and greater understanding of the problems which embattled the twentieth century than had been experienced in the dream plays of Strindberg. Theatre needed a broader arena than the four-walled interior with velvet trappings and the conventions of the Romantic stages. It needed new playwrights to question what was happening to society.

The post-war German drama counted such important talents as Georg Kaiser, Franz Werfel, the Czech Capek brothers and Ernst Toller. Georg Kaiser's *Gas* trilogy is the symbolic history of modern industrialism rushing headlong into destruction. *From Morn to Midnight* tries to capture the futility of life seen from the cage of an embezzling bank clerk.

Franz Werfel, poet and novelist, wrote Expressionistic and non-Expressionistic plays. His chronicle of the Jews, *The Eternal Road,* had been effectively staged by Max Reinhardt in this country.

Karel Capek, in his memorable play, *R.U.R.* conceived a future in which all men would be overcome by automatons or robots.

Ernst Toller, the noblest and most dramatic of the Expressionists, celebrated a spiritual conversion of two kinds, from Pacifism to militantism, and from revolution to counter-revolution. The social-minded physician-playwright, Friedrich Wolf, to the vivid exposition of the social theme by Toller, added the touch of commitment.

Expressionism, German in character, showed itself in the theatre in other countries. France had its apostle of Expressionism in H. R. Lenormand. He made his first mark in the theatre in 1919 with the play *The Failures,* a sketchy clinical study of the world of the theatre behind the wings. His interest in the subconscious deepened with *Time Is a Dream.* Past, present and future are to be seen on the same screen, for one who has eyes to see. An important further exploration in this field of pathology was *The Coward,* presented in 1925, the portrait of an artist who evades service in the World War and finishes by becoming a spy.

We know of Claudel's symbolistic dramas and his specific attempt at a new technique, which foretold Epic Theatre, in his opera *Christophe Colomb* (published 1929).

One of the great Irish playwrights, O'Casey, also turned to Expressionism in a trenchant pacifist protest, *The Silver Tassie*. Other Irishmen bogged down in isolationary Expressionism with failures looking larger than most successes.

O'Neill started with a *tour de force* of social panorama and evolution of a society in terror in *Emperor Jones*, in 1920. In his second Expressionist play, *The Hairy Ape*, O'Neill strains to make acceptable his theory of evolution. He schematized human personality in *The Great God Brown* and repeated the pursuit, both metaphysical and social, in *Days Without End*. In *Lazarus Laughed* and *Dynamo*, O'Neill reached the zenith of the Expressionistic influence in his work. His characters remained schematized, but their prior interest no longer goes towards the tragic exultation of social forces but back to the stream of consciousness of Strindberg's plays.

Germany's avant-garde had moved the theatre towards reality. Expressionism had produced a specific vision, a new *Weltanschauung*. It was this *Weltanschauung* which turned the artist into "the man with a mission," quixotic and difficult to get along with, the unwanted questioner of truth, the unsolicited inquirer into action.

. . .

The French avant-garde, Surrealism, on the other hand, moved the theatre away from reality. As much as Expressionism tended toward objectivity, Surrealism indulged in subjective experiments, reversal of the medium, and intentional misuse of their material by the artists. To some critics this indicated a new freedom and creative vigor; to others, a decadence—"the decline of the West."

Surrealism had such philosophers as André Breton at its head and a galaxy of brilliant young painters, poets and writers, the like of which had not been seen since the Renaissance: among them were Paul Eluard, Louis Aragon, Benjamin Peret, Appollinaire, Cocteau, Phillipe Soupault, Robert Desnois, René Crevel, Michel Leris, Jacques Prévert, Raymond Queneau, René Char, Georges Limbour, Pierre Naville; painters like Max Ernst, André Masson, Pablo Picasso, Hans Arp, Salvador Dali, Joan Miró, Yves Tanguy, Albert Giacometti, René Magritte, Victor Brauner; and the film artist, Luis Buñuel.

Although united under one banner, these artists never seemed to be able to form one bloc. There may have been several reasons for this; one, in all probability, was that they were passing among themselves the "Cup of the Absolute." Convinced of the absurdity of life, of the imbecility of most men, and the delusion of all heroics, the Surrealists acknowledged only the primacy of the imagination. A second reason was that they had remained apolitical and iconoclastic.

Unlike the avant-garde in Germany, the French writers and artists let themselves be dispossessed by history. The Surrealists found a braggart satisfaction in being au dessus de la mèlée.

As late as 1939, when Franz Werfel addressed the P.E.N. Club in Paris and informed it of the Nazi danger (having barely escaped Nazi extermination in his hometown Prague), he was received with derisive smiles. The Parisian writers were still au dessus de la mèlée.

It is an ironic fact that the artists and writers who felt secure were precisely those who escaped by the skin of their teeth from the approaching Nazi invasion. I am speaking of Le Breton, Leger, Seligmann, Mehring and others, searching and finding refuge in America.

What was the contribution of the Surrealist Movement to the theatre? We can count some thirteen Surrealist plays; charming and spirited composition but most of them forgotten today.

The one complete successful Surrealist manifestation in the theatre; Alfred Jarry's play: Ubu Roi, had come as early as 1890 and was an explosion—the waves of which are still felt today.

The great merit of Ubu Roi, was its deep-cutting social satire and the fireworks of linguistic invention, which liberated the theatre from Realism.

Ubu Roi was the eruption of life into the grotesque, into laughter. It was not the kind of laughter which is an expression of joy, but rather of diabolic origin, antilife, antihope, anticulture.

In spite of André Breton's praise of Ubu Roi: "It is an admirable creation for which I would forego all of Shakespeare and Rabelais," Jarry's play was not a glory of French literature.

Surrealism had not fed the theatre. Its protest against mediocrity certainly inspired the rebellion against the boulevard theatres and their commercialism, but did advance the theatre to a dead end.

. . .

The true avant-garde of French theatre came from another source.

Suddenly, impressive placards, blue on orange, appeared on the kiosks and walls of Paris. They bore the announcement of an experimental theatre and called to the young to join a movement in favor of the renewal of the theatre. It was more than an appeal, it was a cry of indignation. Its voice: Copeau.

Copeau had little in his favor to recommend him as a leader of avant-garde. He was a scholar, a man of letters, and a critic.

He was already forty years old. But it was his Théâtre du Vieux-Colombier, its repertory and actors, which inspired the Avant-garde du Cartel.

Copeau built one of the most difficult repertoires any theatre could possibly present. He played Shakespeare as well as Molière, Marivaux, Beaumarchais, Mérimée. He performed Musset as well as Gozzi and Goldoni, and discovered new writers among his contemporaries: Gide, Claudel, Schlumberger, Duhamel, Vildrac, Romains. He did more than that. He created, theatre as an institution, a way of life, an inspiration which went far beyond the mere theatrical experience.

Copeau, besides being an excellent director, was a pedagogue. He borrowed a great deal from foreign experiences; from Stanislavsky, whom he had met in Paris; from Appia and Craig. The curiosity he had for the bold pedagogical techniques and innovations of Isadora Duncan and Jacques Dalcroze, led him to a definite credo of theatre on which he insisted more and more: "The main thing for an actor is to give himself. But to give himself he has to possess himself."

He made studies of dance, mime, improvisation, and recitation; even acrobatics with the Brothers Fratellini at the Cirque d'Hiver in Paris. He thought of a school as being like a religious order.

"We want to institute an order; that is, something that can be understood, something one can join; an order of abnegation, faith and love, illuminated by reason, humanized by common sense, sustained by discipline."

Copeau was a great believer in starting from scratch. "It is not permissible to speak about a Renaissance if we don't begin at the beginning." What he meant was a school.

This reminds me of Piscator's oft-repeated phrase preceding each of his productions, that "one would have to begin at the beginning," whatever the beginning signified, whether it be period, characterization, philosophy, or anything else.

When, under continuous economic pressure despite his success, Copeau closed the Théâtre du Vieux-Colombier, he retired from Paris and moved his family to a little village in Burgundy. He still took thirty students and some faithful collaborators with him to continue a dramatic center and creative work. Out of these efforts came La Compagnie des Quinze, which he organized and directed for five years. The company toured France and from time to time went to Paris.

Copeau put Michael St. Denis at its head. After three seasons abroad, St. Denis created the London Theatre Studio. This, in turn, influenced Tyrone Guthrie, John Gielgud, Laurence Olivier, Alec Guinness, George Devine and others.

In Paris several theatrical companies were organized. Four young directors, inspired by Copeau, established, in spite of the postwar difficulties, a repertory and a reputation which went far beyond France: Charles Dullin, Louis Jouvet, Georges Pitoeff and Gaston Baty.

"The theatre," Louis Jouvet affirmed, "is not only the expression of a people, of a nation, but the truest and most alive statement of a civilization."

Dullin never stopped searching for a spiritual quality in the theatre. "The beauty of theatre is in the faith and love we have for it as well as in the constant search for spiritual perfection and not in the gain of richesse."

As for Pitoeff, his whole existence was the proof and the example of self-sacrifice, a heroic fight against poverty.

Baty joined Copeau in his disdain for material and commercial combinations. In Le manifeste de la Chimère, he stated: "Here we are, a few of us, to found a theatre on faith, enthusiasm and voluntary poverty."

The aphorisms at the top of the following page are indeed a credo:

La Chimère *is not a business, but a work of art.*
La Chimère *has no fortune, but faith.*
La Chimère *does not use art, but serves art.*

But let us not think of these men as idealistic fools. It is said of Dullin that he maintained an atmosphere of nonartiness in his studio; we know of Baty's discipline; Pitoeff's masterful programing; and Jouvet's concreteness.

The reputation of Copeau and the Cartel des Quatre established itself also in foreign lands. A real influence was exercised by the Theatre of the Vieux Columbier in New York during World War I. It inspired in America the forming of different groups of similar faith, such as the Washington Square Players, and the Provincetown Players, and the Theatre Guild, which adapted Copeau's repertory for its first productions. The Group Theatre later is said to have been greatly influenced in its attitude toward theatre by the rules and maxims of The Vieux Colombier.

In Russia, the avant-garde since 1900 was linked with Constructivism and with three names greatly admired in the theatre: Mayakovsky, Meyerhold, and the great film director, Eisenstein.

Eisenstein, known for such films as *Potemkin* and *Ivan the Terrible,* was a film maker and a film teacher. Down with the story and the plot! He discarded other vital elements of the theatre, such as the triangle drama, and brought to the screen the image of collective action.

Mayakovsky—poet, playwright and director—was convinced that the new society would need a new theatre; the masses would enter its doors for the first time. The new theatre had to be pure and active. Mayakovsky thought that the best formula for setting the imagination of the audience into action was to turn away from naturalism. Although preoccupied with much the same subjects as the Naturalists—crime, murder, prostitution, greed—he scorned external truths and physical realities. He constructed other conflicts more deadly, involving the consciousness of extant powers. Stripping away the lies and deceptions, Mayakowsky concluded—unfortunately for himself—that the world was not ready for the task set for it. He committed suicide.

Vservolod Meyerhold's rebellion was theatrically spectacular. He did not create from life, like Mayakovsky, but from art. He rejected naturalism. He wanted theatre to be art and not life. As a consequence, Meyerhold dealt mercilessly destructive blows against Stanislavsky.

Yet his zèle de démolisseur* did great service to the theatre. It took the theatre out of its scenic cage and brought it back to its true function as entertainment. He championed imaginative directors and the dynamic spectacle. He believed that the theatre could become the vital force to carry along all the people with it to a new and creative world.

Whether Meyerhold's role has been overestimated or not, the future will tell. He has been praised and attacked in his own country and influenced a long line of artists around the world who have built on his theory of Constructivism. It is enough to read his notes, not to mention his admirable defense of the theatre before the Comintern, to understand that whatever label one may apply to his work Meyerhold remains one of the rare geniuses of the theatre.

In the history of the theatre, Constructivism showed two faces: socialized Constructivism and artistic Constructivism. In Russia this combination of two tendencies seemed to coincide, but the fact was they actually contradicted each other under a superficial semblance of similarity.

Socialized Constructivism was a pleasant term to the intellectual who dominated Russia after the October uprising.

* Nina Gourfinkel, Gallimard, 1963.

The young generation of artists searched for means of incorporating the creative process (by definition irrational) into the rational concept of Marxist society.

They had learned from dialectical materialism that man owed his character and his existence to the unending dynamic movement of thesis, antithesis, and synthesis. They learned that every phenomenon of life was a synthesis, a combination of a plus and a minus. Constructivism, therefore, became the starting point of a synthesizing process.

This young generation of artists felt that they themselves were results of this dialectical movement. They held themselves responsible—as men and as artists—to continue this dynamic movement. If they had been shaped by the blind movement of economic determinism, they had also learned to manipulate dialectical forces. They hoped with them and through them, the progress of mankind would become consciously self-directed.

They hoped, too, that this progress would change the position of the artist from the luxury object he had been to something as useful for society as a scientist, an engineer, a worker, an inventor. An unbroken chain of responsibility would go from one to the other, from art to science; the goal of all this was to build the future. Art in all its guises was to merge completely with the construction of the future. Just as the bridge-builder finds his freedom in being able to build a bridge, art was to find its freedom in being able to build a new society.

Side by side with this socialized and socializing movement ran the movement of artistic Constructivism, represented by Meyerhold and later by Tairoff.

The Meyerholdian stage performs a "Construction," understood as the Kantian creation: he is separated from reality, his art has a life of its own, it is a universe with its own logic and with its own laws. The freedom of the Marxist artist is consumed in his complete identification with the society; the freedom of the Meyerholdian artist is consumed in his complete separation from it. Only by historical coincidence would their stylized, expressionist forms acquire a definite similarity and be fused with one another.

Meyerhold was the inventor of a theatre which has been called *extratheatrale*, erroneously called the forerunner to the later theories of the Piscator stage. Meyerhold's enormous knowledge and his conviction that deep changes are necessary to revive the spirit of an age made him explore all the sources of the theatrical tradition, Elizabethan, Spanish, Far Eastern and also the large popular sources of the Commedia dell' Arte, that of the dancers, jugglers, and actors of the Russian fairs.

A number of examples of Meyerhold's Constructivist influences in stage designing were seen in America in the mid- 'twenties. Among these were Louis Lozowick's designs for Georg Kaiser's *Gas*, produced in 1926 by the Goodman Memorial Theatre of Chicago; the settings done by Woodman Thompson for J. P. McEvoy's comedy, *God Loves Us*, produced by the Actors' Theatre the same year; the settings done by Donald Oenslager for *Pinwheel*, produced in 1927 at the Neighborhood Playhouse; and the settings done by Mordecai Gorelik for the John Howard Lawson farce *Loudspeaker* which the New Playwrights' Theatre produced in 1927.

Germany's avant-garde had found a difficult refuge in the United States. Although America had adopted the Expressionist School of painting, it was not equally gallant to Expressionist Theatre. The latter was too emotional, too stormy, too remote for American audiences.

And every ship sailing past the Statue of Liberty brought controversial figures of the theatre to American shores.

To name a few: Fritz von Unruh, the great Expressionist writer, George Grosz, Germany's Daumier; Walter Mehring, the sharpest pen in the theatre; Kurt Weill and Lotte Lenya; Ernst Toller, the poet; Alfred Kerr, drama critic; Manfred George, newspaper editor; Ilya Ehrenburg, novelist and scenarist; Fritz Kortner, and Ernst Deutsch, actors, Elizabeth Bergner, Luise Rainer, Albert Basserman, Thomas Mann, Erika Mann, Klaus Mann; and the great French film director, Benoit-Levy. It is regrettable that in spite of the presence of these great writers, directors and actors in America, no avant-garde movement was formed, in fact, never took roots, never started. In the new American theatre, the interest and the curiosity went in another direction: to the second-class European artist for whom art was only a means of self-survival. It seemed as though an easier way of understanding could be created with those men and women who had not yet achieved mastery of their trade in the countries they had come from. They were accepted, and they soon prospered.

The others, even if they had been honored guests in the years before their migration, as had Max Reinhardt, for instance, were welcomed grandly but superficially. They remained strangers.

Only the enlightened few—I speak here of scholars as well as of critics, producers, and people in the theatre with insight as well as power—only these enlightened few, and not truly until the death of Bertolt Brecht in 1956, realized that these men and women who had come here in search of liberty, represented more than the avant-garde of Europe's culture. They were its guardians.

Piscator was given the chance to function as an educator, but never as a creative artist. New York had not yet seen a Piscator production.

Fritz von Unruh, one-time glory of the young playwrights' group of Max Reinhardt, found no producers for his plays, and only a very limited interest for his books.

Ferdinand Bruckner, outside of *The Criminals* and *Chaff*,

both produced at the Dramatic Workshop, had none of his twenty plays produced, and actually starved to death.

Ernst Toller, as we know, committed suicide.

Fritz Kortner started working on film scripts, since it was hard to get an acting job.

Helene Thimig, the wife of Max Reinhardt, the unforgettable actress in the role of *Good Deeds* in Hoffmansthal's version of *Everyman*, written for Max Reinhardt for the Salzburg festival, could only get minor acting jobs.

Lily Darvas, who had been wined and dined when she came here with the original Reinhardt productions, had been fighting for ten years to get a lead.

Bertolt Brecht, according to Mordecai Gorelik, got only one job in several years, as advisor on a film about a Nazi Gauleiter in Czechoslovakia, *Hangmen Also Die*.

11) STUDIO THEATRE

THE STUDIO THEATRE

of the New School for Social Research
66 West 12th Street

ERWIN PISCATOR, DIRECTOR

SEPTEMBER, 1940

Founded in order to create good theatre at popular prices by
reviving seldom-seen classics
presenting new plays and new talent

DECEMBER, 1940

"*King Lear*"—first production. Directed by Erwin Piscator, with Sam
Jaffe in the title role.
"A unique King Lear"—Samuel A. Tannenbaum, Vice President of
the Shakespeare Association.

MARCH, 1941

"The Circle of Chalk"—a Chinese classic, adapted by Klabund. Directed by James Light, with Dolly Haas in the leading role.

"Without doubt one of the most delightful evenings in the theatre." —George Freedley, NY Telegraph

MAY, 1941

"Any Day Now" by Philip Yordan. Directed by Robert Klein. Presenting a new American playwright, who is now in Hollywood.

NOVEMBER, 1941

"Days of Our Youth" by Frank Gabrielson. Directed by James Light. A play about American college life, by a new American author.

"One of the most interesting and enjoyable productions in New York this season."—Wilella Waldorf, NY Post

DECEMBER, 1941

"The Criminals" by Ferdinand Bruckner. Directed by Sanford Meisner. Introducing Lily Darvas, of the Reinhardt Theatre, to American audiences.

"A revealing and timely study of the demoralization in Germany which led to the ascent to power of Hitler's regime."—Robert Coleman, Mirror

MARCH, 1942

"Nathan the Wise," by Lessing, in a free adaptation in English verse by Ferdinand Bruckner. Directed by James Light. The first professional English production of the well known classic.

SPRING, 1942

"War and Peace," the epic play based on Tolstoi's famous novel, by Alfred Neumann and Erwin Piscator.

These are the highlights of the first three years.

After the Dramatic Workshop had been successfully launched (we prided ourselves on having seventeen full-time students), our interest turned towards creating a theatre in which the spirit and the vision of Piscator's experience could function—The Studio Theatre.

For this purpose, Dr. Johnson granted to the Dramatic Workshop the use of the New School auditorium. In doing this, he gave not only a professional face to the Dramatic

Workshop but the beginning of the experimental era, which was to transcend its reputation by inspiring the famous Equity Library Theatre and form the first companies of the great expansion of the off-Broadway movement of the next decades.

WHY STUDIO THEATRE?

Why not experimental theatre? Avant-garde theatre?

Because our Studio Theatre should not serve alone the desire for experimentation, but would have more concrete aims: provide a forum for unusual plays, to create a vanguard, to prepare a theatre of tomorrow, eventually merge with a wider tradition and become a door to Broadway, an influence on mass media in the not too distant future.

It should also be a center for professional actors and actresses where they could gain experience and develop their talent without depending on an occasional stock or professional engagement. And naturally offer an apprentice experience to our student actors of the Dramatic Workshop.

It should be the perfect "theatre for learning."

A center, a theatre for study, a school theatre.

A plant and a playground—where the playwright, director, actor and scene designer would come together and meet with each other, discuss their projects, develop their ideas, question even their skills without fear of the vagaries of commercialism.

Our Studio would above all be the laboratory for the new playwright; the one to present us with the new theatre. But where was he? With the exceptions of Tennessee Williams and Arthur Miller, most of them were rewriting the same play.

It was clear that we had to develop this new playwright, train him, make him explore new creative approaches. This was a matter of time. New playwrights don't grow overnight, not even under expert supervision.

What would we do in the meantime? Put old theatre in a new bottle? Reinterpret masterpieces of Classical theatre lying neglected? Reveal the potency of former Broadway successes and give them new life? While we were waiting for the new talent to produce, should we plunge into revival? This was difficult as revivals were not looked upon favorably by the average entertainment-seeker.

Suppose a great painting hung in a gallery, and three or four thousand people had seen it, and then it was stored away never to be seen again? That's what—so it seemed to us—the American theatre had done with its Elizabethan neighbor; with the treasures of the Restoration, not to speak of Racine, Corneille, Molière, Goldoni, Beaumarchais, to say nothing of Lessing, Kleist, Schiller and Goethe.

How absurd would this policy be if it were followed in the realm of music or the visual arts. No student could really study music in its true balance, importance, and ideas. No critic could revaluate a work in the light of new experience.

• • •

General curiosity had risen towards Piscator's innovations through certain productions on Broadway. In musical comedy his innovations had been used whimsically. People had admired the flawlessly functioning treadmill in I Married an Angel which had created a sensation before we arrived in America.

What other inventions would Piscator bring to inject new life and freedom into the conformity of American Theatre today, critics wondered.

None. Piscator was hardly in a position to do so. Although as Bertolt Brecht had said, "It (was) impossible to list all the inventions . . . that Piscator . . . [had] . . . brought into the theatre," other than technical solutions would have to be found for the new Studio Theatre.

Piscator would have to go back to the beginning of theatre.

He would have to reduce every idea to the simplest denominator, improvise instead of experiment, sketch instead of execute, accept instead of demand.

Even the auditorium of the New School, which could only optimistically be called a theatre, had been conceived as a hall for lectures, recitals, concerts, and light opera. It had its own unique physiognomy: the face of *fin de siècle* Vienna. Joseph Urban had shaped his priceless gem like a baroque pearl, with a platform at the small end of the area. The ceiling dropped in tiers above five hundred comfortable seats like a ruffled petticoat.

This may have been the reason that, except for occasional recitals, the auditorium had remained unused. The Expressionist outcries and the attempts of social revolt had bypassed it.

How could it ever have a future as a Piscator Studio? Only by the greatest stretch of the imagination could one possibly visualize what Piscator could do with it. Yet, its very shortcomings would present a challenge to him; the chance to work intimately and intensely with new playwrights and present plays in progress, rather than completed works. Works not wholly realized in every detail; not conclusive products, slick presentations—rather living tissue, a pulse-beat of our generation: the grasping of new themes, the shaping of new relationships.

"What I always wanted," said Piscator, "is to play without scenery, without costumes, gowns, or props, naked—not physically naked—but naked in the soul. What I truly want is to find the secret behind the mask where the truth lies, the plain literal truth, which is at the bottom of our lives, the real why; the laws. Once we have recognized these laws, we can create accordingly."

One could hear Gordon Craig's or Antoine Artaud's con-

tempt of illusion. But it was more than that; Piscator wanted
at this moment a rostrum for inquiry, a pulpit for protests:
theatre as a tribunal as he had once conceived it—the image
left with him after the first World War.

But could the Studio Theatre correct the image which had
singled him out in many books as an "engineer of theatre,"
rather than an artist? No doubt he had received the recognition of the world with his successes, yes, but with the help of
the great stages of Europe, gigantic arenas, like Reinhardt's
Grosse Schauspielhaus in Berlin, with its audience of 4,000.
Had he not built "scaffolds and catwalks, used machinery
worth millions," created sensation? But what now? What
could he do with the stage on 12th street that Brecht had
already tried in Hollywood and had not succeeded?

> Brecht tried to solve the problem of form, Piscator the
> problem of content [writes Herbert Jhering]. It is surprising
> that the poet had more influence on the style in the theatre
> and the director more on the drama. Most attempts to come
> to terms with the political and social realities of the present
> lead us back to Piscator; most attempts to create a new form,
> to Brecht. Epic drama? Yes—where the theatre conquers
> new spiritual contents and presents new scientific findings
> and philosophical maxims. Collective themes: poison gas,
> war, stock exchange, industry, socialism. The drama is
> dramatic where it fights, indicts, or tries to change things.
> It is nonsense to say that Epic Theatre is the journalistic
> play. It is only a beginning, a transition to poetic drama.

Piscator was ready to begin once more, leaving his fame
and commercial success.

But, by allowing himself to enter the theatrical life of
America through the portals of learning, Piscator invited criticism. By his very choice, he opened himself to attack by the
commercial theatre.

. . .

Theatrical forms have to be checked against reality and not against esthetics. Studio theatres have often been amateur theatres or have grown out of amateur theatres. Piscator's Studio Theatre was to function with professionals—actors, directors, technicians.

The famous studio theatres of the past had often improved in thought and form over the conventional theatre. The ideal combination was school, studio, and professional theatre together, as realized by Piscator in Berlin.

Most studio theatres were protesting against existing conditions. What was Piscator's protest to be?

He protested often, above all, against the renewal of Naturalism as offered on the American stage. In a curious way the "Engaged Theatre" of the 'thirties had faded into a naturalistic theatre in the 'forties. The "cause" so excitedly defended in *Waiting for Lefty* still existed, but had been watered down to the evasive commonplace, the self-deceiving blindness of *Rocket to the Moon*. No flaming idealism supported a theme or play, but in its place a compromise—the compromise ingrained in everyday give and take. Would these feelings and attitudes carry the theatre through the emergency and excitement of war, or would this theatre begin to look like Chekhov's phantom plays of past society, producing characters of no consequence, without hope or future?

Naturalism is always a sign of the intellectual poverty of an era, incapable of communicating ideas. The powerful convention of the "house of vision" (the theatre) with its "art of revealing through the art of concealing" had been an eminent spiritual force in all the ancient entertainment. Did the contemporary theatre reveal anything—except its weakness? Naturalism pinpointed only one thing: a breakdown of tradition. Naturalism could not carry the symbols necessary to stimulate courage and rally the nation at this difficult hour.

The theatre, to survive, needed a dynamic reversion, a reversion which would go to the very sources of the human condition. Destruction of the Naturalist super-marionette world, which a childish faith in the "open society" and a "godsent Democracy," based on a facile optimism which could neither see as evil nor hear as evil.

The admirable wisdom which played godfather to the gods of the Orient and to the gods of the Occident had instructed all guardians of the spirit to direct their thoughts not to rival life, but to go beyond life. The artist was by definition the one who could see beyond life, beyond the ordinary perception—and could create even more than he had seen. Only men of vision were allowed to hold the office of celebrating the spirit. One could find among these seers sages full of knowledge, strong men striving for justice, artists in the service of *veritas*.

The best examples of learning theatres, perhaps, are the early Jesuit theatres, which used the stages as a means of communication and propaganda. School drama was only one part of it. Originally in Latin, the plays of the so-called "Time of the Troubles" slipped into the vernacular. The change was gradual, from the church to the churchyard and later, when the crowds became larger, to the marketplaces.

Under the influence of the Humanists, the "reading rooms," another form of studio theatre, pointed the way to presentations of early literature in the European countries.

Early Russian studios were founded along the lines of the "learning" of the existing Jesuit theatres.

This was particularly true of the Maly Theatre (this term meant small theatre) where the first Studio experiments of Realistic acting took place. The "Maly" grew to an art theatre and enjoyed such reputation as an institute of education that it was said that "in Moscow one went to the universities but one studied at the Maly."

In Stanislavsky's Studio more was accomplished than the preparatory work for his later famous acting "Method." The Studio was a center of training and experimentation in more than one way. It can be considered to have laid the groundwork for the famous Moscow Art Theatre, in which the Stanislavsky system of acting triumphed and developed in a complete symphonic ensemble presentation. But Stanislavsky's restless genius was not satisfied with what he had discovered. Obsessed by the fear that the theatre might be up a blind alley with Naturalism, Stanislavsky created a laboratory for seeking new forms departing from everyday feelings on the stage.

Meyerhold, during his provincial tours, gathered a troupe for which he also was searching out a new path. Together with Stanislavsky he created still another "Studio" dedicated to producing lofty fantasies. Dismissing Realism as a way of art which had outlived its age, he experimented with theatre in a way similar to the experiments of the Impressionist painters, poets, and musicians. The spiritual situation was to be transmitted, not the physical alone. He found support for his theories in writers like Maurice Maeterlinck and Gerhardt Hauptmann. In spite of this, Stanislavsky became disillusioned and withdrew from the Studio.

In 1902 Meyerhold continued on his own with a new "Studio Ecole," where he asserted the power of the director and designer over the stage. He gave preference to the marionette image over the actor by creating his method of "Bio-Mechanics." He found support in his protest against Naturalism in the "Symbolical Theatre" of these years.

It was the dynamic political changes already rocking Russia that changed Meyerhold's direction of experimentation. He developed different strata for the actor, drawing upon the improvisations of the Roman mimes and the versatile masks which could be identifiable for the audience and arouse them from the trivia of their present life. He created a special studio in 1910 for this. He invented and re-invented. As his official position in the Imperial Theatre did not permit him to use his own name while working elsewhere, he chose Dr. Dappertuto as a pseudonym.

Dr. Dappertuto was originally one of the dynamic and fabulous creations which E. T. A. Hoffmann had brought to life —strangely akin in spirit and mind to Meyerhold: the hero of one of the *Tales of Hoffman*, the evil genius who persuaded Giuletta to capture Hoffmann's soul.

Germany, in the early years of the twentieth-century theatre, had a great roll-call of different Dappertutos selling their souls in extravagant productions, especially in Munich, Dresden and Berlin.

It was Max Reinhardt's Studio that exemplified the Expressionist theatre in spite of the fact that this was not according to Reinhardt's taste. His thirst for theatricality, for ceremonial and worldly customs, rites and rituals, in which he had succeeded in such an extraordinary way in his great theatres, were by far dearer to him.

The modern studio theatres of France were not always *théâtres d'études* in the sense of serious research except for the Théâtre Libre of André Antoine, who created his Studio in 1887.

Antoine was a businessman from Limoges, an enthusiastic amateur actor, who had journeyed to Paris. In order to realize his ideas of theatre and resolve the conflict between real life and romantic imagination, he founded a studio which he called "Théâtre Libre." He protested against the "well-made play" of Sardou, so successfully performed by Sarah Bernhardt. Zola, who thought of theatre as a slice of life, came to support Antoine's protest. Although Naturalistic in acting, Antoine inspired his playwrights to go further than Ibsen and Strindberg. Brieux, Curel and Porto-Riche did not deal only with specific contemporary evils and the iniquity of the social system. They were moralists and reformers trying to offer remedies to social evil, such as thirty years later we find in the Brecht Lehrstück.

Antoine's Studio became a model for Otto Brahm's experimental Freie Buehne in Berlin, which opened in 1889. It won fame through the first production of a German poet whom the Nationalists as well as the Socialists and the Communists have since claimed to be their ancestor, Gerhardt Hauptmann.

The Théâtre Libre, providing plays at low admission cost, to some extent also influenced the Berliner Neue Volksbuehne which, making a further step, inaugurated in 1890 an experimental program for the working classes, limited to subscribers who drew lots for their seats.

Antoine's influence in England was clear in the efforts of another actor, G. T. Greif, who founded in London a studio called Independent Theatre. It favored unknown playwrights and became, for several years, quite successful. Shortly after, in 1905, the Abbey Theatre in Dublin opened a stage for the Irish players with the idea of awakening the audience to the fact that theatre could have a humane and progressive enlightening influence.

Gordon Craig, the stage designer who began his life as an actor under the direction of Henry Irving, feeling that the contemporary British theatre gave him no opportunity for a truly creative experiment, founded a Studio and school for the art of the theatre in Florence in 1913. Although he remained one of the great dilettantes of theatre, his teaching influenced the work of most of the best modern stage designers in Europe.

Today Studio Theatres are spread all over England. Some have training centers and schools attached to them. Most of them enjoy skilled direction and produce plays of experimental nature in quality production.

In America, "studio theatre" was often synonomous with "little theatre." The little theatres were rooted in the active and real participation of the life of the community. They drew well-nigh the whole of their moral, intellectual and spiritual life from the environment of which they formed a natural part.

It was Piscator's studio in Berlin which made the total break with all convention. The most spectacular support came to him from the Bauhaus Group in Weimar.

• • •

The Bauhaus, originally a school of design, a collective embracing of the whole range of visual arts; architecture, planning, painting, sculpture, industrial design and stagework, searched for a new and powerful working correlation with the theatre. Seeking a synthesis of art and modern technology, the Bauhaus strove for objective means to relate the individual creative effort to a common background. Gropius, together with Moholy-Nagy, viewed the field of stagework from the designer's point of view, but their experiences acquired theatrical body and life at Piscator's studio.

When in 1922 Lothar Schreyer's plan to form a Bauhaus Theatre failed, a great new standard for a theatre had nevertheless arisen out of the potential experiments of this unique teamwork who had pointed the way to new creative form. Through them, the primary meaning of space was rediscovered and with it a new possibility for the director. The New organization came to be known as "total theatre," or "Piscator theatre," or "Epic theatre."

The aims of the Bauhaus were scenic aims. Stage poetry instead of word poetry—aims relying on space, form, and light. In manipulating these forms, new and surprising effects in mechanical motion revealed themselves. Piscator's Theatre of light, which he developed only in the 'fifties in Germany (in such plays as Sartre's *L'Engrenâge* and the opera *Rosamunde Floris*, text by Georg Kaiser and music by Boris Placher) was one of his own transfigurations of space, form and color.

. . .

However much evidence of his successes and failures one may collect from the scenes of his efforts, Piscator's Theatre was alive with ideas. He believed in the important role of the playgoer, in his participation and last but not least, his education. Hundreds of letters were sent out to solicit membership. No tickets sold at the box office, admission was by subscription. This would make one more bond between player and audience, and would prepare the ground for a future Repertoire. He wrote:

> We shall present plays which will provide the theatre with a new language, new ideas, new approaches. Sometimes uncomfortable plays, "unplayable" plays. Plays of a new and vitalized philosophy to transform the ways of thought and feeling of the public at large. Plays which cannot be done on Broadway, because of their uncertain appeal, or sophisticated intelligence level, or overlarge cast.
> A learning place for you, the playgoer, if you want to assume the responsibility to question and explain social currents and in such reappraisal become an educational force.
> Art can never be a monologue. It is a dialogue with one or many. So we want you, dear Playgoer, to be a partner in our discussions on this haphazardous and unfinished business: Theatre.
> . . . You can offer us an audience of ideal playgoers. You are not the casual playgoer whose criticism begins and ends with opinion, after one carelessly seen performance; one who dismisses a play capriciously, smugly, irresponsibly with "I liked it" or "I did not like it at all."

> Like the music lover who studies the score of Beethoven's
> Ninth Symphony and follows the performance with
> intelligence you will make an art of seeing, hearing,
> understanding.
> I know a stockbroker who learned Greek to understand
> Classic drama in its original tongue. He went to see a play
> which he had read before and disliked. He saw it not once,
> but ten times. Each attendance revealed new ideas. He
> realized that he could not be confident of a single impression.
> This must have been the man of whom Shakespeare said, "If
> only one in the audience understands, that is enough for
> me."
> Shakespeare certainly had no thought of the box office at this
> moment. However, by creating an audience of ideal playgoers
> —you—who will insist upon your right to see the play again
> and again, we do establish a box office which is self-
> perpetuating.
> For this reason we give you an active role in our Studio
> Theatre. You will be a responsive collaborator in our
> practical work; read the play before its performance, attend
> lectures by the staff of the Dramatic Workshop, participate
> in the cast's first reading, see a regular and a dress rehearsal
> of the play.
> With such creative unity, we can come again to the theatre
> of poetry, the word, the language, the idea. You, the ideal
> playgoer, have so much to offer us. Won't you join with us
> in bringing this theatre to life?

And so began the Studio Theatre of the Dramatic Workshop at the New School of Social Research.

. . .

Most of the actors rarely think of the role the audience
plays in the life of the theatre. But whoever has played in an
empty hall has a different idea. It is practically as if the other
part of oneself were missing and as if no theatrical experience
could take place without becoming a joint enterprise between
performer and playgoer.

The history of theatre audiences has been turbulent. They

have undergone as much of a change as the theatre itself.

First governed by religion, then by the state, the theatre has invented many social mechanisms to educate the spectator as an individual or as a "collective." On certain occasions, the individual exercised a definite role in the creation and orientation of theatre; from the Greeks to the feudal theatre of Louis XIV. At other periods, it was the "collective" that animated the theatre with its dynamism, and gave it direction.

Theatre was required each time, then, not just to represent a different life, but to initiate representations of various, even contrary, natures.

With the French Revolution, theatre was born more or less out of the social body. The plebeian had his say—the ordinary fellow, the obscure man. And for the first time, the aristocratic audience was challenged.

Rousseau's idea that a novel art capable of changing man could come only out of a novel society reversed the role of stage and audience. Rousseau formulated a veritable *Théorie de la fête*, which turned the theatre over to the service of the people, specifically dedicated to the citizen who was not cultivated but aroused to political participation. The citizen assumed the role of the theatrical hero. The polemics that arose from these spectacles, civic festivals, and popular theatricals which Robespierre and other leaders of the revolution organized, flung a gauntlet to all the principles of art invested in the theatre, but at the same time they reinforced the national and political character of the audience.

Not for long. The turn of the nineteenth century saw a sweep of the audience chessboard. The ideas formulated by Lessing's *Hamburgische Dramaturgie* and Diderot's *Theatre as a Moral Institution* found a fascinated audience.

The bourgeoisie de-socialized the stage and focused its interest on the pursuit of personal truth and self-realization. The new myth was *nature*—or as near nature as one could get. It corresponded exactly to the literalness of behavior and the accent on truth and simplicity of the period. The velvet curtain became a fourth wall; no communication between audience and stage was permitted. Theatre addressed itself to a narrower and narrower circle of initiates; the circle dwindled to a point when the actors were talking strictly to themselves.

This was brought to a triumph by the Meiningers. Having raised the different aspects of Naturalism to a surprising level of perfection in Germany, they enjoyed a great acclaim during a five-year tour of Russia (1885-90). The German company had aroused the interest and admiration of Stanislavsky, who missed scarcely a performance and later professed that this integral resurrection of an event on stage, this magic naturalism, this illusionism rivaling the real, had marked a new and important stage in his own creative life.

The twentieth century changed all this.

The curtain was torn down, the fourth wall opened. Contact between audience and stage was re-established. A new search for truth, this time coming from the artists themselves, did away with the painted décor, exposed the stage lighting, revealed bare walls, scaffolds and other structural elements. Not less significant was the appearance of the metteur-en-scène, the new Prometheus.

This orientation attained its climax with Epic Theatre; a theatre which could do equal justice to an Aeschylus or a Shakespeare, a Chekhov or a Brecht—a total spectacle that would open new perspectives, not only in the radical transformation of technical means, but also in the discovery of new subjects and new forms.

. . .

The theatre cannot be wholly understood without reference to the audience—even though they both are one. Criticism of the theatre must forever remain superficial unless it takes into account the audience that creates it.

Once upon a time, an image was drawn that has since haunted every artist of the theatre; it is the image of the one man in the audience whom Shakespeare mentioned; the man across the footlights whom you can hardly see, but whose radiation you feel because he is with you at every moment. It was for this man that the great actors, Kean, Coquelin, Terry, the Barrymores, Laughton, Olivier, played.

In some degree, although we may not think any longer of that one man, an assembly of people also forms a unit, once they are gathered together and exposed to the same experience.

But this unit has a mirror quality. It shows many different significant patterns, communicating, not images, but notions of an image—a pattern of feeling, for example—symbolic moods of communication, sometimes nonverbal, but conveying their likes or dislikes. In one word, there are different kinds of audiences.

This is perhaps pursuing the argument quite far into the sphere of generalization, but we know that in its symbolic existence, whatever its kinship, the audience expresses that ultimate good sense which we term civilization.

The contemporary audience has its own archetypes. They are briefly in fashion like the productions they favor: Symbolist, Expressionist, Constructivist, Realist, Method—strenuously theatrical themselves—they are arrestingly sincere now and then, and occasionally memorable.

The audience of the great families, the carriage trade, has become a small decorative minority. Despite their veneer they are neither stupid nor indolent. They are so overfed with cultural obligation that they never have the time to really enjoy a performance.

The theatre invariably corresponds for them to a kind of

moral endorsement. But mind you, they can take it or leave it; this doesn't make any difference to the theatre, either, because the impact of their endorsement is negligible.

The second kind of audience is the majority of the *nouveau riche*—the leisure class. They pay highly for the privilege of sitting in the first four rows. They have worked hard to arrive at this milestone of achievement, where they can sink comfortably into a velvet-cushioned seat and digest their dinner in Roman fashion while being entertained. They don't come for pleasure. They come to look after their investments; time, money, love. They are sponsors. They are gamblers. I have nothing against them. They are the breadbasket of the theatre.

Third, there is the "intellectual" audience—the precursors of calamity—with their following of parasites. Between the last musical and the new dramatic hit, their knowledge doesn't deepen or widen. Halfway between relating a nightmare and reporting an incident, they are positively aware that man is absurd and that life is corrupt. No one should make any sense out of anything.

Their women are lost-and-found celebrities to one another, protégés and freaks, sometimes merely spoiled children. They discuss everything and everyone—Gandhi, Sartre, Genet, Albee; the Bible, de Gaulle, and forever Cocteau . . . and of course Stanislavsky, Noël Coward, and Peter Brook. They know as much about the budget that controls every spectacle as they know about the royalties, and they are as precise as an IBM machine even if they have not invested money in a show. In a single breath, they accept the Royal Ballet, the latest painting of Dali, and the new schedule of the Beatles. They have a termite-like appetite for eating away the good, the true, and the beautiful from the earthly paradise.

The fourth is the professional audience—the theatre people. They all live in a remarkable airy fashion, be it on Park

Avenue, in private homes on the East or West Side, or in old brownstones downtown. If they stride right and left of Central Park, they stand right and left of themselves. They are not contemptuous of money, but find it hard to escape the demands of it. They are great arguers, and they are worshippers of success. They are the realistic organization of the world's most romantic profession.

They are the most difficult audience of all because they never feel like spectators—only competitors.

There is also another audience: the union and white-collar worker audience. Usually they are too exhausted to be as intelligent as they truly are. A night at the theatre is an outlet to them, necessary to their pent-up energies. They have a tendency to defend the underdog, to explain and justify writer, director, and actor, if the reviewers attack them. They defend style and values, even if they do not understand. In one word, they humanize failure.

These were the people who had publicly declared that the Studio Theatre was necessary. It would be difficult to finance the plays we were going to give. But in the end faithful membership would support us. So they said—and that's what we believed.

The last audience, symbol of communication between reality and the theatre, is youth and the young adults. They have one thing in common: their hostility to everything that preceded their generation. They are rather insensitive to all lessons or attempts at education in whatever form—except perhaps the "lesson" of Ionesco's theatre, carrying psychological tensions to paroxysm.

They are traders in hope, but they easily practice fraud in the name of anything. They are the result of neurosis, and bad education. They are miraculous caricatures of their own time, only a little more dramatic. They have their own brand of irony, a brand that only a few years ago would have been called the Witch's Sabbath. They live in extremes because that is the only way they know how to live.

But they are also brave, strong and inventive. They know it is up to them to fight for the creative, vital impulses which are their birthright and which are in danger of being destroyed by modern dehumanization. They know this can only be done through a new kind of education. The theatre is one of these means.

• • •

How can the theatre contribute to the dream of total education which our age must see developed?

I have the firm belief that the theatre could act as the pioneer of this new age where men can still remain practical men, yet at the same time feel the necessity to be part of the world of the creative spirit and carry some of its meaning or possibilities into the life of every day.

It is a curious aspect of the "electrical age" that the theatre establishes a kind of network that has much of the character of our central nervous system. It is not merely an "electrical network," but constitutes a unique field of experience, in which all kinds of impressions and experiences are translated and interact, enabling us to react to the world as a whole.

I say that the theatre could act as the pioneer of this new age of mechanization, fragmentation, automation and all sorts of moveable types. Theatre could act forcefully by understanding and using the energies and products, and by fusing them with information and learning.

The theatre could produce a new type of audience; an audience of participants, independent of the place or kind of operation, independent of patterns of decentralization, independent of the diversity in the work to be performed.

For this kind of audience we would not need the specific

enticements of entertainment. The time will pass when the spectator is tired, exhausted with his rational life or day labor, and vexed with social frictions of all sorts.

He will laugh, as an armchair spectator, at a flashback of his small world, while he, who sits as a fugitive, is in fact a co-creator.

And he will be the co-creator of this new theatre. He will be the *public*. Not a small group of thinking and educated people, dependent on a number of moods and trends that are extraneous to the theatre as an institution, but he will be a partner in World Theatre, one of the crowd—a large, ardent and sensitive crowd of individuals, of men who have paid a high price for being an individual and part of the crowd at the same time.

12) STUDIO THEATRE PRODUCTIONS

Piscator had pleaded for many years that the classics be taken down from the shelves and revived for modern audiences. He decided now, in the pressure of war-darkening Europe, for a play famous for its classic mold: *King Lear* called the "unplayable play" by all the critics from the seventeenth century on.

Most critics distrust revivals. But Shakespeare has admittedly always been considered contemporary. For generations, artists have thrown their passions into the mold of this 300-year-old tragedy and shaped it according to the morals and ethical issues of their day.

Piscator's aim was to interpret King Lear in today's spirit—the spirit of the headlines.

What were these headlines?

Dictatorship, violence, war.

The Nazis were still in Paris. Gestapo headquarters on the Rue de Lauriston sealed the evidence of their tortures.

F.D.R. had signed the first peacetime draft law on November 14; the Nazis bombed Coventry, the blitz was at its height.

What was more closely related to this beginning of Hitler's 1,000-year Reich than the chaotic world of Lear?

Piscator's concept was that Lear showed the fallacy of dictatorship, the wheel that at the end "comes full circle."

In an interview with the New York Times on December 8, 1940, Piscator stated:

> We seek to revitalize the significant literature of another age. This is what we are doing with this great Shakespearean tragedy. In Lear there are the elements of today's worldwide tragedy—the rise of dictatorships—and it is in the terms of this problem that we treat the drama.
>
> Today we see Lear in the company of the dictators who are remaking the map of the world. What he did in dividing his kingdom is in line with the ideology of a tyrant. More injustice follows and that is why we recognize in this 300-year-old tragedy the social forces and political tactics of today's dictatorships.

The use of the theatre as the third eye of history finally struck home with the students. They were ready to accept theatre as a teacher. Hadn't the earlier playwrights made a point of this? Were not tragedy and comedy until the nineteenth century mainly a propaganda of ideas?

Yet could history speak effectively from the stage when history was being made outside every day? Was it not attempting the impossible?

For this we trusted to the Epic Theatre design of the production.

Piscator proceeded methodically in designing his production, being both judge and jury.

Lear's tragedy was no longer a private affair of lust and hatred, nor was it relevant that Lear was of royal blood. Nor did Lear cast his shadow across history. He was not one Lear, but all the Lears.

"How do you love me?" Lear asks Cordelia, and freezes around a core of dead words. He talks himself into irreconcilable despair and hatred. His own tirades blind him to the facts and drive him to delusion. His own statements do not leave him any way out. Words follow words. Slogans, trite phrases, harangues, abstractions, false antitheses come to possess his mind, similar to "The Thousand Year Reich," "unconditional surrender," "the class war," "the permanent revolution." The life of Lear's mind is arrested by the weight of his eloquence. His words carry him forward after the confrontation with the human to the confrontation with the inhuman. His conduct is no longer responsive to reality because he has distorted it. He has driven out human reason and becomes the victim of his own miserable exaggeration. Even his voice has changed. It has become sonorous and hollow like the storm against which he rages. His heroics finally bring him to destruction. At the close of the circle, he is a prisoner of his own making, of his own tyranny, tightly chained to the catastrophe he has himself created.

Rehearsals went on splendidly.

The actors were surprised to find Piscator the most contained and reserved individual within range of the work-light.

"He is inclined to amble rather than walk," was the observation in the wings, "inclined to hold back rather than charge."

Yes, it was true. Only when helping some tyro through a

difficult passage did he put on the actor's cloak. Then there was little that was phlegmatic about him. He would get under the emotional skin of the character, draw out the significant traits with caressing deliberation, and repeat his statements over and over until the player became almost hypnotized by the effect.

But something more happened in a brief time—deeper in its connotation. The strained atmosphere around a foreign director and an American cast changed. An atmosphere of good fellowship established itself, to everyone's delight. Piscator had become one of them, and for the first time, the little Playhouse on Twelfth Street had become his home. Benson Inge, after watching a rehearsal, wrote in the *New York Herald Tribune*:

> A legend has entered the theatre of the New School for Social Research. With fairest Cordelia, it whispers on stage, thou art most rich being poor, most choice forsaken and m-o-s-t loved despised.
>
> Some one dares call "Time for lunch, Mr. Piscator," and the legend, now relaxing with a cigar inside an office niche that overlooks the vast Urban-designed auditorium becomes Erwin Piscator, who removes the robes of his King Lear improvisations and talks of life and its realities.
>
> Piscator is scarcely the "mad monk" one might have expected after learning his turbulent history in the theatre. But that may be because of the fragmentary biographical notes which came through during his last ten and most active years on the stage. At certain periods, they read like a censored modern-day war communique.

The dream of Shaw and Gordon Craig of divesting Shakespearean drama of romantic pictorialism was also the aim of Piscator. Since he had no arena stage for his production, he bridged the gulf between audience and actors by leaving the platform open. There was no fourth wall, no curtain, no naturalistic convention of any kind. The set, consisted of a succession of ramps leading to a revolving stage with a series of diminishing semi-circular platforms that rose like large steps against a gray fish-net cyclorama. The technical supervision was under the direction of Hans Sondheimer, former stage engineer of the Bavarian State Theatre; the lighting by A. Feder; the sound effects by Harold Burris-Meyer.

. . .

King Lear was presented on Saturday, December 14, 1940, in the auditorium of the New School before a small, eclectic audience. One-third of the seats had been removed to make room for the staging of the production. Its sponsors included Eddie Dowling, Clifton Fadiman, Robert E. Sherwood, Paul Muni, Sinclair Lewis, George S. Kaufman, and Oscar Levant.

Sam Jaffe played King Lear. This excellent actor had scored great success in *The Jazz Singer* and as Kringelein in *Grand Hotel* as well as in numerous films.

Margaret Curtis, who had been the Catherine of Orson Welles' *Five Kings*, was Regan; Lisbeth Lynn, the Cordelia, had made her New York bow in Reinhardt's *The Eternal Road*; Herbert Berghof, as the Fool, an extraordinary if uneven talent; and Lotte Goslar, as the Fool's mummer, a superb mime who came from Hollywood especially for these performances.

Among the director's assistants were five unusual young people who went ahead in their fields as directors and playwrights: Betty Lord, Alec S. Nyary, Cyril Schocken, Jack Katz and Chouteau Dyer.

A few agonizing hours later, when we bought the first morning papers, we knew that the critics had failed to approve the daring concept. The reviews were unfavorable.

The audience (who was it that said "The audience is always right"?) understood the pertinence of the play as presented. The enormous cry that emanated from the whole play, the blaze of warning, the prophecy of the catastrophe to come; it was not a play any more but a dispatch from a new front, which was soon to be called World War II.

With his usual perspicacity, Dr. Johnson realized the effect some of the reviews would have upon Piscator. He summoned me to his office with utmost friendliness and told me that this politico-esthetic argumentation of men who had mostly seen only conservative productions of Shakespeare should not influence Piscator; that, on the contrary, he should go on and on completely oblivious to any criticism.

Maurice Materlinck, Nobel prize winner for literature in 1911 and now himself a political refugee, understood the conception of *Lear* and wrote the following letter to Piscator, whom he had never met:

> Dear Sir:
>
> I feel the urge to give you a brief résumé of what I told you at the end of the performance of King Lear.
>
> A great critic of the 19th century, himself a great poet, called King Lear "the Leviathan of Shakespearean seas." This magnificent, stupendous and frightening drama in which the poet plunges us into the very pit of human distress in a torrent of madness, has always been considered unplayable. You have dared to wrest it from the silence of the book, to make it palpitate and shout in all its sublime horror. You have in some way exorcised it.
>
> With material means which were practically nil, by the sole force and sureness of your inner vision projected into the audience by scuptural magic of movement, attitude, grouping, by incantation of colors, play of lights and shadows, your heroic and daring enterprise unrolled—a kind of miracle—before all the admirers of Shakespeare who should bow on deep respect. May your magnificent example find more than one imitator.
>
> Very sincerely yours,
>
> MAETERLINCK

Along with their congratulations on the performance, the Shakespeare Association of New York expressed considerable interest in our plans for future productions of Shakespeare.

Soon after *King Lear*, Fitzi suggested that James Light, the director, become associated with the Studio Theatre.

Light had been one of the leading directors of the Provincetown Playhouse and was a personal friend of O'Neill. He had never attempted to smooth the wrinkles from the writings of America's greatest playwright, nor had he avoided sharing the burden of O'Neill's despair. It had remained engraved on his own face, a totality of comradeship.

In spite of the scope of his interests, James Light had remained intensely personal and subjective as an artist. He had no appreciation for scientific philosophy in the theatre, thought that Nietzsche, Karl Marx and Heidegger were at the base of all evil in the theatre and that their disciples had proved unsuccessful in bringing life to the stage.

He accepted the direction of the second production at the Studio Theatre—*The Circle of Chalk* by Klabund and he wrote for the next bulletin his view of the Studio Theatre.

> To restore the actor to his art, and lost masterpieces to the place, the stage; to bring out modern plays now neglected because they are supposedly uncommercial, the Theatre. At its head they placed Erwin Piscator. No more important or significant figure could be chosen than this great director who has revolutionized the art of the European theatre, and whose influence has so strongly affected our American stage.

The Circle of Chalk was a fantasy, taken from the repertoire of the Chinese Theatre called Yuan-chu-po-cheng, *i.e.*, the hundred pieces composed under the Yuan, or princes of the family of Jen Khan in the years 1259-1368. In his adaptation, Klabund replaced the old text with many of his own lyrics.

Max Reinhardt had staged Klabund's version in Berlin in 1925 with Carola Neher in the lead.

Klabund (Alfred Henschke) was born in Germany in 1891, and died of tuberculosis in Switzerland in 1928. His father was a chemist, his surroundings humble. Klabund was a close personal friend and university classmate of Erwin Piscator. His first book of poems appeared when he was a little over twenty; the verses were described as more like telegrams than the usual forms of versification. However, most of his work was in the true tradition of romantic *Lieder*. He also translated Litai Pe, and Persian poetry. Continually aware of his nearness to death, he became fanatical for life. He felt intensely that the age in which he lived stood between life and death just as he did, but he did not fall in with the easy, erotic escapes of lesser artists. He was a poet of our age, whose fate he suffered and whose battles he fought to the end. His own explanation of his pseudonym was:

> *My name is Klabund*
> *That means change*
> *My mother was called phantom*
> *My father vision.*

James Laver, curator of the Victoria and Albert Museum in London, translated Klabund's *The Circle of Chalk* into English. His version was produced in London and ran for over a year. Anna May Wong played the lead, which Dolly Haas was to play in the Studio Theatre production. And Rose Quong, who played the role of Mrs. Ma in London, came to play the same role in our production.

The story evolves around an illicit affair between a law clerk and the first wife of a wealthy merchant. She poisons her husband and lays the blame on his innocent second wife. She even claims the second wife's child, to whom the inheritance will go, as her own. In the ensuing trial, the judge uses Solomon's tactics to discover the real mother of the child.

Dolly Haas was the interpreter of the real mother, Hai Tang. She fit the part well; critics praised her performance. Her candid beauty made one almost forget how good an actress she was. Perhaps in this conflict between nature and art may be found the reason for the incomprehensible fact that Dolly never had the public appeal of a Katharine Hepburn or an Olivia De Haviland.

For the third offering, the Studio Theatre decided to do a first play by an American playwright. The play chosen was *Any Day Now*, a comedy by Philip Yordan. Robert Klein directed and Charles de Scheim, who played Nick the Bartender in *Time of Your Life*, played the lead. Brooks Atkinson of the *New York Times* (June 10, 1941) did not care for this production. He found it "rough-edged and imitative, and studiously spontaneous in writing and staging."

Philip Yordan, nevertheless, became quite a discovery of the Dramatic Workshop through his second play, *Anna Lucasta*, which became a world-wide success. We had presented an early version with a white cast in a "Plays in Work" production at the Workshop.

It was about this time that several other important artists joined our Studio Theatre staff. Among them was Mordecai Gorelik, who had done notable settings for the Provincetown Playhouse productions and for the Theatre Guild, and was a founding member of the Group Theatre. We expected a great deal from him at the Studio Theatre. Unfortunately, he was deeply involved in his important book, *New Theatres for Old*, in which he included a chapter about Piscator. It was this book which, in fact, limited the possibility of Gorelik's practical work at the Studio Theatre.

Another artist, whose experience combined expert knowledge in the theatre with a taste for experimentation, joined our production staff with *Lear*. He was A. Feder, the lighting expert, who began his career in the Federal Theatre Laboratory.

Harold Burris-Meyer, equally a specialist, came to us to continue his experimentation in acoustics and sound, which he had started with *Lear*.

On November 28, 1941 we presented a play of "inside America," *Days of Our Youth*, by Frank Gabrielson.

It was a play about American college life. It was an ideal play for us because of the large cast it required. For all their youthful determination and the play's warmth, the production fell into a kind of vacuum, the vacuum of those dark days of Pearl Harbor.

"Yes," said Piscator. "It is precisely in times of catastrophe that the artist is needed, that he must seek to discharge his debt to society by seeking to rebuild what is being destroyed, to understand what is transitory, to regenerate what is of true value and to hold on to what is indestructible."

The war brought to the Studio Theatre a play that had been set for production on Broadway—Ferdinand Bruckner's *The Criminals*. Bruckner, at first immersed in Expressionism, became an activist playwright during the late 'twenties, which caused him to lose his German citizenship as soon as Hitler came into power.

The Criminals was a play about pre-Hitler youth and was handled most effectively. There was no better play to show to an American audience the growth and vicious development of the days after the Munich Agreement.

Piscator had invited Sanford Meisner to direct it. Sanford was able to interest one of the truly great stars of European theatre, the former leading lady in Max Reinhardt's productions and wife of Ferenc Molnar, the playwright, Lily Darvas. She had been searching for a role to play in English, and her performance in *The Criminals* brought forth glowing notices for her artistry and further recognition for Bruckner's play.

In March, 1942, Ferdinand Bruckner brought us his free adaptation in English of the mighty Gotthold Ephraim Lessing play, *Nathan the Wise*. Piscator accepted it with enthusiasm.

Apart from the fact that it would be the first professional production in English in America of a great classic German work, it represented to Piscator the play he had been waiting for—the political play.

Nathan the Wise was written by Lessing in 1779 as a plea for religious and racial equality; a protest against intolerance, a most noble and passionate play. It was astonishing, incomprehensible even, that such a message could have come from a country that was proving so reactionary and barbarian; and it was even more astonishing that Hitler's country was once the fatherland of Humanism, the fatherland of Goethe.

It is known that Goethe, who was only one generation younger than Lessing, was completely surprised to find such a voice of protest coming out of "barbarous Germany" of that time.

"In America today," Piscator wrote for the program of the Studio Theatre "the essential conditions to that honest effort to reach the truth, still exist. They are being defended on all fronts with planes and guns and they must be defended at home with that same spirit of scientific humanism which has been the lifework of all artists before and after Lessing and which is both the means and the goal of the human race."

Nathan the Wise was set in the time of the Third Crusade, when religious hostility was particularly savage. According to the story, the Jew Nathan has raised a Christian child as his own. When the young Knight Templar in love with Rebecca finds out this deception, he wants to punish the Jew according to ecclesiastical law, and is dissuaded only by the intervention of a Mohammedan. There are several scenes in the play which convey truth with overwhelming simplicity. The most famous scene centers around the wise Jew's straightforward telling of the parable of *The Three Rings*. The fable originally came from Boccaccio.

> *Three brothers had inherited three precious rings from their father. One of these rings had the magic power to render its owner pleasing to God and man. But which was the right one? The father's will explains that as long as the brothers compete in good deeds and good will, it will never be known. Everyone may believe that he is the true heir of God if he follows His laws and obeys His commandments. But who is the rightful owner of the ring, is as uncertain as who is the true heir of God.*

Lessing had lived under Frederick the Great, who was as well known for his spirtual liberalism as for his political despotism, his fanatical belief in a greater Germany and his obsession with war. But under Frederick, Lessing was not exiled, he could even write *Nathan the Wise*. Under Hitler he would not have been allowed to live. Germany owes a deep debt of gratitude to Lessing, who prepared the way for her later achievements of intellectual life.

It was neither the halting translation nor the pertinent direction of James Light which made this plea for tolerance a theatrical success. The press found it an admirable and moving play in spite of the old-fashioned plot, which was static for an American audience accustomed to action. But it had the great merit of being totally timely. It was brought to the audience exactly at the moment of their understanding. Besides the playgoer could identify himself much more with the destiny of Nathan. His fight was much more comprehensible than Lear's self-made catastrophe.

While Wolcott Gibbs in the *New Yorker* held that he could "not quite see *Nathan* as an evening's entertainment, no matter how much you may admire the sentiments," Brooks Atkinson in the *Times* certified that this was the "first work of intelligence to appear in our neighborhood for a long time."

On April 3, 1942, the Belasco Theatre marquee read: *Nathan the Wise* starring Herbert Berghof. The Shuberts' enthusiasm and understanding of the importance of this play brought the Studio Theatre performance to Broadway.

People were beginning to recognize and examine the merits of the Studio Theatre. With *Nathan* on Broadway, interest was ranging beyond the confines of the New School.

We could sum up the Studio Theatre's efforts in a banal way saying that they had been shedding light on different aspects of Epic Theatre. We could say that *King Lear* was a revision of the classics; *Circle of Chalk*, a play with a realistic message; Bruckner's *The Criminals* an investigation of the human condition; and *Nathan the Wise* a lesson in political theatre.

I do not think that this classification would prove anything as far as the value of the Studio Theatre was concerned.

To me the value of the Studio Theatre was that it functioned like a third eye of history. It drew a perspective. It did not show us just the frozen world of congealed ideas, nor did it reflect only our daily thoughts. It assumed a duty, a most annoying but important assignment—to show the truth.

Dorothy Thompson, the well-known columnist, in a symposium on the Theatre in Wartime on January 29, 1942, hailed the Studio Theatre for setting an example for Broadway: "Why is it that our theatre wishes to avoid the issues of the war?" And she answers:

> How could it possibly be expected not to, since the theatre has avoided every profound emotional and intellectual issue for a long time. It is taking off plays scheduled before the war began—plays that would help men realize the war. It

suspects that its audience are exclusively composed of Shorts and Kimmels. Above all, it wants to avoid tragedy in any form. Thus, it seeks to isolate men from suffering and reality. But no one can be isolated from the suffering and reality of war; therefore, it does not isolate anyone from war but instead isolates men and women from each other.

. . . There is an immense power and comfort to be found in a body of men and women sitting together and sharing a common experience even of suffering. Creative release comes out of the pooling of one's faith, joy, patriotism; and above all, it comes from being lifted onto a higher plane, in which birth and death, past, present and future, assume their proportions in time.

Billboard summed up our efforts in March, 1942, in the following words:

The Studio Theatre, it seems, is gradually assuming the place once held—the place that should still be held—by the Theatre Guild.

13) "WAR AND PEACE"- A REALITY ON STAGE

Since Hitler's attack on Russia, America had awakened spiritually. It was if the country had suddenly discovered the primacy of certain values; above all that War and Peace were not just words—

In the autumn of 1941 a new and harsher wind blew around the Dramatic Workshop. Life was measured by abrupt departures. Students enlisted, were drafted into the services, new students enrolled. Faculty members went, new ones came.

Few believed that peace was at an end. With Pearl Harbor and our entrance into World War II, there was no longer any doubt.

The truth had come to us that the spirit of adventure was different from the adventure of the spirit. Philosophy had suddenly a ring of truth: one should have lived with Tolstoy long ago. Was art not closely linked to religion, to man's spiritual emancipation, to his becoming a conscious creator?

It was if everyone was suddenly released from his own loves and hatreds and enlisted in a greater love—that of the Whole. As if it were possible to correct the distortions and mistakes of indifference and place life again in the right perspective: against death.

Hitler was following Napoleon's road to Russia. Was he not attempting the same course as Napoleon—Moscow, Smolensk, Borodino? Was Tolstoy right in saying war is a matter of chance—and how would chance play with us? Was this history proving that "War is the father of all things," as Heraclitus said, or can man change the great and cruel pattern?

Our fascination with Tolstoy's great work was renewed. War and Peace, presented now, would be more than a play, more than history. It would represent truth in the world of that moment.

Piscator decided not to wait any longer, to abandon all Broadway ambitions for War and Peace, and produce his and Alfred Neumann's dramatization at the Studio Theatre.

Anyone who has lived the extraordinary instant in which a cherished ambition vanished in the light of a more important task knows how much resignation goes into such a decision. Actually to abandon the chance of a commercial production on Broadway might have seemed to many people a foolish choice. But they would fail to understand Piscator, who although aware that the Studio Theatre could only give the skeletal substance of the richly designed production, nevertheless, thought it necessary to do it.

Was he a gambler or was he a stern believer in the message? Perhaps he was both. His deep sense of the sacredness of life always was the winner.

Everything we did now carried a new beginning. Our time was filled with all the big and small things that are involved in starting again. Time did not carry any meaning except the date for the opening of *War and Peace*.

. . .

Now Epic Theatre was no longer to be just a colorful phrase used in the Playwrights' Seminars to describe Piscator's theatre, but was to become a stage reality.

What was Epic Theatre—this theatre "truer to life and fact"? Was it theatre at all? This "play" of freedom and responsibility, tailored by knowledge, ruled by laws that man's mind can discover and should obey? Was it Theatre, all self-existent, ultimate?

Nothing on stage is ultimate, and much thought is necessary to create reality. No doubt, from the playwright's point of view, Epic Theatre enlarges the nature of theatre as it shows a perspective of life. But man does not become unrealistic if he strives for perspective, nor does the theatre. Both change proportion, that is all.

Some stress the value of this perspective as an educational act. But it seems to me that it is more than that. It is also an individual act, the very pinnacle of personal development. Perspective is a shift of balance and accent away from the self, toward the objective look, the "distant look." The Theatre of Illusion, contrary to the Epic Theatre, favors the "intimate look," the image in the mirror, which is always dramatic, full of excitement, vanity, and romantic emotion.

I remember seeing such a look of perfection, which struck me intensely. It was at the Metropolitan Museum in New York. There is an etched relief of a woman on a mirror, the earliest known, found in an Egyptian tomb of 2025 B.C., the portrait of a Sumerian Princess, Kawitt.

There is nothing in her attitude of that emotional outpour, the tensing of the muscles, the troubled expression, so characteristic of the later period; so characteristic of our own look in the mirror; so typical of the Theatre of Illusion. Kawitt, on the contrary, had an exquisite, ironic smile, as if she were capable of laughing at herself. Perhaps it is this look that Brecht means when he mentions the effect of alienation.

The sweep of this thought goes further. Most of the time in Epic Theatre events are narrated—*not* shown. This gives the story an even more objective slant. Events become a matter of history, be it past, present, or future.

The "distant look" is the historical look, the observer's look. History as the narrator of events, as the molder of characters, as the "measurer" of things—as they happen—by cause and effect.

This "distant look" is not without attraction, nor is it new in the arts. It can be found on the old icons, representations of sacred personages, flat paintings, low reliefs, sculptured figures.

Religion says that not one leaf falls from a tree without a cause. Whatever man creates belongs to history—to his own, to that of other people, of other actions, which added up in performance produce achievement, exploits, adventure, evolution. It has long been said that we live in deeds and not in years.

Man cannot evade history because he cannot evade his own experience. Every war is his own, and every peace as well. He is part of the grand scheme, the grand design, the general schemes, and the minuscule enterprises that also are part of his realm of actions.

He cannot escape responsibility for it. Whatever surrounds him is his creation. It is of his own making, positively and negatively as well. But as these innumerable and various actions which constitute his task of living are of his own making, they are changeable. There is no fatality in man's act of expression except the fatality he superimposes on it. Man in his quality of the doer is as changeable as his fate. He is, therefore, as essentially dramatic as in his historical role he is Epic.

The Greek playwrights knew it. So did Shakespeare, Voltaire, Goethe, Gorky, Rolland, Buechner, Shaw, O'Neill, Brecht, Sartre; they are all Epic playwrights because they are thinkers. To them, the Hegelian idea that art is no different from science was acceptable. Science has the function of subduing and exploiting reality for the use of man, including his social existence; art has the function of involving itself in reality in order to change it effectively. The playwright, therefore, is the recorder of history as much as the poet of history.

What is often misunderstood by professionals in the theatre is that Epic Theatre is as much a director's theatre as it is the playwright's. A director's theatre is a theatre in which the director rules.

This sovereignty of the director is not new in the theatre. In each period in which the theatre used all its means to produce a totality on stage, the director became quite powerful. Modern times have known such dynamos, each one completely different in his form of expression: Richard Wagner, Copeau, Meyerhold, Tairoff, Max Reinhardt, Gordon Craig. All of them have been true *meneurs de jeu*; that is, spectacular ringleaders—magicians, tyrants in their powerful single-mindedness.

Piscator has been accused of being a tyrant seeking his own identity, while actually he was seeking to establish an objective reality on stage. He was also accused of being an engineer, an architect of theatre.

When Antonin Artaud speaks of "the architecture" of a play, he is not far from the Piscator-Gropius idea of theatre

Total Theatre. Total Theatre suggests the "universal director," whom Artaud envisioned as well.

No two men differed more in their idea of what theatre should be than Artaud and Piscator. Yet in their theories one can find certain resemblances.

Both artists, Artaud as well as Piscator, thought of theatre as functional. Artaud states in his manifesto that theatre has to function "as precisely as the circulation of the blood."

Piscator expressed it in a Dadaistic way: he wanted theatre to work "as easily and precisely as a typewriter."

Artaud was a better theorist than a practical man of theatre. Piscator was, above all, a director who knew how to put his theories into practice. He reorganized a play in order to experience it in terms of the moralist; Artaud, in terms of the sensualist. Artaud the sensualist, Piscator the moralist—both bound by an intense love of the theatre. Artaud in his "theatre of cruelty" wanted man to transcend "the psychological and physical limitations." Piscator believed the intelligence of man capable of guiding him beyond personal destinies.

Both sought to eliminate the estrangement between stage and audience, between player and playgoer, and to establish a direct contact between them, not a sentimental attachment nor a nostalgic dependence nor a psychological identity, but a give-and-take on a realistic level, provoking catharsis from within. The playgoer should not continue to view the play passively but be consumed by it actively; that is, he should go through an experience that really challenges his conditioned thinking and that provokes change.

It is not easy for theatre people to subscribe to an approach so sober in presentation and vibrant in content as Epic Theatre. If they succeed in doing so, they experience the feeling of scales falling from their eyes and given an undistorted sense of the wonder of "reality."

Thus Epic Theatre rather demonstrates life than pretends

to be life. Its logic is more than appeal to the life of reason in the theatre. It is the link with facts and events.

Brecht used to say to Piscator, "Please stop your damned logical way of acting."

Where does the director start?

With little. Art always starts with little—an image that ap pears. The image of Napoleon at odds with destiny, as in Tolstoy's play. It connects with other images: the Czar, bewildered noblemen, idealists, men of war, peasants, the couples; images of a world perplexed. Even if the first image is not perfect, it is a specific image and should present and express what is true.

Images precede action. They set the pattern in which the direction has to go. Sometimes, the original image—no more than a suggestion—is part of the director's personal experience. It is not yet creation. It discloses itself to him when it is clearly expressed within him.

Then only can the director draw a *diagram of the performance.*

The diagram is more than an outline. It is a real *carte du pays,* a mark of the landscape the director intends to conquer. It must have perspective, define the scale, propose the ground plan, base and method of operation, and take steps to insure that everything is workable. A play in twenty scenes, as for instance Anouilh's *The Lark,* which we can consider an Epic play, has to be as fluid in presentation as the two- or three-act play. The scenes have to follow in chronological order; inner and outer order; separate entities have to form a whole; successive scenes or simultaneous scenes: flashbacks; hypothetical scenes telescoping the events.

The diagram has also to take care of the root activities of the characters, their emotional tangents involved in the situation, the cause and effect of the happenings; tell the story, analyze it. The diagram shows this analysis visually step by step—sometimes designing it clearly as black and white, sometimes pointing it out with a finger, sometimes marking the course of figures, constructive data, maneuvering to pull out the idea as the gold from the mine. A workable diagram must teem with ideas and possibilities; yet it is only preparation and comes to naught without dramaturgy.

Dramaturgy seems an obscure word in the theatrical vocabulary. Few people know exactly what it means.

Yet dramaturgy really signifies "the play's the thing." It is the final and definite essence of the play come to life, the winding up of all the efforts that have been going on before, the putting into practice of everything that has been elaborated upon. In one word, it is the carrying into execution of the whole performance.

It is the final state, in which the director-craftsman and the playwright achieve their closest collaboration.

I don't want to advocate a method, but I should like to speak for dramaturgy, because it permits the director, even if he is not a "genius," to direct a creditable performance.

The next step for the director is to take perspective. Every period speaks its own language and every art form is conditioned by its own experience. This experience is based upon a specific reality. Reality is not just an outer manifestation but the expression of the inner man. It conditions the behavior and thinking of an era. "Modern man tastes of his own world," says the philosopher Arnold Hauser, "in the juxtaposition and blending of things and events." Does this mean that modern man is less involved than his ancestors in his acts of expression? Nothing can be too great for those who erect skyscrapers. Is it a different kind of greatness which confronts us in the theatre?

"Is there an 'ordering light'?" asked Moholy-Nagy, the close collaborator of Walter Gropius. "Is there an 'ordering light' in what we are doing?" We sometimes wonder. Can art and knowledge, these distinct fields of our activities, come together? Yes. There is an ordering light in the theatre—a pilot light for the director to find the concept of his production—truth as it takes shape and gets hold of his conscience: dramaturgy.

Dramaturgy deals not only with the idea, the theme, the story, but also with the plot. While the relation of man and his acts is profoundly dramatic in itself, it is not the plot, the conflict, which determines the action of the Epic play. It is always the basic philosophy, the point of view; be it historical, political, social or moral.

It is also dramaturgy which provides identity for the play and formulates its style, brings together all the inner and outer elements—which allows the ideas to become alive.

Dramaturgy is the rock and fortress of the Epic play—the structure, the strengthener that gives sustenance to the whole edifice. Shakespeare spoke of "Atlantian shoulders fit to bear the weight of the mightiest monarchies." Epic Theatre is a mighty monarchy.

The basic conflict presents itself threefold: the thesis, individually and collectively; the antithesis, the absolute; and the resulting synthesis.

This synthesis, once established for the play, serves as the center from which everything radiates and becomes the "active principle" of the production.

It is good to be reminded here, or so it seems to me, of Piscator's contention that modern theatre should be regarded as a parliament in the sense of the ancients, to see and present "life steadily and as a whole." Epic theatre sees life as a whole and a continuum as well as a cause-and-effect phenomenon.

The Epic play is not written in acts but in small scenes, each one self-contained. The conflict of passion does not drive towards any catharsis. It does not portray any struggle, but rests on a situation, showing it, developing it in sequences. Flashback as well as future visions free the action from time and space and change the spectator into the observer; who, instead of sharing an emotional climax, can analyze the why and the wherefore. Epic Theatre compels the spectator to a world outlook instead of a view from the bridge.

Dramaturgy can work in a positive or negative way for a play.

"Is Clyde Griffiths guilty or not guilty—in your screen treatment?" was the first question the director Sergei Eisenstein was asked by B. P. Schulberg, the head of Paramount Pictures, for whom Eisenstein was to direct *An American Tragedy*.

"Not guilty," was Eisenstein's answer.

"Then your script is a terrible threat to society."

Eisenstein and his associates explained that in their treatment, they considered the crime committed by Griffiths not his alone, but that of the whole society. Therefore, the film was concerned with exposing that guilt. Apparently, Dreiser thought so too, when he brought the material to a tragic conclusion in his book, an ending unthinkable without a definite social attitude. Paramount Pictures felt that this concept denied the American dream. Eisenstein's script is still gathering dust for Paramount Pictures.

Piscator's dramaturgy for Schiller's *The Robbers*, as he produced it at the Staatstheater in Berlin, transformed the classic into messianic drama. The fight between the two von Moor Brothers, normally accepted as the fight between good and evil, became under Piscator's direction the fight between the established order and the revolt. Karl von Moor, the hero, became the rebel-reformer of humanity. Franz, the antagonist and villain, grew into the criminal guardian of materialistic life. Their quarrel was no longer merely a quarrel between two human beings, one egotistical and one self-sacrificing, but the fight between two social attitudes, two social groups.

To design his performance, the director of Epic Theatre has also to consider *composition*.

Composition on stage is the agreement of the part with the whole. In itself, composition is nothing and cannot be grasped that way. Only as organization of the whole does its importance reveal itself. It is the concrete structure, form and design of the ideas that must be conveyed to the audience. It is also the "path of the eye" of which the painter speaks, the path that leads us into the depth of the act as well as along the road. This path can be presented only by a line of movement of the characters or by grouping them in an emphatic way. Composition is also music insofar as it fashions sound and voice. It is performance when it combines execution, touch and expression. It is action as it takes advantage of the images of perception and brings them together in dramatic sequences.

Composition, of course, "does not tell the story." It is the technique employed, capable of expressing feeling, mood, and the quality of the subject. There are opportunities for composition not only in the grouping of the actors, but also in the handling of spatial unities, block forms, machinery, and through the greatest magician of all—space.

Space, theatrically seen, means not only spatial arrangements of the stage, but it means space as a human experience.

"Space is a reality," says Moholy-Nagy, the magician of stage vision. "A reality, once it has been comprehended in its essence, can be grasped and arranged according to its own laws. . . . These laws," he continues, "have to be studied so as to use them in the service of expression."

Space is more than a formative possibility. It is seen first in the extensions of height, breadth and depth; as line, as plane, as solid or volume. But its manipulation is, curiously enough, not fixed.

In the transient action of the play, space develops a four-dimensional quality within which every physical entity may be located. Every physical environment, or any circumscribed portion of it, has one temporal and three spatial coordinates. The temporal gives us the duration, the interval between two points of time. Man, of course, is its chief phenomenon, the organism of flesh and blood—the measure of all things.

Every performance is connected with concrete and abstract time, the customary moment or hour for something to happen, to begin and to end; and then with the endless variety of this fixed time and the possibility of fitting it creatively into a coherent system—the unified production.

The unity of time with space and action has played and still plays an important role in the "well-made" play, based on the Aristotelian concept. The Epic play, except in rare cases when events span several decades, need not extend beyond the normal stage time of about two hours. However, it exceeds it in imaginative narrative time.

There is another aspect of design for production that should be mentioned here: the motorization of the stage.

The mobile stage is still a question of money but also, more importantly, a question of its permanent imaginative value. How long can treadmills, turntables, changing, moving, and rotating levels, escalators, motorized bridges, elevators—the complete, even the ideal motorization of the stage—sustain the playgoer's interest?

> We must learn to use the physical world of the stage as freely as a painter uses his palette. Film and television hold tremendous possibilities for the theatre. Also, the use of music and sound effects can lead to contrasts within the dialogue—such as the spoken and the subconscious thought.

> *Only in this way will the director really come into his own
> and help to create a theatre that will be of our modern age.*

This Piscator said in his book more than thirty years ago.

Every good director also has to know how to handle lights.
In no other area of the stage has so much progress been made
as with lighting. "When one day the actor can walk on
light," said Piscator, "he will become as light as air. He will
float on space. His body proportions and plasticity will
change."

Light is indeed the stage's first painter. In the past, light
was directed onto the stage from above, from the sides, from
different wings, from the proscenium, left-stage, right-stage,
from floats and from behind the scenes.

But light that frees the foot from the floor creates a
different dimension of the character. Light is no longer a separate element, but blends with the actors. It creates new laws
of movement and gesture, and probably new dialogue.

Color also plays its part. Epic productions demand much
color variation. Colored light is used to underscore and point
up the action. The color wheel is frequently used in order to
accentuate the dynamic quality of staging.

But technique may turn against the director. Machines and
gadgets seem sometimes to have lives of their own.

A bizarre incident occurred in connection with Piscator's
production of *What Price Glory?* at the Staatstheater in Berlin.

The two protagonists, American soldiers who were both in
love with the same French girl, had been fighting with each
other for her favors. They were ordered to leave the village
and march to the front. This march to the front was Piscator's *pièce de résistance*—the death march of *What Price
Glory?* To reinforce the despairing quality of that march, he
had installed a large treadmill, extending from upstage center

toward the audience, which was to activate their march—their march to death. The stage grew darker and darker. As soon as the two actors, Hans Albers and Fritz Kortner, felt the treadmill moving under their feet, they reacted to it. Their weary bodies stiffened and their march rhythm tightened. Their guns lifted triumphantly, mesmerized by the rhythm of their own movement. They flung their caps into the air in the rapture of victory of a triumphant military class.

The critics the following day observed with surprise that Piscator had finally succumbed to patriotic enthusiasm.

Another almost tragic accident occurred during a Piscator performance of Gorki's *Lower Depths*. The first act lies in a tenement section of the city. The scene was set by Piscator on different levels, with a continuous movement of elevators bringing one group of people down while the preceding group disappeared into a trap below the stage. All the levels were united by an enormous black curtain which covered the actors' bodies and left only the heads visible in the semi-darkness of the dawn.

At one moment the trap door got stuck while another elevator from above started moving. If it continued and the trap door did not open the group on the lower level would be crushed. At the last moment, while the orchestra members turned their heads away to avoid seeing the tragedy, of which the audience was completely unaware, the trap door finally opened.

Seen from this perspective, the Epic Theatre director should take into account another facet: *technology*. He should be a good engineer of the theatre. The modern playgoer responds positively to the new theatre construction of glass and metal and the technical inventions. He likes to have confirmed on stage what surrounds him in his daily life—the machinery of civilization. He is proud, in this way, to share the alpha and omega of the newest creations.

It is the director's job to determine the technical means with which to activate his performance and which will also find intellectual as well as spiritual response in the playgoer.

· · ·

Piscator had conceived, for *War and Peace,* a stage split into five acting areas. At the rear was a platform made of glass ascending to an area which he called *the stage of destiny.* Here the historical characters appeared—Napoleon; the Czar. Here also the battle of Borodino was shown; one could see Lilliputian soldiers being advanced and retreated by a Gulliver—Pierre, the central character of the play, the battlefield's observer.

Covering the center of the stage at audience eye-level was a circled area which Piscator called *the stage of action.* Here specific dramatic scenes were played; the whole subjective life of the characters was unfolded here. On this platform, Andrei said goodbye to his father and wife before going into war. He came back here to find that his wife had died. It was also here that he introduced to his father the captivating Natasha with whom he, now a widower, had fallen in love. Here he offers to forgive his enemy Kuragin, who has seduced Natasha in his absence.

The drama has scenes played in consecutive sequence and also scenes played simultaneously. For these, three stages jutted out towards the audience; small platforms constituting different areas.

Right and left were *stages of reflection or meditation* from which Andrei, Natasha and Pierre voiced their private thoughts and stream-of-consciousness reactions; their private thoughts as well as Tolstoy's thoughts—that is, the Tolstoyan philosophy the dramatists wanted to convey.

Then, downstage center, there was a *small bridge* going into the audience, which served the central character of the play, the Narrator: the spokesman for our time and also the antique messenger, who prepares the way for the scenes and brings the tidings of events. Perhaps, enlarging our vision, we can think of him as common sense, public opinion.

This five-part model stage gave Piscator the opportunity to explain to the students his idea of Total Theatre as Gropius and he had seen it.

Piscator drew directly on quotations from Gropius, to define Total Theatre:

> In the Total Theatre . . . we have tried to create an instrument so flexible that a director can employ any one of three stage forms by the use of simple, ingenious mechanisms. The expenditure for such an interchangeable stage mechanism would be fully compensated for by the diversity of purposes to which such a building would lend itself: for presentation of drama, opera, film, and dance; for choral or instrumental music; for sports events or assemblies. Conventional plays could be just as easily accommodated as the most fantastic experimental creations of a stage director of the future.
>
> An audience will shake off its inertia when it experiences the surprise effect of space transformed. By shifting the scene of action during the performance from one stage position to another and by using a system of spotlights and film projectors, transforming walls and ceiling into moving-picture scenes, the whole house would be animated by three-dimensional means instead of the "flat" picture effect of the conventional stage. This would also greatly reduce the cumbersome paraphernalia of properties and hanging backdrops.
>
> Thus the playhouse itself, made to dissolve into the shifting, illusionary space of the imagination, would become the scene of action itself. Such a theatre would stimulate the conception of playwright and stage director alike; for while it is true that the mind can transform the body, it is equally true that structure can transform the mind.

Attempts had been made before to give history a meaning on stage. A meaning is not revealed merely through time and space, nor through the mere personal conflict. It only takes on complete significance when integrated into an infinitely vaster drama—that of the universe.

This spiritual vision of the universe is usually a technical composition in a Piscator production. In our present situation, it was not possible to be concerned with scenic invention. The Studio Theatre was no better equipped than at the time we produced *King Lear*; and we had not heard the last of the *Lear* thunderstorm that drove the critics out of the theatre. We had seen technique become a dead end because it had to function in such narrow confines and under great restriction of budget.

War and Peace at the Studio Theatre would by no stretch of imagination be the production Piscator had envisioned for Gilbert Miller.

Why did Piscator take the risk then to present the play?

There were several reasons: the first and most important was that the sum and substance of *War and Peace* Tolstoy's "telling substance" had proved true: war was an object of chance. In spite of all warnings, in spite of the tragic experiences of other countries, in spite of the efforts of the League of Nations, war had continued to flourish, even take on gigantic dimensions.

The other reason was that the Studio Theatre production would be an ideal chart for the students to understand and study Epic Theatre.

"To clarify and clarify again . . ." Piscator used to say. Interpretation is nothing, knowledge is what counts.

To understand, he went back to the sources again and again, accounting, verifying—telling.

I thought at first that so much clarity would be damaging to the theatre, and that the underlying text, the unspoken word, could bring more clarity than all this directness.

I found out that it is not so; that language is a spider's web spun by intelligence, in which reality and lie are both caught; that one cannot be clear enough in the theatre, nor simple enough; that truth is not wrapped in ceremonial robes nor can speech be led outside of the action. True poetry sits in the heart of the debate as war sits in the heart of peace.

"The choice of *War and Peace* for a dramatization was not accidental." It was years ago that Piscator had written this to Gilbert Miller. He was writing the same words now as the foreword for the program of the Studio Theatre performance.

> In 1938, the Spring before Munich, the world knew the Nazi danger, but it did not see the disaster. And we who had felt the first blow had not found the means of transmitting our apprehension to those that had not yet felt it.
>
> It was then I thought of War and Peace. Tolstoy . . . shows in Pierre the development of an idealist from a pure Pacifist to a fighter; in Napoleon, the man who misused the aims of the French Revolution—Liberté, Egalité, Fraternité—for his own imperialistic ends. To me, as I re-read Tolstoy's work, Pierre, with his good will, his confidence in human dignity and his belief in the progression of the good, seemed the true representative of all the people who are natural enemies of fascism.
>
> Today, the thoughts of Pierre may seem too passive, but it is this very passivism that clarifies the difference between the regimented jingoism that makes fascist countries jump into a war, and the spiritual preparation that democracies need before they can convince themselves there is no other way out. There comes a time, nevertheless, when even men like Pierre, however disinclined, begin to realize that peaceful thinking and living are not enough to maintain peace. This seemed to me the important message, and it is the principal reason why we present the play at this time.

"Is there that much in a play to think about?" a student asked.

"Drama with a 'pointer,' you know," said another teasingly.

"It has a popular boy-meets-girl appeal; Lisa loves Andrei. Andrei loves Natasha. Natasha loves Pierre."

"It can never be done," said another youth, just as Piscator entered. "Why do you think Gilbert Miller dropped it?"

. . .

Piscator started staging; everything was in turmoil. Scenes emerged, were tried out, rejected, redone. He never seemed to go back to what had already been established, as is customary, but began with material that was at the bottom of the pile. He dug for the content again and again. From this sprang, new ideas, new ways to deal with the material. But from this also sprang the breath of life that pervaded his rehearsals and, whenever he succeeded, this breath found its way into the performance.

The play's structure caught the actors unprepared. This was not a play, yet it was a play. These loose scenes going on successively, sometimes simultaneously—were these a play? The students were certain it would be unworkable. Most of the play was narration, fragments of dialogue describing highly complex situations and even more complex characters. Time seemed to be of no importance. A character is seen in his home, then gets wounded on a battlefield and returns home years later. Stage time—five minutes. And what about settings, illusion? A drawing room opens up on a battlefield?

The Czar and Napoleon meet on the same platform of destiny. Moscow is burning while Andrei dies in his room hundreds of miles away. Where are we? In Russia? Where is the snow? The sleighs, the samovars, the ikons, candles, draperies, the Volga, the gypsy music? How little flesh and blood does this stage require? How bare an atmosphere?

Yet as the rehearsals went on, it became clear to all that,

although they still did not believe the story could come out on the stage, and did not trust its dramatization or its translation, they could not deny that the play had caught their interest. There was a concentration, a driving intensity in the staging, which captured their attention—a new dynamism in opposition to the unobtrusive, stylized bare platforms.

Those who objected to the approach did not realize that what may have been offensive to the sensibilities of the present, would not offend those of tomorrow, that simplicity, austerity—abstention from sentimentality—did not eliminate beauty, and that every work of art has its own aesthetic quality.

We would have to agree on the term, aesthetic quality. Is the aim of art merely enjoyment? Is not beauty on stage also shaped and molded by a concept or a purpose? Are not the mechanized arts beautiful, the whole machinery of the modern age? Ford wanted to make his cars functional but also beautiful. We have only to agree on what we understand by the word. Beauty of form, beauty of idea, or beauty of expression. There are people who say we are in need of beauty more than ever but what does it imply? Pleasure of the senses, the exaltation of the mind, or the solidification of the spirit?

. . .

War and Peace was presented in the late spring of 1942, in May, as an experimental performance with an excellent cast.

Hugo Haas, who played Pierre Bezuhov had made his debut in America the previous winter in The First Crocus, had been one of the foremost actors in Prague where he had played a variety of roles. He had also been a director and an actor in films, and had directed one of the first anti-Nazi movies, Skeleton on Horseback. Dolly Haas as Natasha had made her first American appearance in the Studio Theatre production of The Circle of Chalk. Ben Ari, the assistant director, who also played Alpatitsh and the insane man, had been prominent in the Habima. Mildred Dunnock played Maria. She had begun as a voice in the Max Reinhardt-Franz Werfel *Eternal Road* and had the most beautiful diction on the American stage.

There was also Warner Anderson (Andrei Bolkonski) who had last been seen opposite Lily Darvas in the Studio Theatre production of *The Criminals;* Fay Baker (Helena), an understudy for Lillian Gish in *Dear Octopus.* Edmonia Nolley (Dunyasha) had had varied theatre experience, including acting, directing and writing. Her Broadway career had been primarlily that of a theatre domestic: the housekeeper in *Children's Hour,* the cook in *The Man Who Came to Dinner,* and companion nurse to Margaret Sullivan. Kenneth Dana (Dorn) had played in many productions, among them *Rope, Five Star Final, Dead End,* and *The American Way.* He had had his own radio program *Thirty-five Questions from Broadway.* Paul Mann (Anatol) an experienced Canadian, had been featured earlier in a Studio Theatre production of Ferdinand Bruckner's *The Criminals.*

. . .

The critics' opinions were once again divided but, all in all, positive. It was not a smashing success and Gilbert Miller had not come repentant to ask us for permission to do the play. He was seen at one of the performances, but disappeared without a word.

The New York Herald Tribune said "War and Peace was a bold, earnest, and conscientious effort to get as much as possible of the letter and spirit of the mighty tale of Tolstoy into serviceable greasepaint terms . . . a gallant try . . .

"By mounting the play in rapid, almost cinematic, succession on two levels and all corners of the Studio Theatre's stage, Mr. Piscator managed to provide a great number of scenes and an overwhelming amount of text. The acting is satisfactory, if something less than brilliant. Hugo Haas as

Pierre, Miss Dolly Haas as the enchanting Natasha, and Warner Anderson as Prince André. As Prince André's pious and slightly sanctimonious sister, Miss Mildred Dunnock seemed to me particularly in character. The settings are simple and attractive and the production of War and Peace moves smoothly and conscientiously enough, the one defect being that the epic quality of the novel ungratefully eludes capture."

The New York Sun liked the scenes flowing into and out of one another under spotlights, behind gauze curtains, and the symbolic black velvet flats. It spoke about Realism blended into Stylism, soliloquy and narration to help the story along, with a vivid picture every so often in the telescoping of time and space.

George Freedley, although he admitted that as a "theatrical experiment" War and Peace was of unquestioned interest, he was not in sympathy with the version that we offered.

Robert Coleman, on the contrary, thought War and Peace was a formidable challenge for a commercial producer with a big bankroll.

Wilella Waldorf, of The New York Post, with her sensitive judgment at all levels, discovered the true merit of our adventure. "The season on Twelfth Street presented recently Erwin Piscator's production of War and Peace. It is doubtful that any stage could do justice to Tolstoy's novel, but the very fact that the Studio Theatre had the nerve to try, merely goes to show the sort of thing one may expect down there."

The strangest compliment we received was from Burns Mantle in the Daily News, who wrote that "the settings, the lighting, and the melding of the many scenes are the chief attractions of War and Peace." Our one-man technical department (together with twelve students) certainly enjoyed the review.

The play continued to be successful with the audience. No

one seemed to be shocked by the experimental approach nor did the playgoer reject Epic Theatre. Of course, if we think of Brecht, we can remember that he was actually only understood after his death and following much indefatigable spadework by the critic Eric Bentley.

Yet for all the good will of our audience, we could not attract the interest of Broadway and transfer the play uptown. We closed it after our usual run of four weeks.

Was this then to be the end of *War and Peace?* Could Piscator, after years of planning write the results off as an experiment gone wrong? What was the strange alchemy that excited the public, but left the critics cold?

• • •

In the search for another play we found Daniel Lewis James's *Winter Soldiers*. Mr. James had received the Sidney Howard Memorial Award for the play from the Playwright Company and $1,500 to assist the New School in its experimental offering.

Winter Soldiers was a play dealing with the siege of Moscow. It opened on November 28, 1942 with a large cast and eleven scenes along a route which led a train from Zagreb in Yugoslavia to the gates of Moscow. It was quite successful with critics and audiences alike.

This success did not bring us luck either—quite the contrary.

The reviews had attracted Equity's attention to the Studio Theatre. The unions felt we were in direct competition with Broadway. This was flattering but disastrous. Our seating capacity was not large enough, even when sold out, to pay union fees to actors or crew. Although the students were taking care of running the play and the actors gave their services, still, the cost for every production was so high that we could not dream of balancing our budget.

Equity threatened to withdraw permission for professionals

to play at the Studio Theatre. Piscator was able to raise enough money to pay actors the Equity rates and to continue with the performances. Then the other unions also cracked down and demanded their share. Any work done on stage— even by the students, whether it were carpentry, lighting, stage design, properties, and even the box office, would have to be union.

During the winter of 1943-44, we were haunted by the crisis which threatened to close the Studio Theatre. We were still believing in a miracle. We hoped against hope to raise the money.

When I say we, I mean the we that creates itself beyond the rules and accidents of language. Something that exists in any creative relationship, and that shows beyond the symbols and the structure of facts.

Everything takes on a pattern when people are working on the same project together—like building a bridge or a highway. These undertakings are no different from producing a play.

There are synoptic works which unite separate areas of knowledge and experience and give a new meaning to the isolated exploration. One begins to read them like a neglected book, first as a surprise; then one gradually perceives that there is something worthwhile in this work which one has searched for for many years. War and Peace was one of these works.

There is a unity that comes from common effort. A "bond" between people which does not represent an absolute ethic in itself, but becomes vital within the frame of reference of the We. There are few better stimulants and causes.

We had made friends since we had come to the New School, and we had earned audience appreciation. The Studio Theatre had many staunch supporters. We turned to them now through Fitzi's clarion call.

When we had come to the end of our list, we realized that we had received many admirable letters, but that the money we needed had not come in.

One of the strong supporters of the Studio Theatre, who had also sponsored Piscator's entry into this country, gave a compelling performance by calling several meetings with people he had hoped would help.

Many of them, outstanding people, had good reason to keep Studio Theatre alive, specifically a group of writers and producers. They were unconcerned, however, about the impending close of the Studio Theatre. This was serious.

One thing was forgotten in this hasty evaluation of the situation. It was later brought out by our Public Relations Department. Namely, that the Studio Theatre had brought an inestimable gain in dollars and cents to the New School, not only by establishing a "greater public image," but through reviews, new items and radio announcements, which appeared almost daily; the publicity was worth thousands of dollars.

Alvin Johnson did not come to our defense this time.

There was something, so we felt, like a play within the play, some kind of activity unfavorable to our fight for keeping the Studio Theatre alive. Ambiguous reasons were given to us; members of the Board apparently objected to the strong public appeal of the Studio Theatre and thought it had no place in a school dedicated to Social Science and Politics.

Inquiry makes little sense in such a case. We could assume what we wanted. And we did not like our assumptions. The cautious behavior of the Board was less discouraging than the indifference of the faculties. They were no longer partners, no longer, presumably, did we have any common basis to talk or understand each other. Everyone seemed overcome by the magic of fear that lack of money produces.

The New School was not wealthy. There had never been

money enough. Now with three faculties and a theatre department running, money was definitely scarce.

Besides the Studio Theatre was considered a losing venture. With a bigger budget so as to take care of the union's demand the danger was great that we would fall into debt.

This was the end for the " greater public image."

The wheel of Piscator's good fortune had come full circle several times. The most powerful shock had been the closing of the Piscatorbuehne in Berlin on June 15, 1928.

It seemed like yesterday. Only this was much more incredible. How could anything finish that had not even had the opportunity to begin? Had all devotion to the project, all thinking and planning led to nothing else but this end? The small sum we needed was a drop of water in the sea of money lost daily on Broadway. Why had no one come to our rescue? The Studio Theatre had not failed, on the contrary, it had given a new impetus to the theatre at large. The History of Theatre told us of similar events, where the lights of the theatre were turned off on the marquee. The guardians of theatre—where were they?

". . . unluckily for me I find myself in difficult straits at present. I urgently need your help . . ."

This is an extract from a letter the sick Artaud wrote to Louis Jouvet in April 1939.

"I have something to say, so let me start mumbling it. . . . I am much easier to get along with than they say. . . . I only want to agree. . . . and I beg you to believe in the urgency of this. . . ." This goes again back to Artaud—and to all the Artauds, Majakowskis, Meyerholds, Piscators—all those who have been experimenters and rebels in the theatre. It is said about Stanislavsky that there were times when he begged his colleagues with tears in his eyes to listen to him. Meyerhold defended the credo of his art before the judges of a disinterested court until his death.

> The number of my experimental productions is small, I can count them on the fingers of one hand. Aside from this, as master—and I have the audacity to consider myself as such—a master must have the right to experiment. He must have the moral right to test his artistic ideas, irrespective of the outcome. He must have the right to commit errors.

The denial of the right to experiment—was that why Ernst Toller hanged himself, tired of being made to test his ideas irrespective of outcome, tired of writing without a publisher, producer, or an audience, weary of betrayal?

I, too, felt weary, but Piscator did not. There was something good in this for him.

They had not done so frightful a thing, they had not thrown out the baby with the bath water. There was something more to it, something more than the old pattern of money and ambition.

Doesn't everything depend on LAW? There are various laws working in the visible world of the vegetable and animal kingdom, there are other laws working in the visionary world of art.

The closing of the Studio Theatre of the Dramatic Workshop was not the end of it.

14) PRESIDENT THEATRE

The President Theatre on West 48th Street had had many lives.

It had been everything—from a cinema in seven languages to a distillery. It had housed serious theatre groups and had presented showcases for amateurs, novices, drama and comedy clubs, balancing its inequities from one bankruptcy to another.

It had the distinction of lighting its marquee with bubbles of reputation, the short-lived Caruso Theatre and a one-year blaze of the Hindenburg Theatre.

After the Irish hoisted their flag for a short period, it ended up as the Midget Theatre, with a true midget cast performing an unforgettable melodrama called *No Mother to Guide Her*.

Under several managements the theatre had functioned as The President Theatre. In March 1938, it was sold at auction. The bid was $122,000 for the five-story building, which was considered a steal.

In 1945, when we saw it for the first time, it offered a rather unique view. Its Baroque frame, dressed up in Italian pink tinting the neighborhood, suggested a tempting package of real estate to the prospective buyer.

We did not buy it. However, we were ready to lease it as quickly as possible. Although on the outside rather gaudy, the President was a real theatre with an excellent stage, good equipment, a dimmer board, dressing rooms, and 299 seats facing a glowing red velvet curtain.

There was a good reason for our haste to sign the contract. It had become clear in the meantime that the episode of the Studio Theatre had only been a prelude to a larger event in the world of changes; the break-up of the Dramatic Workshop from the New School.

In spite of the closing of the Studio Theatre we had continued using the auditorium of the New School for our March of Drama. Unable to play with professional actors, we used the students in readings, which in progressive experience turned readings into scenes and scenes into acts. An audience of surprised playgoers discovered a wealth of theatre for the first time. What had seemed merely further study became a sporting proposition, a serious, alive way of learning, which had a cultural end.

As we occupied the auditorium almost daily for rehearsals, as well as for performances, the auditorium became the object of much conniving.

Not only had we been working against financial odds, but we were also pressed for space. We had not realized that space at the New School had become a rare commodity. While the Dramatic Workshop had been growing in student body (from 20 to 7,700) the former University of Exile, now proudly called the Graduate Faculty of Political and Social Science and the recognized backbone of the school, had grown as well. It was only natural that its members demanded use of the auditorium for their lectures and meetings.

While we were still trying to find some compromise, another competitor for the auditorium bid for possession; the new Ecole Libre des Hautes Etudes, a veritable who's who of Franco-Belgian culture, with Nobel Prize winners, former prime ministers, and even one prominent screen star on their roster.

As the situation had become untenable, I was asked to find a theatre or hall which would become a refuge for the expanding activities of the Dramatic Workshop with its seminars and productions.

Little did we know what challenging, perplexing and extraordinarily successful years were to follow our change of location. They can hardly be described. At the present moment, all that counted was that we had a theatre again.

• • •

The irony was that even at the *President Theatre* we were not able to play with professional actors without satisfying the union's demand. This no longer upset us. Our student body had grown not only in number but also in talent, well-trained talent by now. We could now use them to advantage.

We made some repeat performances of the most successful classical plays that we had presented at the New School, such as *Twelfth Night*, *The Imaginary Invalid*, and even *Hannele*.

But our true interest lay in a "theatre of ideas," provocative theatre, prompted by life—contemporary life.

It is a hazardous task to stimulate the audience to think; to discern and discriminate; to make it take a look at itself; to make people distinguish between the true and false. However, it is an even more formidable task to get them away from ordinary plays, ordinary forms, and to uncover for them different dimensions of reality.

The modern novel has explored much better than the theatre the phenomenal changes of time and space. James Joyce and Dos Passos, dissimilar in approach and style, have examined modern man in his new surroundings and puzzling transformations, and have shown the simultaneity and continuity of our lives. They stripped the antiquated values from their texts, retaining only the accoutrements of the concrete and the abstract of narration: situation, character, and action.

The novelists grasped the political and creative forces and shaped the postwar tensions trying to find roots for the action of man, not in an episodic accessory sense, but in an Epic vision, creating a continuity of life and art.

What had the playwrights done to inform us about life? Recently they had, for the most part, exploited sensationalism and focused on unhealthy problems or on the evocation of the most personal emotions. Others exposed the smallest canvas they could find; enjoyed the black and white of photographic truth.

Where were the great themes of our times, themes in which we could recognize the politics of survival and salvation, themes with the morals lying in the depths of order as well as in anarchy, themes prompted by doubt and betrayal, regroupings of economic reality, new forms of corruption and aggression? Where were the new plays and who was writing them?

If theatre was here to stay, it had to reflect contemporary life; give true shape to our weaknesses and our strength; our running progress and walking. It had to help us endure the period of marking time. So it is that in war or in peace, man can make changes and can change. This was to be the age of the "new man"—the protagonist of our theatre.

We knew that there were new plays written every day. Our own curriculum had stimulated playwrights to go ahead, but we knew too that in spite of showing much talent and more ambition, these plays were mostly cautiously dramatized autobiographies. We had to draw upon existent mature writers from other countries.

Consequently some of the most significant plays of the modern world theatre had their first American performances on the stage of our 48th Street Theatre.

Jean-Paul Sartre	*The Flies*	April 1947
Armand Salacrou	*Nights of Wrath*	December 1947
Robert Penn Warren	*All the King's Men*	January 1948
Wolfgang Borchert	*Outside the Door*	March 1949
John Matthews	*The Scapegoat*	April 1950

Were these Epic plays, the inquiring playgoer might ask? Not in the didactic sense of the word. Brecht's satellites and admirers will not mention them as Epic, let alone give them a place in the sacred fold.

Why had they been chosen to inaugurate a Piscator season at the President? They had something in common: Piscator's philosophy. But there was more to it. They embodied his *feu sacré*.

All these plays were in a peculiar way related to political strife and warfare. They held a lesson learned in our time: to reduce the aggressive drive to a tolerable necessity, live peacefully together and work for a common end. Such goals may seem dangerously inappropriate to some theatre people and humorous to others.

Yet this teaching is not new and was always Piscator's deepest credo. He liked the theme; a theme upon which to build a new society. This is one of the reasons Piscator was never seeking only the "well-made" play. He sought themes, themes involving individuals to the degree that their personal destiny would reflect the tenor of the whole. He sought the representation of a bond between man and man which could be called Christian, although he was not of any church. He sought representations of the bond of love and friendship which could embrace the whole world, reach out to all humanity and exert a pressure in the right direction in spite of the world's madness.

That gave rise to the primary element in Piscator's approach, the element that separated his theatre from Brecht's. Brecht's approach remained fictional and circumstantial. It was balladlike; episodic, like the song of a minstrel. Piscator's epic concept was grounded in a reality bigger than himself, conjuring up some of the kindred spirit of the Homeric poem.

Brecht, so often referred to as the creator of Epic style, tied his theatre to the fable and narrowed the stage. Piscator, searching for the commandments of the great builders of humanity, unfolded in epic dimensions and opened up the stage.

The President performances were never Total Theatre such as Piscator had produced in Berlin in the 'twenties. Life did not allow him that luxury. Yet even in the restrained circumstances he was facing now, the focus remained; human evolution. Evolution, the natural companion of reality. Evolution would make a modern play into a classic or draw from a forgotten drama, a subtext worth being produced in our time. Not episodic but Epic.

To the literal-minded, Sartre's The Flies was a modern version of the old Orestes legend. In fact it was also a remarkably bold denunciation of tyranny and despotism. The tragedy of Orestes returning to find his homeland violated parallels the tragedy of the occupation of France by the Nazis. Zeus, symbolized not merely the god of the flies and death, not only the greatest of despots and deceivers, but also Hitler. Nor was Orestes alone the hero "engaged" but every French soldier, every *poilu*.

This was a striking twist to give the myth of Orestes, but a wholly predictable one for Sartre. Once a prisoner in a German concentration camp, Sartre had escaped and found his way home to Paris where he had joined the French Underground. He had never forgotten his captivity. *The Flies*, as presented by Charles Dullin in 1943 at the Théâtre de la Cîté in Nazi-occupied Paris, proved more than an existentialist credo. It was a manifestation of a pledge to the Resistance.

Although Sartre dressed up his characters in antique robes, it must have been clear to the German headquarters that this play was an open defiance to the Nazi oppressors. Perhaps it was not "stupidity" on the part of the German high command in Paris to allow the play to be performed to crowded houses but on the contrary diplomatic flair. Let us not forget that the occupation forces in Paris were recruited from the elite cadres of Germany. Their special mission was to impress the Parisians with the German heritage of culture, perfection of manners, and tact. Also, the Germans, avid lovers of French culture, may have remembered Beaumarchais' revolutionary *Figaro* and the unprecedented acclaim it gained because of its interdiction.

. . .

Piscator opened his production with a documentary film showing the German army entering Paris. One saw the victors passing beneath the Arc de Triomphe, marching in goose step down the Champs-Elysées, their triumphant faces challenging the mournful faces of the Parisians.

The film was intended to be an opening shot at the audience, fired from the stage.

During rehearsals and again at the first previews a difference of opinion arose which swept audience and cast into debate; they felt that in introducing the play in this fashion, Piscator was violating its classic mold.

An alarm was sounded to Sartre in France. A few days later, we were informed by cable that Simone de Beauvoir, his appointed emissary, was en route to New York.

Piscator offered to show the play in two different versions, one evening with the documentary and one evening without. This, he hoped, would also bring a reaction that would justify his choice.

And so it happened, in successive preview performances.

The evening without the introduction of the film proved a moderate success. The audience had come to see a Greek play. They saw it—a modern adaptation of the tragic story, which everyone had expected. Even the second act, with its catharsis in murder, did not make the evening into anything more exciting than just a good modern treatment of a classical theme.

The second night, introduced by the film, awakened the audience to the fact that something other than only the Orestes story was being played here. They gasped, but suddenly they understood Sartre's bravery in having this play performed under the very noses of the Nazis. Piscator had added a dimension: Paris under the Occupation.

The shot aimed at the audience proved successful on opening night, April 17, 1947.

Simone de Beauvoir expressed her happy surprise at Piscator's concept. "It is one of the few theatrical experiences which lift the theatre beyond its self-satisfied mindlessness and gives the audience an active role again."

Even the critics praised the play and production unanimously.

"The staging of *The Flies*, under Erwin Piscator's supervision," one wrote, "offers an exciting change of pace from conventional productions. . . ."

Sartre's strangely ambiguous Zeus, in his effort to create order in the world he began, blunders by being vain—he gives man the freedom which ultimately destroys him. The "free" Orestes, although only a "mite in the scheme of things" does not recognize Zeus any longer as his king. "The king of the gods, king of the stones and stars," is not his king, "not the king of man." He is responsible for his life. He does not need a king anymore.

In spite of the passionate theme, there is a cool breath going through the play which never allows us to admire Sartre. His dialectical genius is not unlike Brecht's. It comes however, not only from the influence of Hegel and Marx, but from an earlier world nourished with philosophy as much as with science, the Cartesian world.

Sartre's equation of freedom is a point in case:

Freedom, as human civitas firstly.

Then, freedom as responsibility. Man is what he does. To save himself and others he must become responsible for his actions. There is no other way out.

Freedom as the goal in man's struggle for existence; not as an aspect of existence but as life's totality—neither moral, emotional, nor physical, but the struggle of choice, the strategic struggle.

. . .

The program for The Flies read: directed by Ransom under the supervision of Erwin Piscator.

It took his associates some time to understand Piscator's system of "supervision," which was mistakenly regarded as the employment of a stage manager.

"Supervision" was Piscator's way of saying: "We work collectively, as a group, together, as a unit and as one person."

Theatre *is* a collective, the most challenging—also the most ambivalent, since in the final analysis one will has to prevail: "a relaxed will" as John Gassner would say.

. . .

I have often thought that the lack of understanding with which Piscator met at times was a consequence of his overall approach to theatre. He possessed the ability to raise any kind of theatre to the level of Epic Theatre. Only those who really worked with him knew that he could also undertake other forms of theatre, old or new. If the resources to experiment had been put at his disposal, Piscator would have swiftly and profoundly advanced the codified practices of Broadway, which, conservatively estimated, was fifty years behind world theatre.

. . .

If Paris labeled Jean-Paul Sartre "the father" of Existentialism, Armand Salacrou, close to Surrealist experiments, modernist constructions and the theatre of dream, was well labeled the dramatist of "anguish and despair."

One of Salacrou's earliest plays, *L'Inconnue d'Arras*, had attracted my interest in 1924. Madame Zukerkand's sister, a Viennese lady and translator of Marcel Achard, Alfred Savoir, Géraldy and many others, directed my attention to Salacrou. It was my first great challenge as a "professional," and I embarked eagerly upon the translation. Salacrou's play was performed subsequently in a number of German theatres.

Now, twenty years later, it was my pleasure to meet with Salacrou's work again, and this time to translate his latest play into English for Piscator.

Nights of Wrath had been running in Paris for almost two years. It was a play about the French Resistance, showing a quite different aspect of it from Sartre's *The Flies*.

Salacrou's characters were average people, thoroughly middle class; good patriots, good citizens who enjoyed work, love, and home until the war confronted them with reality—and their true nature.

Bernard Bazire, Salacrou's protagonist, gives shelter to a lifelong friend who has been wounded while blowing up a German supply train near Chartres. Realizing that this hospitality endangers his family, Bazire is faced with the choice of turning his friend out or endangering the safety of his family. He struggles with his conscience; but, impelled by his wife, he surrenders his friend to the town's collaborationist. The friend is tortured and finally put to death by the Gestapo in an action that also involves the death of other members of the Resistance.

In *Nights of Wrath* Salacrou portrays those who were neutral during the war, neither collaborationists nor members of the Resistance. They remained faceless until the critical moment—the moment of choice, the moment when the answer "yes" or "no" determines the destiny of another human being.

Salacrou in this play asked an important question which was directed not only at Europe but at every man, everywhere.

Is passiveness treason? Is it a crime to remain indifferent in the face of violence? How much does a man deceive himself about his courage and forthrightness? Then, how dangerous is the mind in its tendency to compromise, its willingness to adjust to anything? How irresponsible is this attitude?

Having shared in the resisting side, Salacrou has contempt for the man who would compromise; but, he does not attempt to dictate or impose a world view. He strives instead for convincing theatre.

Therein lies perhaps both the success and the limitation of Salacrou's theatre. His primary gift is in powerful theatrical action. His characters cry out. They are dramatic. His truth is clear and specific, but loaded with theatrical devices. His challenge is less a rebellion than a trick. Yet, his poetic intention and his sardonic wit have often since been used effectively by other writers, specifically in the Theatre of the Absurd.

As a production, *Nights of Wrath* remained an eloquent appeal to all to recognize the fact that no person or nation can remain neutral or indifferent in the face of disaster. I was praised by the press for directing the play skilfully. The students were moved by the inherent reality of the theme and acted it with astonishing sincerity.

. . .

Robert Penn Warren, the poet-novelist, had begun in the winter of 1937-38 to work on a verse and prose play called *Proud Flesh*.

When he returned to America in 1943, he decided to treat the material as a novel. The book, entitled *All the King's Men*, published in 1946, won the Pulitzer Prize.

Dealing with the South of the 'twenties and 'thirties, when it was ruled by political bosses and their corrupt machines, the story centers on Willie Stark. A simple "country hick" wanting to do good, Stark realizes that he can achieve this only through power.

It deals with Jack Burden, the "Southern gentleman" who has no motivating drive in life and becomes a willing tool for Stark, the man of action.

And it deals with the cunning crooks around Stark who raise him to the Governor's chair.

It deals with the people who loved Stark and those who hated him and those who, like the judge who realized the good Stark tried to do, but who could not abide his methods.

It deals with All the King's Men.

While visiting Piscator at Lake Placid in the summer of 1947, Warren showed him his earlier treatment of the material, *Proud Flesh*. Enthusiastic as Piscator was about the novel, the verse play left him cold. Much of it was exposition, beautiful lyric writing: highly complex situations with critical scenes occurring off-stage.

The tragedy of the modern political man, who has to compromise, and his defeat through the acceptance of this, had not materialized in *Proud Flesh*. Epic Theatre could tell the story of compromise.

Warren defended himself at first against Epic Theatre. He did not want his play to be either historical or biographical. He did not want any political idea to become the central theme. He wanted the facts of a man's life dressed up as poetic images. He did not want any lesson for society, any criticism of it. He wanted his play merely to interpret a world in which all paths lead to corruption, not to attack that world. "I do not wish to duplicate the world. We cannot duplicate the world. We can merely live in it."

He kept insisting in long discussions, facing the Adirondack sky embracing the lake, that he had been interested and attracted by the fate of Huey Long, but that he wanted to forget him. Willie Stark to him was purely fictional; so *All the King's Men* was fiction. To repeat, somewhat amended, an oft-used phrase, "Any resemblance to actual persons, Mussolini or Hitler, living or dead, is purely coincidental." Warren was sure he did not want any political consideration, direct or indirect, to invade his play.

Yet politics was the very air that had nourished his life. He had grown up in Louisiana, and for anyone living in the South in the 'thirties, "politics was nearer than hands and feet," in his own words.

Little as he wanted to enrich the play with new ideas, he did not want to have it simplified either, and become merely an exposé of the corruption of the times. "I know that the play, if it is to be honest, has to do some justice to the reality

—I mean reality . . ." He never finished the sentence, although he repeated it often enough.

What was the play's reality? A state explosive with violence, corruption, sadism, perverted aspiration, and dwarfed intelligence.

A reality, he was afraid, although of legitimate and valuable concern, that would deny him stage poetry.

Nevertheless, the collaboration between Piscator and Warren began. Both artists had something in common which made a creative relationship possible. They both worked in structural terms: the one in terms of dramaturgy, the other in terms of pure poetry.

And slowly *All the King's Men*, in Piscator's directoral hands, became political theatre.

First, as he explained in his program notes: "The fate of modern man is a political fate . . . quite different from the Greek mythological fate or the Christian divine fate or the Medieval heroic fate."

Piscator did not completely achieve the wholeness of the characters he had desired to provide in Penn Warren's play. When Louis Kronenberger wrote in a review (*PM*, January 23, 1948) that Warren's dramatization at the President "cannot be regarded as a sound play," he was right.

Piscator agreed with him. No, it was not a sound play. It was a dramatized novel with a great theme. Yet did it not exemplify, by a stretch of the imagination, a moral truth, the key term being the reality of a human being who in adversity capitulates? The conflict and the crises of choice never appeared in the play. Whatever the message, it was not stated directly. Instead, Warren in telling us the story reconciled the rational with the poetic and elevated his characters to myth.

Was Huey Long a myth? A Myth of our time? Warren, I am afraid, allowed us to think that the aim justifies the means.

The play captured the attention of the press, and attracted a discriminating audience. It did honor to the tenth anniversary of the Dramatic Workshop. Dr. Johnson wrote:

> What I see in the Dramatic Workshop, after ten years of development, is an educational set-up that reproduces the conditions of the actual life of the theatre more efficiently and adequately than any theatrical or dramatic educational set-up that exists in America, or has ever existed in America. I say this with full recognition of the remarkable work of Professor Baker at Harvard, later at Yale. Professor Baker turned out scholars, some of whom produced dramas of distinction. What he offered was education so brilliantly amateur that it verged on the professional. Piscator is so brilliantly professional that he verges on the amateur.

Wolfgang Borchert's play, *Outside the Door*, was the first unusual play to come out of postwar Germany. It has been classified as an Expressionist play and so it is, if we consider Expressionism as part and parcel of the international movement of experimentation that characterized the European theatre at the turn of the century.

I myself think that Expressionism is not dead—for it is too rich, diversified, and progressive to fade away. It only went underground and then burst forth afresh with Ionesco, with Friedrich Dürenmatt, with Max Frisch and Fritz Hochwaelder. All their writing, diverse as it appears, has roots in Expressionism.

When Borchert wrote his play, it was evident that he could not develop it in the naturalistic style. The transformation of all human values after the war, the unrealistic evaluation of cause and effect, and the absence of aim, the bartering for survival, had taken the theatre out of what had been called reality.

To me, Borchert's play is timeless. It is the expression of a haunting poetic intuition which experiences the outside world before it can find itself.

Borchert does not present only the soldier Beckman, who is one of those "outside the door," but, in the play's expressionistic magnification, he presents all those "outside the door."

The other characters are similar in their anonymity. The wife who has betrayed him; the friend who has forgotten him; the girl who calls him a ghost; the one-legged man who beckons to him; the colonel who is as gay as he is brutal; a woman who is freezing in a warm room.

Beckman had two strange partners who are part of the elements of his own madness; the Other One, who knows the ways of the world and the River Elbe, an honest river that stinks of oil and fish.

"It is a decadent play," said John Gassner. "I've read it and I dislike it intensely." There was a moment of silence and Piscator arose.

"Let's walk around the block, John," he said. "What I want to say needs a clear head."

Piscator was not altogether surprised at Gassner's reaction. Hadn't the author himself described his work as a "play no theatre wants to play and no audience wants to see"?

Borchert, like Georg Buechner, died in his twenties. He had written the play in 1946, shortly before his death. It had been said about him that, had he lived, he might have become another Buechner.

The play, Piscator explained to Gassner, had a message for a new generation, a message he could defend—but one which America might have no use for.

Nevertheless, the play was performed:

In it, a soldier Beckman stands on a pontoon. It looks strange. There is a single dark sound, a splash, and his silhouette is gone. The wind blows. The Elbe flows on. The streetcars jangle. A man has jumped into the river.

He won't be the first one nor will he be the last. But, in Beckman's case, death doesn't want him. The river gives him back. It is a "stubborn" river, which does not want a creature to slip away in its arms just because he feels "outside the door." The river laughs at Beckman's suicide and spits him out.

Turned away from the wind and the water, Beckman meets with the "Other One;" the One of yesterday . . . the One of the schoolbench . . . the One of the skating rink . . . the One he met again in the snowstorm of Smolensk . . . and in the shelter of Gorodok. The Other One . . . of Stalingrad. The Other One, who is also himself—the One of tomorrow.

But Beckman does not agree that there is a tomorrow. And although the Other One assures him that there is a tomorrow and that there is good in all the evil and light in the darkest darkness, Beckman denies. He chases the Other One away. To him the Other One has no face, although he may speak with a thousand voices and laugh while he cries. He will never believe him again. Hadn't he provided him with false hopes of a home, wife and children? They had not even recognized him as he came back with his goggles for eyes and a gas mask for a face. They have shut the door and left him outside, no more than a stone in the street; a part of the acres of rubble.

The Other One sends Beckman out into life. An old battle-experienced general teaches Beckman to play, on a giant xylophone constructed of men's bones, "The Entrance of the Gladiators." He meets some women; old ones with gray hair and hard, crackling hands; young ones with lovely, longing eyes and many little children, and they whisper out of the darkness where he stands: "Corporal Beckman . . . where is my father . . . Corporal Beckman . . . Where is my husband . . . Corporal Beckman . . . Where is my son . . .

Where is my brother . . . Where is my bridegroom . . .
Where . . . Where?"

And Beckman asks his Colonel—could he not add the responsibility for these few dead soldiers to his own thousands?

> Can you live, Colonel . . . Can you live, Colonel . . .
> Can you live one minute . . . without screaming . . . Can
> you sleep nights? . . . Yes . . . Then it does not matter
> to you . . . Then I can sleep too—if you would be so kind
> and take back my ghost and at last I can sleep again.

But the Colonel gasps at the strange young man. Another
door closes.

Beckman goes to a nightclub. There he is set up as a clown
to sing to the customers the song of those "outside the door."
He does it so well that here too the clients are frozen in fear,
and the door closes.

So, finally, he makes his way back to his mother, to the
sanctum where he was born. But there are strangers in his
home. The Beckmans are gone. They have moved away; Plot
5 in the Olsdorf cemetery.

The door bangs shut.

Alone, Beckman is again approached by the Other One.
Life goes on, he hears the Other One say. Why should not
Beckman live when all the other ones around him live? But
Beckman is dead. He has frozen to death standing outside
the door. He has been murdered by the murderers and is
dead among those who know that their deaths were like their
lives—senseless.

Is there no answer to this? No answer . . . Anywhere?
NO ANSWER . . .

The New York Times reported:

> Outside the Door has been written with a genuine intensity
> possessed only by those who have known torment and
> pain . . .

The next important play we had the good fortune to present to our growing audiences was an adaptation of Kafka's *The Trial* by John F. Matthews.

John Matthews came to us after teaching playwriting at Northwestern University and the University of Cincinnati. At the Dramatic Workshop he quietly developed writers who were turning out some good material. His earlier experience in radio as actor, writer and producer made him an astute judge of working procedures for playwrights. He was also the author of several notable plays and had scripted films for Warner Brothers. Even if our contact seemed casual during the years of his presence at the School, we were sure that he was one of our most inspiring teachers. We were not surprised when he brought us his dramatization of *The Trial*; a version tremendously superior in content and in true understanding of Kafka's world to the Gide-Barrault theatricalization.

In dramatizing Kafka, Matthews had made a timely choice, even to the title he gave the play: *The Scapegoat*. (Kafka himself had never given a title to his novel, but had referred to it in conversation as *The Trial*.)

Yet Matthews did even more, astonishing and angering some of the Kafka fans, but proving his superb sense of theatre. He took a poetic license rarely used in the dramatization of a novel. He updated the play.

The Trial had been written by Kafka some time after the First World War. John Matthews presented his story with overtones of the Second World War.

Kafka's literary utterances, although profound and original, tempted and puzzled many playwrights. To Max Brod, to whom Kafka willed his published and unpublished work, it must have been torture.

When Kafka instructed Brod that he wanted everything "in the way of diaries, manuscripts, letters (my own and others), sketches and so on to be burned unread," he certainly meant it.

Kafka, having spent his childhood in the flamboyant baroque city of Vienna, had shifted the center of his activities to Prague. After taking his degree in law at the German University in Prague, he started to write, but made his livelihood in an accident insurance office.

Soon he found himself uprooted, in more than one way. The birth of the Czechoslovakian republic left him, as a German writer in exile, undesirable. Being a Jew in a Catholic society made him a foreigner. Politically denounced, he found himself thrust "outside the door."

Years of sickness and misery followed, until his early death, in June, 1924, at the age of forty-one.

Kafka's wish to destroy his work produced a torrent of arguments by people who perceived in Kafka nothing more than a neurotic artist. Brod, who had listened with fanatical veneration to every word Kafka pronounced while he was alive, was no willing accomplice to his friend's desire. Being a friend but also an astute professional man, Brod knew that Kafka's work was not a trifle to be burned to gratify the wish of a dying man to exorcise his demon, but something that was meant to remain alive—of the same scope in both matter and means as the great modern creative works, such as those of James Joyce, Marcel Proust, and T. S. Eliot.

Undoubtedly Matthews must have known of Max Brod's conflict of conscience. Every attempt to publish these works or to dramatize them became in Brod's eyes a minor crime, a corruption by society. After twenty years of the closest unclouded friendship with Kafka, Brod was sensitive to the slightest distortion, even in the most excellent translation. The smallest scrap of paper he discovered, even a postcard forgotten in a drawer, became important to him.

What complicated Matthews' position even further was

that Kafka's literary output was classified in America as presenting a world of fantasy and irrationality.

Nothing was farther from the truth.

Kafka's triumph was of a religious order. Never had he advocated an evasion of spiritual life. There was no trickery or sophistry in his theory of escape. Kafka believed in evasion as the necessary means of survival for the man born to the new era he prognosticated: the "totalitarian age."

Joseph K in Kafka's *The Trial* underscores this view more strongly than Gregor in *The Metamorphosis*. Gregor is deprived of freedom by committing himself to self-evasion. K is deprived of freedom by a society which has grossly advanced upon him. Both try to find a way of outwitting the murderous circumstances that take control of them by giving in to them—as, for instance, K identifying with the summary courts in the perpetual sessions in *The Trial*.

The endeavor to win "through self-denial" is one of the startling, highly calculated and bedeviled devices of Kafka, never a mere trick; it probes deeply into man's striving. The fight for survival involves the process of atonement, and Kafka's characters—often in self-parody—practice it tirelessly. One might think that Kafka as a writer operated on the assumption of the "numbness" experienced before a catastrophe, a numbness that annuls all defense in combat.

This apathy became an inescapable reality for all of us during the war years, not only in the death camps but in such instances as the American paratroop company in the Battle of the Bulge silently digging their own graves before their execution.

Kafka's characters are not enigmatic figures; on the contrary, they act most logically. It is the state of permanent crisis that delivers them from thought by forcing them to act out their destiny; an act of heresy, choosing willful destruction, carrying into effect a downward self-transcendence.

So it happens that the nonpolitical man, finding himself politically involved, effaces himself in the hope of survival.

Kafka's characters are unreachable for entreaty or response. They are in trance-like states at the abyss of the human.

But, although falling prey to their enemies, they remain untouched by them. One wonders whether this is the reflective belief that this enemy, like all evil, will disintegrate through its own rottenness—or whether they, the victims, in the face of a menacing and arbitrary existence, simply perform the necessary rites for a more viable order of existence on whatever level.

There was an echo of Hitler's "final solution for eight million people" in the Piscator production of The Scapegoat. Also, something of the destroyed illusion of a man who had believed himself improvable and improving but had found that "the war to end war" had not changed man's inhumanity to man.

If apathy had smothered without recourse or exit the victims of Gestapo-controlled Europe, Mr. K could meet the same fate here, everywhere, anywhere.

Why?

John Matthews gives us an answer.

The Scapegoat is the story of "the nameless terror" that was the European heritage after the Second World War. The fear of things that might happen is the cause of all our anxiety.

"The nameless terror" is not only a gap in our awareness, it has proved a historical fact. As a gap, it drugs us. It sent men without fight to the concentration camps. As a fact, a historical fact, it ignores the shapes of civilization of the preceding decades and all the progress there has been.

The Scapegoat is man eternally pursued, eternally put to trial, eternally crucified, always judged by those who have no judgment. But, Kafka, profoundly conscious of the real and the symbolic, epitomizes here a principle that expresses the essence of religious truth: the recognition that the reality of the spirit does not depend upon the rational as truth. On the contrary, the reality of the spirit moves fluidly and profoundly, without doctrine. It loses vitality when it becomes a fixed belief.

Matthew's scapegoat is a slave not of a totalitarian state but of his own guilt feelings, which unavoidably lead him to punishment. As he has assumed his guilt, he prepares also his degradation, which leaves him a poor chance of survival under the law of the fittest. In fact, if he were to survive, he would be not only meaningless as a human being, but misleading. In giving himself up to the justice of the anonymous authority, he avoids becoming a freak of nature. His basis for salvation is to die as "the scapegoat" for all human evil. In terms of medieval witchcraft, he has to become "the cause of evil itself." And, in order to follow the unavoidable process of private guilt becoming collective guilt, he cannot remain only the cause of evil, but must bear the effects—he becomes the representative of evil—standing up for evil himself.

• • •

With *The Scapegoat* we presented our fifth important production. Our growing membership was proof that Piscator had created a demand for this kind of theatre. The inquiring playgoer had followed with great interest these substantial— almost too substantial—plays. The students never stopped wondering at the continuous productivity of the white-haired man who looked so young and who, despite his engaging smile, loved theatre "heavy with meaning."

A true theatrical personality implies several selves. By now, most of our associates had experienced Piscator, the philosopher and disciplinarian. There was another, quite different— the "totally other," who showed himself more and more, es-

pecially in rehearsals; the true theatre man who found his
deepest life in play.

Piscator, the actor, "held the mirror up to nature" now, a
mirror in which he could see himself and the life he created.

This takes us to the very kernel of the Piscator experiment.
For all the philosophizing frame of his mind, for all his growing humanism, his naturalist's objectivity, his intelligent sympathy as the interpreter of events, Piscator was an actor
turned director. His perfect spontaneity, his absolute freedom
when he was on stage, his rich imagination transcending all
relative conditions, his continuous being in movement—
pulled by the tension between the opposite poles of Epic and
Dramatic—bespoke a life of the stage enriched by the actor's
universe. It bespoke a make-believe containing all possibilities, from the agony of Macbeth to the sacred obsession of
Hamlet. His great theatrical feast, which he had developed
for himself and which he never stopped renewing, came to
him from a different platform, as well.

That is why he had started early to regard himself as much
an author as a director—author meaning "creator," the person
who controls the direct handling of the stage.

How does it take place, this passionate equation of author
and director?

The stage has often been said to be an arena of combat for
the two. For Piscator the stage was just another living presence, a third actor, so to speak; an actor not immersed in
thoughtlessness and wild emotion but aware and ready to ac-
knowledge every technical and practical means to bring the
theatre close to its purpose.

This idea of the stage as a collaborator may be an exagger-
ated one, but is at any rate a vital and perfectly acceptable
image. The director becomes in that way a modern Daedalus,
the ideal artist of mechanical skill and workmanship, the
craftsman on whom the artists depend, the tinkerer of supe-

rior skill and common sense who knows that the theatre is fifty years behind in technology compared with the mechanical wonders that surround us in our daily lives.

But technology not for its beauty or its thrill, Piscator proclaimed, but "technic as an artistic necessity." Piscator was sure, as a director, to extricate the meaning from the text and impose it as form. He laughed at people who think that technology will kill the poetry of the stage.

"Tell me first," he said, "what is this poetry of the stage you are talking about?"

"The word—the poetry of the word."

"For thirty years people have complained that technology," he writes in his article "Technic as an Artistic Necessity," "has killed the dream, and that the spoken word was the loser."

> What word? How many good words are being written that have such shape as to make unnecessary optical effects on the stage? But even if great plays existed today (greater plays than those that attract our attention) there never was a time when audiences were so spoiled with regard to optical effects as they are today. Films and TV are proof of that. And, while these means become ever more perfected, the theatre becomes increasingly impoverished with regard to its optical achievements, without making up in intellectual content what it lacks in technology.
>
> Yet this impoverishment is not necessary. I do not mean to say that colossal scenery must be built. The stage should merely participate in technical developments. The word "technology" was never infamous in the theatre. The unity of time, place, and action practiced by the Greeks is only a result—its origin was technical. Time was given by the sun from its rise to its setting (there was no artificial light; the stage was the place it shone on: and the action was the action that could occur at this time and in this place, i.e., without rebuilding.)
>
> But technology, in the final analysis, is only a means of

> spiritual expression, and must rise above itself. Where it
> fails to do that, it is in the way, whether in films or on
> stage. The search for the application of technical means is
> only the attempt to find the clearest expression; the shortest
> way of communication. The technical itself must become
> art.

The truth lay even deeper, in reality itself, as we had realized when formulating our program.

Few Epic plays were masterpieces.

It amused Piscator no end when artists, scenic designers, playwrights and students came to him with definite ideas about Epic. "Epic Theatre is still very young," he said to them. "You must not treat it so impatiently. There are few Epic plays. Yet there will be more and more, and you are going to write them and produce them."

For the moment, to be more explicit, he divided Epic Theatre into two catagories: the truly Epic plays, which had broken with the tradition of Aristotle and established a loose style of scenes disregarding the inevitable catharsis, and plays which lent themselves to Epic Theatre production because there were elements in their conflict of a basic social philosophy, which allowed an astute director to treat them differently from the conventional play.

To show an example of what he meant, he came back to War and Peace, to All the King's Men.

Yet I have seen Piscator staging a production of Bernard Shaw's play Androcles and the Lion in an Epic way. Shaw's play supports an idea which is ideal for the concept of a director of Epic Theatre: oppressor versus oppressed. Shaw's comprehensive foreword to the play, with its abundance of ideas on religion, history, morality, and sociology, contains many elements of Epic Theatre.

Another problem came up to torment our playwrights, that of Piscator's inclination to "rewrite." Although American playwrights had learned, since the beginnings of motion pictures, to adapt themselves to group work, they still felt that in the theatre they were to be sole master.

This, in my mind, is simply amateur arrogance.

If we consider that one generation produces at its best a handful of geniuses and that the rest of the royalty-taking scribblers are perhaps good craftsmen—excellent craftsmen (one might take them for geniuses were it not for their lack of true invention)—we cannot feel sympathy with the playwright offended because his script has been touched by another more skillful hand. He reminds me of the charming, often repeated story of Piscator's collaboration with Walter Mehring, one of Germany's true poet-playwrights. As usual, Mehring's play was changed by Piscator in structure as well as in execution. Mehring, alert of mind and an admirer of Piscator, obeyed and rewrote during the night what was destroyed during the day. One morning—it was shortly before the opening—he arrived with his right arm bandaged. He had acquired an infection, he said, and was incapable of writing any more changes. Piscator smiled indulgently and ordered a secretary to assist Mehring.

What was the fundamentally new hallmark with which Piscator had transformed the old stage?

The attempt to serve a spiritual concept with the most modern means of expression. This call for justice for all—dressed up in a fresh innovation—has been a unique and powerful call. A new function of the director as the choraegus of the stage has been added (to remember Toller's world in Hoppla, We Live, build on multi-storeyed iron scaffolds, as though life were a factory). Rasputin was played in a giant sphere that turned like an armed turret with bridges, stairs and gangways, transparent screens, projectors, and with everyday life reaching through cell walls.

• • •

If Piscator had engaged himself in the theatre of war and the impasse of history and sociology, sometimes not to his own advantage, his technical genius had passionately enrolled his forces of imagination in a renewal of the stage.

Like Dos Passos, his closest kin in the Epic area as a writer, Piscator used methodological means as a director: documentation, blueprints, inner and outer montage, technology, film, dance, loud speakers, posters, anything to free the material and expand it in time and space. He renounced the intellectual and psychological structure of the whole, the premeditated dialogue and the preeminence of the spoken word. The language of the play turns "optical"; it addresses the eye directly through mime, gestures, the basic *gestus*, and a new kind of scenic realization. Scenery is not a stage designer's individual creation, but the craftsman-artist's attempt to give visual structure to the director's thought of the whole production, the essence becoming visual.

If only we could find a play that allowed his method to come through, his polytechnical method, which sometimes left one amazed when he explained it—amazed and yet believing!

With each production we saw Piscator's staging change. Each time he formulated a concept, which he then worked out visually as well.

It is the paradox of the artistic life of Piscator that this master of the stage, this modern Daedalus of the theatre, lit his most beautiful fires when he was inspired by other aritists, like George Grosz, for instance.

If the acccptcd theme of *Schweik* was that "the human race is a race of victims," both artists, Piscator and Grosz, developed this theme to its maximum possibility by creating a dramatic-dynamic totality of the stage. They successfully opened up a new dynamic realm, that of the stage itself, in the total integration of thought, sound, color, light, form, and motion.

Such collaborations are rare. In "a school that is a theatre," Piscator had to start from scratch to fulfill his purpose. Many things remained abstract until exemplified by him.

He felt rightly that he should do a play at the President in which he could use all his technical skill. "Technique as an Artistic Necessity" became the slogan for the next month, during which he prepared the production of Nicolai Pogodin's *The Aristocrats*.

. . .

"If the death of Chekhov tore out a large part of the heart of the theatre," according to Stanislavsky, Nicolai Pogodin, being a great, new, fresh talent, must have put some of it back.

Pogodin was a newspaper man who had turned playwright, to the advantage of Soviet drama. He was no ordinary Bolshevik, but one of the romantic and poetic fighters of the Revolution, who never could conceal his disapproval of the bureaucrats. Together with Afinogenev, Kirshon and Vishnevsky, he became one of the ideologically useful writers of the new Soviet theatre, known to us mostly through his play *The Aristocrats*.

What attracted us to the play was that it was not only a provocative study of criminology, prostitution, and wreckers of society, but a richly human document dealing with the re-education of prisoners at the Baltic-White Sea Canal project.

Pogodin created valid characters who upheld the credo of generations and believed in the perfectibility of man. He claimed the same aspirations as Voltaire and Diderot and even Schiller in their plays, in his belief that reason and education could change society.

The production of *The Aristocrats* was the living proof of

"technique as an artistic necessity," which Piscator had so often proclaimed.

The stage was open and bare. The background consisted of four screens attached to steel pipes and mounted on dollies, which assured the mobility of the production. Not only did each scene have a specific screen arrangement with a series of slides to be projected, but the slide and screen positions were changeable within the scene. A turntable allowed the stage and the screens to move independently, or both to move together or in opposition. Furniture and props were placed in front of the screens and maneuvered in the manner of the Chinese theatre. They formed walled rooms, rows of trees or merely backgrounds for the slides to be projected upon. While one screen showed a slide setting the scene, another showed the map of the territory; a third projected statistics relative to the progress of the canal, and the fourth a picture of the workers and their slogans. Some scenes, such as those in the forest, required simultaneous projections on all the screens, thus creating a total illusion.

These projected images, fragmentary or total, provided a dynamic background for the action. While the disassociation was sometimes upsetting for the actor, it extended the play's scope and clarified its lesson.

It would not be quite fair to think of *The Aristocrats* as a fragment of history, formalistic in execution. On the contrary, in Piscator's production this play became a living experience of our day.

In rehearsing *The Aristocrats*, the students were quickly aware that Piscator's defense of content versus form was more than a personal whim. He was driving relentlessly for the meaning of the play with a kind of trenchant logic. "Look at me," he said. "I am the one who always points with his finger. It may be considered impolite, but it is the theatre's first gesture. I do not call it pointing *at* something. I call it pointing *out* something." He explained further that this demonstration was not new in the theatre. Euripides scolded Aristophanes for the same *gestus*.

Nor is it limited to theatre. Painters and musicians do the same. George Grosz used to point out a topic of his composition with his pen or with his brush. So did Toscanini, who stabbed a note as if it were a personal enemy. Poets and writers point at life with irony, with ridicule; then single out the position, play an idea to the breaking point.

The Aristocrats proved excellent entertainment. For the students it was a rare experience of group work. The whole student body was needed to master the technical intricacies and difficulties of the production and to maintain the performance. When not involved as actors, they had to enlist for stagework. Our turntable, although our latest acquisition, was medieval, rotated by foot. Each dolly had to have a special operator, guiding it in synchronization with the group working on more than a thousand light cues.

The Aristocrats remained in our repertory. It not only provided the audience with a contemporary play of topical significance dealing with a different society from ours, but it also provided the Dramatic Workshop with the rare example of a communal enterprise in theatre such as was once fostered by the Church.

. . .

After seeing *The Aristocrats*, Wilella Waldorf in the *New York Post* named Piscator "the Wizard of the little theatre on 48th Street."

And, as a wizard, he was busy sorting out the many lights of the theatrical sky and putting them all together again in meaningful brilliance.

It was after the tenth anniversary of the Dramatic Workshop that Piscator turned his attention again to the March of Drama.

Together with Chouteau Dyer, who had inaugurated the first successful student performances given at the New School, Piscator developed a repertory of plays at the President Theatre, taken from John Gassner's lectures. They were weekly performances of scenes, which, in chronological order, presented an illustrated history of theatre.

It was Fitzi's idea to make the March of Drama Repertory a paying proposition.

The President audience was admitted by membership in the same way in which the Studio Theatre had operated— membership was solicited by direct mail, not only to the potential playgoers, but also to various groups. The Board of Education graciously offered their help now for Repertory of the March of Drama. They suggested that our theatre should work in association with teachers of English of New York City and vicinity. In giving them the choice of a specific program of plays designed to complement their English department studies.

As we could not sell tickets at the box office, Fitzi had another bright idea. Why not enroll the playgoer as a regular student in the Dramatic Workshop? The courses and seminars would provide him with a general knowledge of the drama, an understanding of the cultural and social forces to which the theatre had responded and continued to respond. In addition, he would attend the performances every week.

The repertory for the first season included:

Steinbeck	Of Mice and Men
Sherwood	The Petrified Forest
Shaw	Androcles and the Lion
Shaw	The Devil's Disciple
Pogodin	The Aristocrats

Pirandello	Tonight We Improvise
Hauptmann	Hannele's Way to Heaven
Molière	The Imaginary Invalid
Shakespeare	Twelfth Night
Lope de Vega	The Sheep Well
Klabund	The Circle of Chalk
Aristophanes	Lysistrata
Gogol	The Inspector General
Dreiser	An American Tragedy
Gorki	The Enemies (adapted by Piscator)
Dumas fils	Camille

From Gassner's lectures on the American galaxy of the last two decades came *Hello Out There, Awake and Sing, Winterset* and other plays.

Soon we had a huge repertory. It was obviously a blessing for the young actors and directors who had come to the school to learn their trade in a practical way. Many of the audiences watched mere students turn into professionals before their eyes. Several off-Broadway groups, largely made up of actors groomed by the Dramatic Workshop and its March of Drama repertory, won great acclaim in their own right from the public and the press.

It is difficult to imagine young actors with greater freedom from self-consciousness and inhibition or with a better chance to learn the skills of the theatre, than those studying presently at the Dramatic Workshop.

During the summer of 1948, *Theatre Arts* summed up the achievements of the Dramatic Workshop over the past eight years, under the title "Broadway Incubator":

> Today the Dramatic Workshop . . . is an established institution offering two-year majors in acting, directing, stagecraft, and playwriting, full programs of study in film, radio and television. A faculty of fifty including John

*Gassner, Lee Strasberg, Edward Mobley and Joseph T.
Shipley staffs 375 full- and 450 part-time students; four
buildings house two theatres, practical workshops with
professional standards—the intimate 250-seat President
Theatre and the spacious 800-seat Rooftop People's
Theatre.
The Dramatic Workshop's March of Drama Repertory is
a history of the theatre illustrating the culture and society
portrayed in every age, presenting plays from Aristophanes
to O'Neill. The thirty-odd productions stem from Gassner's
March of Drama lectures and demonstrations—twenty
plays currently, three to six new ones added each year . . .
New Plays in Work and the Playwrights Seminar introduce
their students' plays; March of Dance traces its development
from antiquity to modern times. By serving as this training
and proving ground, the Dramatic Workshop of the New
School has provided the theatrical touchstone paving the
way for many, including Pulitzer Prize Playwright Tennessee
Williams, Phillip Yordan, Marlon Brando . . . and
Elaine Stritch . . .*

And, not to be overlooked, Rod Steiger, Maureen Stapleton,
Ben Gazzara, Walter Matthau and others.

The day Alvin Johnson and Erwin Piscator set up the
Dramatic Workshop at the New School for Social Research,
he envisioned the eventual growth of this unit into an institution organized for teaching and study in the higher branches
of learning in theatre, like a college of theatre—a university
of the theatre.

Our temporary charter from the Board of Regents had
reached its last year satisfactorily and the Dramatic Workshop
could, provided certain economic requirements were also fulfilled, acquire university status, qualifying the students for
bachelor's, master's, and doctor's degrees.

This was not without an ironic counterpoint. Piscator, as a
boy, had rebelled against school and abstract teaching. He
left the university dissatisfied because he did not believe in

academic training. Now his theatre experience had brought him back to the university.

There were no hours for Piscator. The days ran ahead of him in a constant expansion of his creative work. He explored ruthlessly what had been achieved up to now, gathered new facts, observed, experimented. He filled notebook after notebook, defining modern Theatre: notes for the director, the playwright, the actor, on the creative process in theatre increased one's understanding and active intelligence.

What these notes reveal above all is his three-fold, all-embracing quality—that of the artist, the humanist and the teacher, which focused his talent in a special way. He was aware, from the first moment an idea struck him, of all the implications and possible developments of this idea just as one might say a tree is aware of its branches and cannot develop in one direction but has to grow in many directions at once towards the warmth and light of life.

Therein was the strength of Piscator's work—the poetry of truth, which strictly speaking, set the stage for him as much as his love for steel, wood, any kind of pure material. He was instantly aware of any sham in life, yet he was theatre through and through.

When Piscator jumped on stage during a rehearsal something electrifying happened in that moment. Suddenly—I have experienced it innumerable times—one could see more than a stage character; one saw a particular human being—all alive, all real—with his past, present, and future.

It was neither his authority nor his knowledge, nor his knowhow, which brought about the desired change in the false attack an actor made on a role, but his tremendous humanity, his absolute faith in man. And although he knew so well that evil is only good distorted, he suffered by it in his every contact (artistic contact is the most intimate of all). In the darkest moments, he could show the great laws of becoming, the laws of change: the good.

We witnessed the expansion of the Dramatic Workshop as an institute of learning with its theatres and related media—radio, television and film. Had the objective been achieved, that of a "school that is theatre"?

Yes, because it defined theatre, not only by its nature, but because it showed its participation in a given culture: theatre as the visual mirror of a purposeful cooperative human society.

New visions are not always immediately recognizable unless they are firmly anchored, articulating the means of expression. "Practice Music, Socrates," said a voice to the despairing philosopher from outside his cell.

"To practice music" in the Socratic sense held no displeasure for Piscator. He liked to be reminded of music, common music, popular music—the progress of men.

What about other progress—technical progress?

It lay not in the few experiments we had demonstrated with our limited facilities, but through our teaching closer understanding of the significance of technical progress in the theatre, which led to greater freedom and a better use of the liberated energies of those engaged in it.

The Dramatic Workshop could also be proud of several noteworthy contributions outside of the School. It had created a Studio Theatre; it had produced plays one could not see elsewhere; it had created a theatre of discussion and ideas. It had built repertory theatre which produced more than fifty plays and enriched the theatre fare, plus presenting its notable new plays, premieres at the President.

Hundreds of scripts had been received by the school's reading department for New Plays in Work. Our own student playwrights, encouraged by Piscator, were turning out works

of exceptional originality under the chairmanship of John
Gassner and Joseph Shipley.

. . .

Tennessee Williams had come to the Dramatic Workshop
while we were still at the New School. He was attracted by
Piscator's legendary authority, his *mise en scène* and directing; directing not as a subservient and minor artist, competing with the playwright, but as an autonomous artist—a bold
and spectacular professional who demanded of the playwright
a new employment of the stage, and who allowed him a never-
before experienced freedom of continuity and simultaneity.

The Theatre Guild, of which Theresa Helburn was a director, had produced his first play, *Battle of Angels*. It had been
a failure—in Boston. Tennessee returned to the school and,
although he continued writing, he was forced to ask for a job.
He thought of becoming Piscator's secretary and wrote to
him about it. Piscator replied, advising him against engaging
himself in anything other than writing.

> I have your play on my desk in Yonkers. Every page I turn
> reminds me of what talent is. As much as I should like to
> have you in the School in a definite capacity, I think it far
> more important for you to be perfectly free to write your
> plays and that you have the opportunity to do so. Let me
> know your plans and ideas.

The world had since witnessed the triumph of Tennessee
Williams' *The Glass Menagerie* on Broadway, with Laurette
Taylor unforgettable in her last great theatre role. This play
bore evidence of Piscator's teaching and Williams' earlier association with the Epic trend. The loose-scene arrangement,
the stream of consciousness, which became identified with
Williams' characters, were charged with emotion but had
overtones of a world bigger than reality—the Epic world. The
Narrator was, of course, a familiar figure, an Epic commodity,
informing us of what we ought to know about the past, the

present and possibly the future of everyone concerned in the play.

The rational overtones in Tennessee Williams' play did not change its poetic beauty, but clarified the content. *The Glass Menagerie* is now considered a modern classic. Tennessee disappeared from the Workshop to our regret, but we were sure that wherever he was he would not stop writing.

We heard from him again after our production of *The Scapegoat*. He wrote to Piscator from his retreat in Key West, Florida:

> I am embarrassed and conscience-stricken, as I should be, by your gentle note of well-deserved reproach. I shall not say anything about my travels or the awful concentration required by my work, but only that I am as interested as ever in what the Dramatic Workshop is doing and continually more and more impressed and admiring of its accomplishments and its endurance in the face of so much that is adverse in our present circumstances. I am not in New York or I would certainly have seen your production of Kafka's great book. I hope to see it when I return in a few days. I have heard nothing but fine and exciting things about it. I feel it is one of the most significant works of our time.
>
> Soon as the terrific strain and tension of this new play is over, I hope we can communicate more fully. I am proud to be a board member and I hope that somehow or other I can manage to participate more than I have in the past.
>
> My continual felicitations, my warm regards as ever.
>
> Tennessee

. . .

The G.I. Bill of Rights and Vocational Training for the Disabled had brought the Dramatic Workshop hundreds of new full-time day and evening students. To further their activities Piscator initiated the Veteran's Memorial Stage under the chairmanship of Leon Askin and Eric Rhodes.

Leon Askin had worked with Piscator in Europe and had

proved himself in America an excellent actor and perhaps even a better director. It was his idea to create the Veteran's Memorial Stage at the Dramatic Workshop and invite Eric Rhodes, the distingushed Hollywood actor and captain in the U.S. Army, who had spent three and a half years in USAF Intelligence, to help him with the veterans.

The New Playwrights Seminar, conducted for professional playwrights, was entrusted to Dr. Joseph T. Shipley, critic and scholar, who had championed Piscator's work from the early days at the New School. Dr. Shipley, the only practicing theatre critic with a Ph.D. in criticism and comparative literature, was president of the New York Drama Critics Circle, and is still vice-president for the U.S. of the International Association of Theatre Critics. His opening night reviews on radio have been broadcast for twenty-five years. He has also reported on the New York theatre for periodicals in India, France, and England. His study The Art of Eugene O'Neill is one of the earliest appreciations of that playwright, and his monumental Guide to Great Plays is the standard work in the field.

The procedure in the New Playwright Seminar was new. After a play had been read by its author, it was criticized by the group. A decision was made as to which scenes should be rewritten by the author. Corrected, these scenes were then submitted to the Repertory acting class, analyzed by the acting teacher and students, and rehearsed with a director. Finally, the whole play was presented again, this time as live theatre by the senior acting group, for another discussion by the professional playwrights in the Seminar.

Under the direction of Sidney Kaufman, a film department was set up at the Dramatic Workshop. Its purpose was "to provide trained personnel for expanding motion picture productions in New York and to create a center for study of the cinema as a cultural and social force."

The Workshop was also directly responsible for a number of experimental Off-Broadway groups. These included On Stage, Studio Seven, The Inter-Players, Off-Broadway Inc., the Dramatic Workshop Players, the People's Drama, We Present, and The New York Repertory Group, Inc.

Besides the many graduates who worked in theatre and educational programs throughout the country were those who had become well-known: Marlon Brando, Chandler Cowles, Elaine Stritch, Jack Garfein, Gene Saks, Rod Steiger, Michael V. Gazzo, Nehemiah Persoff, Tony Curtis, Virginia Baker.

With 225 full daytime and 450 evening students, the Dramatic Workshop had become an outstanding institution. With its income of $350,000 to $400,000 a year, the Workshop had reached a status unique in the City of New York for a specialized school.

A fund-raising campaign was planned to secure the School's financial status and allow the Workshop to purchase a building of its own.

These were the prerequisites for the crystallization of the Piscator experiment—the State recognition of the Dramatic Workshop as University of Theater.

We were successful beyond even Dr. Johnson's expectations, as so we thought:

> . . . If there had been a Piscator in the days of my youth, [writes Dr. Johnson] with the command of the theatre as reality, with the vast variety of experience and competence, I would have begged, borrowed or stolen to be with him, and under him I think that then my fate would not have been that of an obscure political scientist . . .

This private expression of esteem changed into a peak of official recognition, which enhanced the second part of the letter:

*I welcomed Piscator to my enterprise at the New School.
I knew that I could not keep him long under my roof.
What he was doing deserved a roof of its own. It could not
thrive permanently under any School however new. It had
to be itself. As itself, the Dramatic Workshop is an
outstanding educational venture in American life. It goes
forth to conquer with the ardent good wishes and the
undying confidence of one who had some small part in its
launching.*

We did not know that Dr. Johnson's letter had its roots, not
alone in admiration nor in esteem, but in something much
more far reaching.

It was a warning, one which we did not hear.

How could we hear a warning when there was so much to
be done; for beyond the goal of a University of Theatre—
there was already a greater idea which drove us on: theatre
as an institution—yes, actively, and practically, a people's
theatre.

15) ROOFTOP THEATRE: A PEOPLE'S THEATRE

"There are people," said Romain Rolland, in 1903 "who want to bring to the people theatre as it is, whatever it is, and others who want to see theatre coming out of the people, as a new art form, a new theatre."

We felt that we had fulfilled the first task and that the second should be taken up as one of the most significant challenges the Dramatic Workshop would encounter.

Our membership had grown tremendously. We carried, for better or for worse, a faithful following along with interested newcomers. Reflecting on our past successes and failures, on our slim chance of reaching Broadway with our kind of "uncomfortable plays," we thought once more of our first meeting with Dr. Johnson.

Now a new voice, which had not lost its power and which could not be tied down either to the search for "success," or *l'engagement militante* could generate its own power now. The voice—a *rêve de jeunesse*, for Piscator—was Theatre as an Institution, a People's Theatre.

We must have had a foreboding of the immensity of the task.

The People's Theatre is a commitment to history. Sometimes a silent one, sometimes an anonymous one. It comes out of the need for communion between man and man.

The object of a people's theatre is to show the truth for whatever its value—to teach what appears to be beyond learning and to enlarge the realm of natural education. To create a unity between stage and audience, to pool different branches of knowledge and organize a mutual exchange of experience. It also expresses and represents, in the final analysis, the struggle between two competing powers of authority, church and state.

It is an active dialogue between the playgoer and the player. Each theatre has to conquer a new theatrical horizon. A minor play may prove effective and important because its simplicity and liberal élan drive the lesson home. Theatre thus becomes an extension of life and as such, an education for life.

The virtue of a People's Theatre is not rooted in esthetics, but in something else, which has been part blessing and part curse from the beginning of time; morality.

Could America provide a proper climate for such a theatrical experience? Her lightweight texture of social conformism and the widespread disinclination to be prophets' voices did not make a foundation for a theatre that wished to lay bare such themes as hunger, sexuality, aggression and fear.

In some vague but indestructible way, the theatre in America had remained middle-class. The voices of history do not attract the average theatregoer. The great outpouring of social theatre in the 'thirties had had no permanent influence upon the theatre. The faceless theatre which followed made it its business to forget the "lost generations," those who had fallen by the wayside in the wake of two World Wars.

What were the financial demands a producer would have to meet if he wanted to create a People's Theatre? What was needed?

The same things as at the time of Lope de Vega: four wooden beams and a platform, which later Romain Rolland translated into:

> All I need for a theatre of the people is a large room with a floor sloping down to a high, wide naked platform. In short, the only condition necessary for this theatre is that the stage as well as the hall can be opened to the multitudes; a hall and a stage both filled with people and actions of people.

Was this all that was necessary to wipe the world clean, to make it as innocent and fresh as it had been on the day of creation, to endow it again with the purity of the elements, the simplicity of sky and earth, of man and animals, of life itself? Would the theater then express the love of the earth and the people?

Who is people?

It is Hemingway's bullfighters, hunters and fishermen; Odets' taxidrivers and clerks; Saroyan's pied pipers; Tennessee Williams' anti-heroes and lilies of hell; Arthur Miller's salesmen, proletarians, adventurers, capitalists, fathers and sons.

A People's Theatre, or so we are told, is known for anonymity and ordinariness, for "sale of values." Nothing could be further from the truth. Only a fool would believe that a low admission price, within the reach of every man, is a sign of second-rate theatre. On the contrary.

The European People's Theatres, although they suffered great setbacks under Hitler, have flourished again in great beauty and in a new affirmation of life. The Volkstheatres of the great cities in Germany have been rebuilt and reopened with the most sophisticated programs. The New Berliner Volksbuehne, having lost its original home in the East, is now housed in one of the most beautiful gardens of West Berlin. An attractive new building, in the tradition of Walter Gropius and Sharoun, was designed by the young Fritz Bornemann, who also had built the stunning new Opera House. Apart from its architectural beauty and outside slickness, the Volksbuehne possesses every innovation of stage technology, miracles of light and sound, which makes the American stage look rather poor in comparison.

In France, Romain Rolland's famous book, *The People's Theatre*, became instrumental in providing new ideas to decentralize the Paris Theatre. Firmin Gemier's Théâtre National Ambulant had been extremely successful for years. Jean Vilar, who in defining the idea of a People's Theatre rather pompously, said to his audience: "*Je vous assemble; je vous unis,*" filled the enormous Trocadero evening after evening with widely acclaimed performances of his Théâtre National Populaire. Roger Planchon, who had moved his Théâtre de la Cité to Villeurbanne, a suburb of Lyon, found an enthusiastic audience waiting for him. The Théâtre Phillippe Gerard, under the direction of Roussillon and George Wilson went to Saint Denis, a suburb of Paris, while Gabriel Garran took his Théâtre de la Commune to Aubervilliers, also near Paris. The great popular theatres in the provinces such as the Théâtre Populaire d'Aquitaine of Bordeaux, the

Centre Dramatique de Sud Ouest of Aix-en-Provence, and the Théâtre Populaire de Lorraine proved equally successful. Jo Thettard's theatre at Caen, Grenier's at Toulouse and Fornier's Théâtre de Bourgogne further confirm the facts that Peoples' Theatres are not what Romain Rolland called, "an article of fashion, a game of dilettantes . . . but the expression of a new society, her thought and her voice. . . ." This doctrine was formulated in the nineteenth century. It is now established. A new art has been created for a new world.

Many are the attempts and successes of Peoples' Theatres in England. Bristol's Old Vic has become world famous and is now known as England's National Theatre.

America did not have a true Peoples' Theatre at the time Piscator began thinking of one. The Institute of Outdoor Drama had launched several open-air, amphitheatre productions such as Williamsburg's *The Common Glory*, Roanoke Island's *The Lost Colony* and *Cherokee*, North Carolina's *Unto These Hills*. The Federal Theatre had served a different purpose than to create "new art for the people by the people," and the City Center's Jean Dalrymple recreated simply Broadway successes at popular prices.

The theatre of social significances of the 1930's should be mentioned as should the Theatre Union (1933-37), the Neighborhood Playhouse (1915-27), American Negro Theatre (1940-49), The Civic Repertory Theatre (1926-32), and the Margo Jones Theatre (1947-59) with its grand design to have productions all over the country. The Phoenix Theatre started later on in the direction of a peoples' theatre. Today we have the Minnesota Theatre Company, The Theatre Group at UCLA, The National Repertory Company, the APA and Joseph Papp's New York Shakespeare Festival in the Park, to mention a few.

In a world in which all concepts of art are shaky, television is a means of communication which has introduced new images of human relationships and provided the American community with a grand medium of imformation.

Is it life's theatre?

It is not a dialogue theatre nor a literary theatre, but it is the theatre of events. It stimulates new lines of investigation in social science, religion and history. It simplifies highbrow ideals by showing indismissible facts of human existence, and it is also a third eye, piercing the magic circle of the Theatre of Illusion.

If television is guided carefully, I do not doubt that it could become the ideal instrument with which to express the genius of the nation, to display the pattern of the national culture; not only the inherited culture, but also present cultural contributions, which determine the culture of the future.

The great overall concept of People's Theatre has hardly been explored, nor have its past riches and power, which go beyond *theatre as a social and moral institution*, beyond repertory theatre back to the theatre's original function of being a *feast festival*.

For thousands of years, festivals, people's celebrations, occurred casually or periodically in all cultures. As a holy day, a day of joy, and a theatrical event, the festival reached its greatest peak during the French Revolution.

New festivals were introduced by the politicians and excited the imagination of men of theatre and audiences alike. We know of the *Feast* of "*The Supreme Being,*" the *Feast of Nature,* of *The Human Race,* of *The French People,* of *The Freedom of the World,* of *Fame and Immortality,* of *Youth,* of *Manhood,* of *Old Age.*

Theatres and churches became too small for the tremendous audiences, and the great festivals were celebrated in the open air, under the heavens, using the whole of nature as a stage. Rousseau in his dramatic way, called out "to give the spectacle to the spectator, make them actors, so that everyone can see himself and love himself in the other, so that at the very end audience and performer are united as one—and the better for it."

Only a short time later Robespierre echoed Rousseau. "Man is the greatest object of nature. There is no more magnificent or moral spectacle than that of a great people assembled together."

It is part of the fate of modern theatre that its feasts are set apart from religious observances. "We do not lack technique in the theatre," Peter Brook states, "we lack the ritual element, the voices of the old myths and incantations."

We know that any good play contains many facets of ritual, and only the mediocre artist robs us of the excitement of the abstract which brings us close to the secret of great theatre.

If ritual in the theatre reminds us of the feast, it can and does stand for more. In its inward meaning ritual ranges from expression of sheer artistry to the sanction of moral conduct.

Morals are the true agents around which the ritual of life assembles; they are the true issue of religion and politics. Since the beginning of time the theatre has stirred a movement between the two poles which holds all drama. The morality of protest and the morality of order.

Protest and order. Guardian and rebel. Citizen and artist.

Morality seems to most of us to have been handed down by the God of Abraham and Moses. Yet, it actually grew around the rural hearth and the rustic altar of the primitive. Morality was imposed by the condition of human life. Duties were imposed by the natural structure of family and tribe. There was the Lord with whom a covenant was made for the young and old, who would govern their destiny according to their right or wrong-doing. The same measure of right and wrong was applied to health and prosperity. In one word, reality and morals worked in perfect harmony—until one day intellect came in.

Then morality was fashioned into a political weapon. The Greeks claimed that virtue was not goodness or kindness but knowledge. No man knowing the good could do evil. This blend of duty and interest became quite forceful. A priestly Socratic aristocracy declared man a thinking, reasonable being. Knowledge became identical with self-knowledge as the only way to know truth.

This view of life, which made of morality a triumph of self-affirmation, was killed by the Reformation. Luther avenged himself on his enemies and oppressors by radically protesting against all accepted values. Knowledge was declared sinful, an aggression on the rest of creation. The moral order proved again superior to ideology.

Humanism tried to balance both mind and soul. It took generations to heal the wound mankind had received from the Reform and to release politics again from the captivity of religion.

With Descartes' *Cogito ergo sum*, moral duty became identical with the will to live. Unfortunately, the Cartesian philosphy ignored the common man and Descartes' idea became the property of the select few.

The new speculative eighteenth century knowledge, plunged into philosophy and put its mark of distinction again upon reason as the highest maxim of self-preservation.

This legacy of reason exercised a decisive influence on morals in the nineteenth century. Inspired by three of the foremost men of letters in France: Rousseau, Voltaire and Diderot, and by extension, Germany's Lessing, Mendelssohn and later Schiller, *theatre as a social and moral institution* emerged. It became, not merely an image of a new order, but also a means of social and political action.

Diderot, a moralist *par excellence*, but also an astute play-wright and all-around theatre person, introduced morality as an active of the human mind in his famous *Manifesto of the Theatre*. It is still one of the great documents in theatrical history.

Diderot, for the first time, brought out the Apollonian-Dionysian duality in the theatre. Apollo is the lucent one, the God of Enlightenment, the observer, the narrator. He is the symbol of everything that makes life possible and worth living. He represents the cognitive modes of experience; the laws of cause and effect, of simultaneity and continuity—the Epic world.

Dionysius is the reveller, the actor, the intoxicated one. He is the product of all formative forces rising directly from nature. He is nature's dream, the subjective, dramatic world.

Enlarging also upon the symbol of "morality of order" and "morality of protest," Diderot introduces other symbols. His leading character is not man who is good, but human nature that is good. Only the miserable conventions of society pervert man.

Diderot pushes his concept of theatre as a social and moral institution to the extreme. He affirms most radically that theatre is here to inspire man with a love for virtue and a horror of vice. "Every dramatic action is an object of morality," he says. He brings theatre back to religion, but the faith upon which this religion rests is not a metaphysical faith but a scientific faith. As reality, truth gives the direction, the meaning, the limit, the raison d'être, to life.

He dreams of turning the churches into theatres and speaks of the stage as of a pulpit and of the actor as a preacher of morals. He reminds the poets and writers of his time of the responsibility and the great role they have to fulfill, to design the future of "the new man:"

"Honest and serious plays will succeed everywhere, more

surely even with the corrupted people. It is in going to the theatre that they will save themselves from the company of scoundrels, and it is there on the stage that they will see the human species as they are and learn to judge them."

It is also Diderot, who for the first time speaks of theatre as a political instrument, "to help an intelligent virtuous government to prepare its people for the reception of the laws."

"All people," he insisted, "have prejudices that should be destroyed, vices to be punished, foibles to be denounced; they are in need of great plays, great performers and performances in which they can recognize themselves. The Theatre is the most extraordinary of all instruments of general communication, if the government knows how to use it. In this way, a change of law can be prepared and the elimination of a bad custom be achieved."

Hitler certainly used these theories born out of a humanitarian philosophy to evil's advantage in his nightmarish *Feast of the Thousand Year Reich.*

• • •

From Diderot's church plays to Piscator's political theatre is only a small step. Piscator, too, is a reformer whose final vision of theatre is a forum, "where the ideas which trouble men are debated and fought for."

If Diderot began the great "controversy on theatre" Voltaire continued it and elevated the theatre to a position worthy of man's highest ambition. A substantial advocate of freedom and equality of man, his participation in the *Controversy of Morals* led to the first victory of the new order over the Church. It was a colossal victory in more senses than one.

• • •

Theatre people too easily forget that society had branded theatre with the mark of infamy. Poets, actors, singers, comedians, dancers, muscians; anyone who engaged himself on the public stage was regarded as an outlaw from good citizenship and was treated as such.

Homer was banished from the ideal Republic. Plato was called a "corrupter of the senses." The children of Bacchus, although combining their talents in religious celebrations, commanded little respect. Cicero did not accept the theatre as a school of good manners. Seneca vehemently expressed his belief that those who frequented the theatre were not only idlers, but sick citizens if not dead ones. Ovid agreed that there was nothing more pernicious than the theatre.

The Christian concept of life, in spite of its celestial inspiration, defamed the theatre as a temple of demons and exposed those in it to defamation as though they were engaged in a profession of shame.

Tertullian denounced the theatre as an enemy of virtue and a distraction which alienated the faithful from God. The fathers of the Church; St. Cyprian, St. Chrysostom, St. Jerome, St. Augustine and St. Ambrose condemned not only the theatre, but pronounced a formal ban against those who attended it. At the Council of Arles, when the Church realized with a shock that many of their faithful were ardent theatre lovers, she threatened them with excommunication.

After the sack of Rome, in trying to retain believers and to gather new sheep to the fold, the Holy Order, ignoring any past antagonism, offered the theatre its protection. It even invited the players to perform in sacred precincts. Great churchmen declared that dramatic presentations were not only inoffensive in nature, but also necessary to human growth; that mystery and morality plays were not licentious in themselves if inspired and supported by the Church.

New quarrels followed injunctions and complaints. In 1598 the Church denounced its patronage and remained hostile to the theatre while the battle continued actively in Italy, England and Spain.

England, however, provided the theatre with patron-protectors, such as the Lord Chamberlain's Company and the Lord Admiral's Company. Shakespeare himself belonged to the Lord Chamberlain's Men and later enjoyed Queen Elizabeth's patronage.

In France royal protection seemed to grow with the interest in the new theatre. Corneille and Racine, in spite of the dangerous antagonism of the Church, had introduced a new theme—profane love. The Jesuits and Jansenists, already in rivalry for the grace and salvation of the faithful lost no time in denouncing the theatre as a serious menace to morals.

By an ironic turn of events, the theatre, not content to remain within its own realm, trespassed on the realm of the Church. The subject in question was false versus real devotion. The name of the play—*Tartuffe*.

The clergy took up arms. Molière, to justify *Tartuffe*, maintained that the theatre proved its morality precisely in denouncing the vices and abuses of the times.

But neither Molière's defense of the theatre nor his other masterpieces brought good fortune to the children of the theatre.

Molière was excommunicated and denied burial, despite the intercession of Louis XIV.

The Church returned to the narrow disciplines of its former years and revived all its canons against actors and theatre people. Sermons were preached everywhere, the theatre was denounced as the work of demons. Bossuet, the greatest religious orator of his time, succeeded in having all theatres in France closed; furthermore no actor could be baptized or married, or given last rites in the Church.

On the occasion of a jubilee in 1690 during which most criminals were granted forgiveness, a petition was addressed to Pope Innocent XIII to set actors free. The Pope sent the petition back for jurisdiction to the Archbishop of Paris with the recommendation to keep them out of the Church. Again the actors remained *hors la loi*.

At the beginning of the eighteenth century the dissension on morals took on a different character. The quarrel up to then, excluding times of antiquity, had been exclusively on theological terms. The New Order brought with it new ideas and stimulated the minds of men, still secretly but nevertheless forcibly. The Church felt itself attacked. During the Regency the theatre became one of the most licentious *divertissements* to which all classes abandoned themselves. The Regent himself brought back the Italian comedians who had been chased out of the country by the old king in 1695. The Church kept silent. Busy as she was with politics, she could not trouble herself with the theatre.

Le Temps Nouveau was the time for fighters and thinkers. A definite distinction was made between religious morals and temporal morals. The theatre was declared free from the first, but was linked to the latter, to the people as a whole, to the collectivity. It had no need anymore to justify itself before the Church, but drew its own legitimacy from the services which it rendered to the social body.

. . .

The reform movement continued to change the theatre into a respectable institution. More and more people from all walks of life became interested. Finally, in 1751, the new Encyclopedia, the collective work of eighteenth century thinkers, edited by La Société des Gens des Lettres and representing the most advanced theories of the century in literature and in philosophy, came out with the up to then unheard of dictum that "dramatic art derives its beauty and its legitimacy from the morality which it teaches."

Marmontel, one of the founders of the Encyclopedia, went further then Voltaire, saying "The theatre is to vice and corruption what the tribunal is to crime, a platform on which the evil-doer is judged and punished." Almost imperceptibly, complicity between the theatre and modern philosophers had started.

The Encyclopedists proved to be the strongest and the most dangerous enemies of the Church. In taking up the causes of the theatre they attacked the authority of the Church. In order to keep the faithful together and to preserve its respect for authority, the Church had no alternative but to counterattack—not the progressive philosophers and their strong coterie, but the weaker enemy, the theatre.

Voltaire was not content to defend the performances alone. He also pleaded the cause of the actor, launching a discussion which was to continue for almost a century. He left no stone unturned in his efforts to rehabilitate the profession, calling it an art "which is authorized by law, recompensed by the sovereigns, and sought after by all men" (*Lettres Philosophiques*).

Voltaire's position was to a great extent shared by the other Encyclopedists. They saw the theatre as the only platform of propaganda for *freedom of thought*. Slowly, imperceptibly, the life of reason had taken possession of the stage and had begun to wage war against superstition, fanaticism and abuse. The quarrel of the theatre had shifted from theology to philosophy and finally to politics. The theatre had become the house of the new learning and of the new freedom.

It was Rousseau who brought the controversy of morals to a climax:

"*J. J. Rousseau, citoyen de Geneve, à Monsieur d'Alembert, de l'Academie royale des sciences de Paris . . . sur son article Geneve dans la Septieme volume de l'Encyclopedie, et particulierement sur le projet d'établir un théâtre de comédie en cette ville.*" Thus the fine pen of the great writer began to draft a manifesto against the theatre, deadlier than any up to then: *La Lettre à d'Alembert.*

255)

What happened?

Rousseau, who had the misfortune to question himself about his role and destiny once too often, had returned after twenty-six years of absence to his native city, Geneva. The old city of Calvin had received him with open arms and a most flattering welcome, which not only brought him back to the Reformed Church, but also reinstated him as a citizen of Geneva.

Rousseau was happy. He never had had a taste for the brilliant, voluptuous, refined, aristocratic society of Paris, against which he had become the official antagonist after his first speech before the Academy of Science and Art; he had only one desire in 1754—to live out his days in Geneva. By a singular irony of destiny, Voltaire came to Geneva only a year after Rousseau and installed himself in a lovely summer chalet which his great wealth transformed into a paradise. While the aristocracy hurried to greet him at his new residence, "Les Delices," the pastorate and the bourgeoisie of Geneva looked at this illustrious guest with a certain dismay and trepidation.

Here we must explain something about Geneva.

Of all the Swiss cities, Geneva, although a free city until the Revolution, was the least tainted by foreign influence. She would have been invulnerable except for a kind of civic schizophrenia.

First of all, there were two Genevas: aristocratic Geneva, eager for and envious of the life and pleasures in Paris; and democratic Geneva, which tended to maintain a kind of antique simplicity.

The fact was that religion dominated politics. The city, filled with industry and riches and throngs of visitors, was divided into two camps: those that loved its austerity and had never left Geneva; and those that had lived under a foreign culture and had brought back alien tastes. Among the imported luxuries was one that had been definitely lacking in

Geneva, the theatre. The Reform had banned all plays, from Mysteries to farces, and, until the end of the seventeenth century, there was no question of theatre in the city. Finally, the French Ambassador, Comte de Lautrec, succeeded in obtaining a permit from the city fathers to open a theatre.

What could a man like Voltaire do in Geneva to escape boredom?

After his quarrel with Frederick of Prussia for editing the King's verses, and his refusal (at least, with no permission granted) ever to enter France, he had finally come to Geneva, which was practically a meeting point of four distinct jurisdictions.

During his residence at Les Delices, he enjoyed what was probably the greatest pleasure of his whole life: writing plays and acting in them, serving as his own stage manager.

On August 10, 1756, d'Alembert announced his visit to Les Delices. He had been invited to write an article about Geneva for the seventh volume of the Encyclopedia. In their conversations, Voltaire did not hesitate to tell him that he wanted to force the hand of the city fathers and the pastors of Geneva to get permission to open a theatre. After several evenings of passionate discussion on the subject, d'Alembert —pressed by Voltaire, but delighted with the prospect— promised to sneak into his article a covert plea in favor of theatre in Geneva.

What happened to Rousseau in the meantime? By an equally ironic twist of fate, he had left Geneva just before Voltaire's arrival. With the stubbornness of a boy, and mortified by the reception Voltaire had received, he decided to stay away from Geneva. He was certain that the author of Zaire was going to pervert this city which, to him, had conserved all the memories of the greatness of the Reform. Because of Voltaire's presence, Geneva definitely was lost forever, for him. Two years later, he did not even accept the post of Bibliothequaire offered to him by the City of Geneva.

To chase Voltaire from Geneva and to appoint himself champion of his native city, to continue his crusade against civilization, became Rousseau's aim. He had found an admirable challenge for his arguments when d'Alembert's article on Geneva, including his *Défense of the Theatre*, appeared in the Encyclopedia.

Any theatre person who reads Rousseau's letter to d'Alembert cannot but deplore the use of poetry and the beauty of style which went into the writing of this most hostile of all theses. Its hypocrisy is even worse. Although politically an enemy of the Church, Rousseau, in attacking the theatre made common cause with the clergy. He set himself in full opposition to his own party, the Encyclopedists.

> *The theatre is an amusement born out of idleness, discontent and neglect of the simple and natural taste which characterizes the good citizen.*
>
> *The spectator seeks only pleasure in the theatre, or that which favors his leanings towards passion. The argument for the utility of tragedy is most hypocritical. What can one learn from Oedipus, except that man is not free and that heaven punishes the crime which heaven wants him to commit? What does one learn from Medea except that the furor of jealousy turns a mother into a monster?*
>
> *Comedy is worse. It is a school for vice and bad habits. It turns kindness and simplicity into ridicule. It disturbs the whole order of society. . . .*

Rousseau did not stop at that. His aim was to prevent Geneva from having a theatre.

Cunningly, the poet examines the practical reasons for opposing the establishment of a theatre in Geneva. Material reasons: Paris, with 600,000 inhabitants, can hardly sustain its three theatres; Geneva, with 24,000, could certainly not support a single one. Could a theatre live, therefore, by the patronage of the rich? Or would it be up to the citizens to help by paying more taxes?

The voice which attacked the theatre so cruelly was not the voice of only an angry man, but of a man who had achieved the stature of a myth, a saintly figure who had established a new credo of the age: the belief in the excellence of human nature and the equality of man.

From this moment on, the polemic of the theatre confounded itself with the drama which agitated the minds between 1750 to 1770—the dead-end fight of the rebellious encyclopedists against the authority of the Church.

La Lettre à d'Alembert created a great sensation. Paris and Geneva debated it among themselves. The Geneva clergy was clever enough to accept Rousseau's gesture as an act of civicness. Progress had passed away like a dream.

Even at the advent of the French Revolution, Rousseau did not change his mind. The defender of the principles of liberty, equality and fraternity, which he himself had helped to affirm, committed, finally and openly, political heresy.

It is said that those who, in the overcrowded Assemblée Nationale, had risen to speak up for the theatre became quickly aware that the writer of the *Contrat Sociale*, who could describe so well the passions of the human heart, was not aware of the passion raging in his own.

At the once-crowded Assemblée Nationale, even Rousseau's partisans, fighting for the rights of theatre people to be citizens, realized that they were fighting in vain. They were running up against the animosity of their acknowledged master, Jean-Jacques Rousseau. In order not to jeopardize the doctrine, they had to withdraw their demand.

The declaration of equality, fraternity, and liberty had obviously not been written for the people in theatre.

It was not until a hundred years later (1850) that the Congregation of the Council of Trent finally accepted the actor as a free member of society and lifted the ban of exile and excommunication.

. . .

It had been obvious for some time that the President was not nearly large enough to accomodate our audience nor to house our student body which now totaled over a thousand students. We needed to find a theatre large enough to accomodate our repertory theatre.

In succession, we examined every possibility that the real estate agents presented to us—everything from an abandoned firehouse to a Mecca Temple.

The gargantuan house on 55th Street, decorated in pseudo-Byzantine manner, was certainly large enough to house several enterprises. Its big stage, well-equipped, and its rehearsal rooms and studios, offered an ideal place to launch a Peoples' Theatre. We paid many visits to this once sacred edifice, had many dinners with the lessee of the house, and listened to his ambitions for establishing in it an Italian opera company. I do not think he clearly understood our interest was in theatre.

Finally, we decided against the Mecca Temple because of the great number of union members, who, it was estimated, would be involved in any repertory set-up we planned. It seemed that low-price theatre was impossible without some kind of subsidy. What we needed was a theatre far off Broadway.

It was suggested that I look on the lower East Side, where I had discovered some loft space in which we had installed our film department. My next search ended at the doors of the nation's most famous remaining Yiddish theatre, the National Theatre on Houston Street.

The history of the National Theatre may best be recalled today through the names of the stars who appeared there and whose theatre life brought it fame: Luther and Stella Adler, Boris Thomashefsky, Davis Kessler, Morris Morrison, Rudolph Schildkraut, Bertha Kalish and the unforgettable Molly Picon.

To this list must be added another star—Gypsy Rose Lee. For it was here, in the second theatre on the premises, that the Minsky brothers presented Gypsy in their famous burlesque.

Old Minsky's men were not satisfied to sit back in their role as patrons of the arts. They saw the whole building as one theatrical enterprise. And so they opened on the fifth floor another theatre, the Rooftop, dedicated to an appreciation of the "finer things in life."

Needless to say, we were eager to sign contracts; all the more so, since the adjoining building could house some classes and seminars of the overflowing Dramatic Workshop.

There was no doubt in my mind that the climate on Second Avenue at Houston Street was conducive to our plans.

· · ·

Once more, we faced confusion brought about by our inability to sell tickets at the box office. Why not make admission free to the public? Carefully we weighed the pros and cons of each issue.

Today, it is interesting to note on a bulletin board in Central Park at the Delacorte Theatre, ADMISSION FREE. But, in 1947, we should have foreseen that this plan of "theater without admission" would meet with resistance from every one of our sponsors, the bank who wrestled with our loans, the Board of the New School, the faculty, and even our own members.

Nevertheless, we went ahead with the Rooftop Theatre.

The windows were opened wide to let in fresh air; the dusty old curtains were torn down and thrown out; a new stage was built, with two fore stages, right and left. The dressing rooms that had served the burlesque queens were stripped and the begrimed brick wall and the back of the stage was scrubbed to its original rosy color; the cycloramas were washed white. The balcony had been condemned as unsafe for occupancy, but it served as an ideal place to install our new lighting equipment.

The establishing of a repertory was the next logical step. No English-speaking repertory theatre existed in New York. No more active and theatrically minded audience could be found to participate in such a project than those who had supported the National Theatre on Second Avenue. We had to bring some plays down from the President and add new ones. At the Rooftop, our program would address itself to a wider audience and would necessarily have greater variety and more popular appeal.

Nevertheless our repertory of world drama represented quite some face-lifting for the old Minsky burlesque house.

"World drama" sounded wonderful, but it was in fact to be our March of Drama Repertory. Here at the Rooftop, with its big stage, excellent lighting and popular audience, we could bring back to life the performances which we had begun presenting in the New School auditorium.

It was amazing how the Rooftop, in secrecy, had begun to answer the call of a Peoples' Theatre. We were convinced it was destined to become as real an institution of the New York scenes as the famous Café Royal on Second Avenue, and would become a landmark like the Brooklyn Bridge.

It was even more amazing that with little publicity and with a small turnout of reviewers accepting our invitations for each performance (a New York critic has no obligation toward a school) the public found its way to the Rooftop Theatre.

Yes, the idea of a Peoples' Theatre became more a reality

from day to day. Meetings were held, petitions circulated, letters signed, programs and brochures written, new membership came in.

Never had Piscator's words that "theatre can be played anywhere, in a marketplace, in a subway station, as long as there is an audience" been truer.

There were those who came because of their European heritage. It reminded them of their youth. There were those to whom that kind of theatre appealed because it was a means of learning to understand other countries, other cultures. And there were those who looked at the Rooftop Theatre as another kind of mission, a refuge, a warm place which would allow them to feed their imagination, a kind of church, which would not preach to them or ask them to give up what they liked most. A play was certainly as good, if not better, than a sermon.

To most of the audience, the Rooftop was a place where the audience could see theatre for which they would have to journey uptown to Broadway, often to find that they had paid more than they could afford for mere entertainment.

At the Rooftop they could see all the plays of the writers they had heard of and seen reviewed in the newspapers; Sherwood, Steinbeck, Odets, Saroyan, Anderson, Williams, Miller. But they could also see Shakespeare, Marlowe, Lope de Vega, Pirandello.

And, if they missed a play it would not matter. It would turn up again. Was this not Repertory?

Soon Second Avenue became proud of its People's Theatre. They had, of course, seen many of the plays in Yiddish, but now that their children spoke English, it was good to see them again. And, they could afford it by making a few more men's suits, baking a few more chrusciks.

The Rooftop audience had all the makings of a warm and

knowing community, a marvelous audience to inquire into life.

They recognized one another at the second or third play. Most of them had six plays allotted to their membership, and they had time to get acquainted. They nodded to each other, more familiar after each performance, and finally spoke to each other. And if it happened that some wine sots dropped in one evening, it did not matter. They too became happily intoxicated with the events of the stage.

The actors also came to know the audience and learned what it means not to be subject to indifference and raw criticism, but to a climate which allowed them to grow, and in turn compensate the audience for their interest.

. . .

For Piscator, the Rooftop Theatre was also a means to inform the audience. He stated unequivocally in our programs and "letters" to the playgoer that the task of a people's theatre was as much to inform as to communicate.

Like summer lightening over the city, Piscator came to grips with a play that was ideally suited to his plans. It was a play about anti-Semitism, *The Burning Bush*, written by Geza Herczeg and Heinz Herald.

The play had been written almost ten years earlier, but it is not unusual for plays of merit to go without production for many years. It dealt with an outrageous miscarriage of justice occurring in a small Hungarian village in 1882, an idea which came from Geza Herczeg's earlier career as a political reporter.

Herczeg had emigrated to America and had established himself as a screen writer in Hollywood. Among the many films he wrote was the Academy Award screenplay, *The Life of Emile Zola*. He recalled that when writing this film he remembered the case of Tisza-Eszlar, a celebrated trial, which took place some years before Dreyfus was incarcerated on Devil's Island. In fact, Herczeg saw this trial as a direct predecessor to the Dreyfus case, to the Lueger arrests in Austria, to Hitler's savageries in Germany.

Herczeg, together with Heinz Herald, based the play on the actual courtroom records.

No pertinent fact was altered. *The Burning Bush* is the story of a political frame-up in a Hungarian village, Tisza-Eszlar, a small community where Jews had settled in 1882. A Christian girl is missing. The rumor is that she has been kidnaped and the Jews are accused of murdering the missing girl. Fifteen of their number are arrested and thrown into prison.

The case well suited the reactionary factions in Hungary, who wanted to discredit the Liberal government. No effort is spared in preparing the case for trial. Perjury and forgery are freely employed. The son of one of the accused, a boy of fourteen, is taken into custody by the police and elaborately coached, with threats and with cajolery, to give evidence for the prosecution against his own father.

The brilliant cross-examination by the defense finally exposes the shocking conspiracy. The prosecutor is withdrawn from the case. The four judges, although all strongly anti-Semitic, have no option save acquit the prisoners unanimously.

Being an inventive director, Piscator found that the best way to stage the play was also the simplest: to show a court trial on our open stage with the audience participating.

The Burning Bush became "theatre as a tribiunal." He organized his production on the basis of previous experiments, where he had recaptured the conflict of the past and turned it into a lesson for the present.

The play responded to "the magnifying glass" of good dramaturgy.

First *the stage began to narrate*—the story of the fifteen innocent accused, the shocking conspiracy exposed by the defense; other events provided facts and figures of the happenings and clarified participation; lies, intolerance, injurious proceedings that happened during the original trial.

The narrator explained the subject matter; the presentation exposed it.

Second, *the stage began to teach*—and it taught a lesson quite unforgettable for anyone who saw the play. Piscator took the position that the trial of Tisza-Eszlar was the beginning of the wave of anti-Semitism. The unanimous acquittal of the prisoners in Hungary was oil in the fire, which started anti-Semitism in the whole of the monarchy.

In consequence of this trial in Hungary the reactionaries resolved to carry the municipal elections of Vienna of which they already had 98 seats (out of a total of 138), with unusual fanatical vigor. Anti-Semitism was no longer a personal expression of religious bias, but had clearly become a political movement; a movement which bore the seed of aberrations of the Church.

On the eve of the election, in January 1895, the Pope, following advice from Cardinal Rampolla, agreed that the best antidote to the feared Socialism would be a clerically controlled fusion of the "Christian" socialists with the group of anti-Semites.

The election resulted, compehensively, in a triumph for the Jew-haters, who then elected a new *Burgermeister* of Vienna, Dr. Karl Lueger, himself a violent anti-Semite. His slogan, "It is I who determine who is a Jew," had become world-famous by the end of the monarchy.

The spectacle of a clerical anti-Semite majority in Vienna strengthened obvious opportunities for anti-Semitism in France. The staggering series of financial catastrophes that culminated in the Panama Scandal allowed anti-Semitism to come forward again. It showed most powerfully in the army, where the reactionary classes were fully represented. The Dreyfus case, which proceeded on a tissue of forgeries and crimes, was an unscrupulous attempt to prove the national hypothesis of the "dangerous Jew." It was the result of the clerical and royalist battle against the hated Jewish officers and precipitated European crises.

Emile Zola, on behalf of Dreyfus, formulated the case against the army in an open letter to the President of the Republic, with the result that he was prosecuted for libel, convicted, and had to flee the country.

The Dreyfus controversy went on and provoked the wildest passion among the reactionaries. National-Socialist Germany continued the conspiracy years later and succeeded.

Third, *the stage began to show the issues;* morality is vital to our survival. Any person or people or nation which does not speak up on behalf of the wronged in behalf of morality condemns itself.

"Mr. Piscator is the chief flame in *The Burning Bush;* the authors burned down to a flicker," wrote Brooks Atkinson in the *New York Times,* December 17, 1949.

Arthur Pollock on December 19, 1949, added that "*The Burning Bush* offered Mr. Piscator one of his best opportunities for production in this country."

One morning Piscator was informed that the President account books showed a deficit. It was not a big one, but it was astounding that it could have occurred under the watchful eyes of two administrators, a treasurer and a diligent accountant. Piscator's dismay was not lessened by the fact that there were no reserve funds on which to operate.

What had happened?

Piscator's days and nights had been consumed by his artistic activity. He was not unaware of difficulties. He had a dependable administrative organization to cope with them. Of course, the theatre is not a grocery store. Theatre is a gamble even in its business—a gamble dealing with our psychological and creative life and its tensions.

There had been an unusual ring of enthusiasm surrounding all our activities during that summer of 1950. It had the characteristic feature of overconfidence which goes with the passionate credo of those who say "everything is fine," when it is not.

In the past, when a production or one of the theatres showed an operating deficit, money could be juggled from one performance to the next to cover the immediate problem. There was always the prospect that the next play would bring things to balance.

Now, however, we faced a different situation. A large part of our income was derived from the Veteran's Administration and their methods of dealing with hundreds of tuition fees to be payed "later." Thus, our deficit extended to the Dramatic Workshop.

It was clear-sighted Clara Mayer, who clarified the situation. Loyal to Piscator's efforts and ambitions, she tried to attract his attention to the distress that was being voiced among the board members. She also tried, on the other hand, to explain to Piscator that he was on his own; that the board members should be thought of as figureheads.

The "moving road" of the Orozsco mural, that emblem of liberty and justice on the New School walls, had stopped the pleasant journey.

To Piscator, the evidence of castastrophe was uncontestable. So it was, also, to Miss Mayer. What could be done?

Monday, Tuesday, Wednesday, Thursday, Friday, Saturday, Sunday and again Monday; fifteen hours a day and how many sleepless nights. . . . Clara agreed.

They filled the vast gap of their silence, filled the whole room, and no one had an answer.

Clara sat there for some time, erect as a soldier on furlough, uncomfortable yet quiet.

Piscator had never taken defeat seriously when it had been only economic. He had faced debts much greater than the present ones.

He pleaded hopefully that new money was coming in. It was true. There were new members, new groups, even new organizations, experincing the benefits of our kind of Theatre.

Clara answered, with a gentle, dismayed shake of her head. These sums would be too small, absurdly too small, to cover the existing deficit.

"You mean to say that there is no one in this big city who will understand what has been created here and why it should survive? Is this the end?"

She remained silent—although she knew that this was true, that Piscator was no dreamer, that the School had met its budget, that performances were packed, that audiences faithfully followed our activities and that there was a need for a People's Theatre in New York.

"Yes, Piscator, but, it does not alter the fact that to continue you must have money."

Clara Mayer rose quietly.

Piscator lifted his head. Clara Mayer walked out of the room.

He suddenly remembered Mrs. Urban and her astonishment when he had told her that his film in Russia had taken three years of his life. He knew that the experiment in America had taken ten years, but he did not want to admit that they could be lost, the most creative years of his life.

It had all started in mutual confidence, with mutual respect, but without any true financial foundation, without any reserve, thus without the possiblity of formulating long-range plans. Everything was centered on the hope of great things for nothing, hope that the public and the appreciation of the press would influence those financially able to sustain the effort.

This hope had been nourished not only by ourselves but by ourselves, by theatre people, playwrights, by the members of theatrical and educational organizations, who followed us enthusiastically, and the progressive press who had supported us.

As the days passed and the situation did not improve, irritation set in. Official polemics started. The New School blamed Piscator for having extended himself beyond his financial capabilities, for his confidence in attempting to run two theatres with students.

He answered that his students were often better than the average professional and that as actors they had the best possible training, as they continuously appeared before the public. Asked what we would do in the light of the possible debts, he replied: "The same as I did before in Berlin when my theatre went bankrupt. I took another one, a bigger one."

And, indeed, Piscator was looking at a larger and more comfortable theatre on Second Avenue—the future Phoenix Theatre. It had a greater seating capacity and, therefore could attract a greater income. As he explained his plan to the members, it was evident to us that many people could be persuaded. Piscator was confident that they would not let him down.

And the members did not let him down. It was the mother organization, the New School, that failed him.

. . .

Theatre means living together and being together for better or worse. This does not mean only the actors and the artists, but the spectators as well, and moreover those that serve the theatre in administrative and promotional capacities. They all have a rendezvous on the evening of a performance. Without this total collaboration theatre does not exist.

It is unfortunate that among this dynamic clique, among

those that created the slogan "the show must go on," there are individuals that believe the theatre can be sold like bananas—that you can buy theater people and establish teamwork and organize success.

To the real theatre person, Theatre is a question of life and death. A "man of the theatre" needs a climate in which he can produce the living reality of Theatre.

It is not for nothing that the French hail a good director as *animateur, anima mundi*—the soul.

Piscator was such an *animateur*.

He believed confidently he could stop the castastrophe; that his Dramatic Workship would not close. It *could* not close, neither the People's Theatre he had housed under a rooftop, nor the President Theatre.

Since its opening in the fall of 1950, the Rooftop, and the President, had produced more plays than a small government theatre in Europe; classics, the best in modern theatre, and a number of distinguished new plays. Currently in repertory at both theatres were the following plays:

All the King's Men - Warren
Androcles and the Lion - Shaw
A Marriage Proposal - Chekhov
A Texas Steer - Hoyt-Carter-Selden
Chaff - Bruckner
Circle of Chalk - (Anonymous Chinese) Adapted by Klabund
Hannele's Way to Heaven - Hauptmann
Imaginary Invalid - Molière
Inspector General - Gogol
Juno and the Paycock - O'Casey
Lysistrata - Aristophanes
Middle Man, What Now? (A musical revue) - Dramatic Workshop students

Mourning Becomes Electra - O'Neill
Nights of Wrath - Salacrou
Of Mice and Men - Steinbeck
Princess Turandot - Gozzi
Shadow of a Gunman - O'Casey
The Sheep Well - Lope de Vega
Tonight We Improvise - Pirandello
Twelfth Night - Shakespeare
The Aristocrats - Pogodin
The Cause of It All - Tolstoy
The Devil's Disciple - Shaw
The Flies - Sartre
The Good Hope - Heijermans
The Little Foxes - Hellman
The Male Animal - Thurber and Nugent
The Petrified Forest - Sherwood
The Taming of the Shrew - Shakespeare
The World We Make - Kingsley
Waiting for Lefty - Odets
What Price Glory? - Anderson and Stallings

It was at this time, while we were desperately seeking ways and means, that Fitzi died.

She had withdrawn to her farm early in the summer and there she died. Fitzi had been so intimately connected with everything going on that we thought that she was still with us, that she still occupied her little office, tucked away in a corner of the unused balcony. It was from that office that she conducted her activities with an air of great stillness . . . a stillness beyond maturity.

Sometimes during a turbulent rehearsal we would look up at the balcony where we knew she was sitting endeavoring to attract an audience for us. In those moments, it seemed as though we desired that peace of hers to quell the anxiety in our own hearts. I do not believe anyone could have more perfectly manifested Pushkin's words: "There is no happiness in the world, but there is stillness and freedom."

Many friends came to her funeral. Someone spoke about Fitzi's rebellious heart, about her courage and her tenderness. Fitzi had used her tenderness. She had used it during all the years of the Dramatic Workshop. The young students were her children, whom she wanted to see grow and live, and who grew and lived, scarcely realizing what was happening to them, scarcely noticing her at all.

With her passing, more than a life went. It was the passing of an era.

The drive for membership still had to go on. Memberships had to be renewed. More money had to be raised. More promises would have to be cashed in. Our situation became desperate when the creditors sent in a lawyer to look after their interests. At the same time, one of the teachers instigated a strike on the day the School was scheduled to reopen for the fall term.

Most of the students did not cross the picket line. And what had probably been thought of as an appropriate moment for seeking higher wages became the moment in which we lost the chance to establish enough credit to keep the Dramatic Workshop alive over the winter.

Still, Piscator did not give up.

With the help of some of the creditors, the President was reopened and so was the Rooftop. As for the Dramatic Workshop, the strike had left us with a dwindling student body.

One day we found the windows of the Rooftop open. We had hardly known that there were any windows. They had always remained closed. There were seven on each side of the stage, rather big now that we could see them with the curtain drawn open which admitted a lot of light. Too much light for our dusty stage and our tired eyes.

But who had opened them?

There was one little man with eyeglasses walking about. We were told that he had come in earlier, and had stuck little white papers on the beautiful costumes which we had stored in the back of the balcony that more recently served us as a storage room as well.

He continued in spite of our arrival to stick other white papers on anything else he could lay his hands on: chairs, sets, props. He worked with such zeal, as if this gesture were his salvation.

I presume it was salvation to his employers, our creditors. I really didn't know how much the Macbeth Crown of the classic repertory was worth in dollars and cents, but the little man seemed to assess every false stone.

This was the end of the Rooftop and the President and the end of the great hope that had guided us until now: the hope for the *Dramatic Workshop* to become a university of theatre, "the school that came to stay." Our unfortunate economic situation would never allow the Board of Regents to transfer our provisional charter into a permanent one.

The school that came to stay had been a dream.

The Piscator experiment was over. In spite of Piscator's sacrifices to the neglect of the creative side of his profession— the neglect for the sake of teaching that had taken him out of commercial theatre for ten years.

Arthur Pollock wrote sensitively about this. We were grateful to him to have taken a moment to record the situation accurately:

> In the beginning, Erwin Piscator must have had other dreams than that of a university where the students might learn the art of the theatre. Today's theatre is one he helped to shape by his imaginative work. He was an innovator.
> Since his coming to this country, Piscator has confined himself almost wholly in imparting what he knows to others,

working through them. We haven't yet seen the complete Piscator, not even the potential one. The American theatre would have profited if Piscator would have been turned loose to improvise, discover, create.

16) THE SCHOOL THAT CAME TO STAY

Theatre people, like the legendary phoenix, rise from the ashes of their defeat, not always perfect, but hardy enough to take flight again.

Like all legends, the one of the fabulous bird sacred to the sun, remains the *beau ideal*; its death is not taken into account.

Like the phoenix—"The school that came to stay—the Dramatic Workshop with its two theatres, the President and Rooftop Theatres—had become a myth.

The encounter between two civilizations had proved in the last resort, an encounter between two irreconcilable spirits. No epilogue could alter the facts.

The Cyclops eye—the eye that never glows with the artist's fire—does not know the glance of reverence. It saw nothing to this end of a mission that Aphrodite had looked upon so favorably.

The image that remained was that of something unfinished. What is someone to do with a dream that had drawn him on and then closed as though it were springing a trap? Should one interpret it as a verdict? Did it mean that Piscator's experiment had become a closed chapter with no onward future?

I do not believe so.

If I understand this experience rightly the short years of the American dream were only a brief time span drawn from the ongoing flow in the depths of one man's expansion into the theatre; an experience that was not conclusive proof of anything, because Piscator was still moving ahead.

There was much hope to be drawn from the source from which the dream had come. Even as a closed experience, the Dramatic Workshop will have much to say to the Theatre of the Future.

This hope came later. Days and weeks were filled with anger and resentment: the anger of frustration. The dream had stopped before it had given a complete message.

In a few months, a few days, perhaps, the whole tragic irony of the closing of the school that came to stay—the school that was theatre—with its great hopes, would be forgotten; but not its covenant.

Events flew fast from then on. The lawyer designated by the Board of Directors to represent the creditors was not a lover of theatre. Every sum of money that came in was paid out to those to whom money was due, instead of being prorated to establish a fund with which the school could continue.

This generous, but to us disastrous, gesture included every bit of property that the school possessed.

"Is the theatre dying," one critic asked, "to allow a thing like this to happen?"

No, the theatre was not dying and never will.

It is men who die when they lose faith, when they refuse to commit themselves to the fight for their beliefs.

It is men who die away, when they do not understand that human progress is learning by steps, of which none is final; that mistakes are rungs in the ascending ladder of the Epic way.

Theatre today should be a radar—a detecting device that emits and focuses a powerful scanning beam on the universe; an alarm system—enabling us to discover social and psychic changes in time to prepare ourselves to cope with them.

As an ideal instrument, the theatre is capable of sustaining its society. The first poet was an artist who animated nature and personified its forces. He became the scientist when his community looked upon him as a witch doctor and later as a miracle worker who exorcised disease. Then organizing the performance of the communal activity, he also had to be a social philosopher.

Theatre as a radar station can care for these needs so as to maintain, amidst the most disruptive events, an even course towards a permanent goal of the *polis*.

The Dramatic Workshop had been such a radar station.

Looking forward to the future, I am fortified in my conclusions: I see the future bright. Never before has the theatre had so much opportunity.

Never has it had a more distinguished role to fulfill. Through mass communication—radio, television, and film— the theatre has reached out to the smallest villages, has entertained and educated people. It has become a highly respectable and respected institution, financially and otherwise. But this is not all. The blueprint of the Dramatic Workshop was an even more vital one. "Theatre as an instrument of better life" is not only as a mirror in which we see what we are and, sometimes, who we are, not only a polished substance that forms images for reflection, but also a speculum showing not only how men live, but how they ought to live. Whatever form it takes, any public performance is social. I would like to think that the implication of these words will spread throughout our culture in a clear way—with the understanding that everything is a part of a whole, a whole that is social, a whole that is man.

"Great theatre? Fight for ideas? Morality? Be your own social institution and as to morals, dispense with them when you can. Raise money, more money. Money! Get that into your head." These were the clichés flung at us during the long drawn-out period of our bankruptcy.

Then came the hectic personal activity that always goes with the end of something. And there was, too, that disturbing feeling of saying goodbye to a great community. The community called the American Theatre, Broadway and Off-Broadway, to whom we had belonged for a decade or more, for better or for worse. We had lived together through great moments and small, witnessed progress, saw talent rocket into the sky and talent go down the drain.

We enjoyed what we did.

Now the joy had gone.

Things do change when money becomes scarce. This was no surprise.

Fear had made a grand entrance at the Dramatic Workshop with Doubt following later. Except for a few people, loyalty went out the window. There are always the few. And they are always the same ones. You know them in advance by intuition, intimately as you know yourself. Then, numbness sets in—like drunken sailors staring at you from the other side of the bar—mixing with the enemy.

. . .

"Make more money liquid," said the lawyer. "Sell what you can." We tried: tables, desks, typewriters, curtains. We did not have much luck selling things, so we decided to unburden ourselves and give away what we could.

I do not recall who fell heir to the enormous wealth of costumes we had acquired during the years of repertory. They had been made with much sacrifice and love. But, I know, and always will, to whom we donated our magnificent array of lighting equipment; Klieg lights, projectors, dimmers, switch-boards went to the Actors' Studio.

I called the Studio and told them of our intention. A couple of days later, some boys arrived in a truck to fetch what was there. I added several items of our own property for which we no longer had any use—such as Piscator's directing lectern from which he had, during the past twelve years, guided a repertory of almost one hundred plays. I dedicated it to Lee Strasberg.

I never heard from Lee Strasberg about this small offering.

In closing the doors of the Dramatic Workshop, we knew we would never be the same. We had surely borrowed some features of the phoenix. True theatre people know their ventures must not be trusted to one place. In the welcoming address there is always a whisper of the farewell.

And farewell it was. Farewell to a fine and exciting venture. There would be new things to say—new things to do. And new things have been said—and done.

. . .

Here our search is at an end as well as our process of recollection.

The moving path of Piscator's American experiment is for others to continue. He had shown the way and given us the first results.

It was sheer irony that the blueprint for a new theatre which Piscator had drawn up in America came to life from the day he went back to Europe.

After a few years as guest director of the most important theatres throughout Europe—producing the plays of his choice at the Schillertheatre, Germany's most beautiful repertory, Piscator was offered the opportunity he had been looking for; the direction of War and Peace.

For twenty years the play in the drawer, War and Peace, had been his silent companion. Many times it had been the handmaiden to various other causes.

When in 1955 War and Peace was produced at the Schillertheatre with almost unlimited means, vast technical machinery and the finest repertory acting group Germany had to offer, it was truly Total Theatre.

Fifty curtain calls, a standing ovation for Piscator welcoming him back to Berlin, a sensational foreign press headed by Kenneth Tynan and an indifferent German press dominated by Friedrich Luft.

I had gone to Berlin from New York for this first night. It is difficult to describe my feelings as I sat there waiting for the performance to start. Before me the open stage—with the difference that it was produced in the fullest dimensions of design seen to date.

. . .

I remembered the first performance of War and Peace in New York at the Studio Theatre and the fullness of heart which emptied in the course of the long evening. I remembered my rebellion at those well-meaning advisors who, during the intermission, had told me that every successful play must have a beginning, a middle and an end; that the leading figure must have no way out, that everything should lead to a catharsis, the cause of which must be self-evident—and that it has always been customary to weep with the weeping, and laugh with the laughing; or better, as Brecht said, to "laugh with the weeping and weep with the laughing."

What was it to be now—on which side was I going to weep or laugh? What choice did I have but to sit and wait?

Only slowly, as the narrator kept talking and the simultaneous scenes unfolded one after the other, showing the dramatic characters of this great Epic in action on their five different stages coming to life—only when Pierre Bezuhov played the battle scene with the lead soldiers on stage amid the great silence of deepest attention that comes over the audience when it is truly aware—only then did I quiet down.

It was not the clumsy, idealistic Pierre nor the progressive, dashing Andrei, nor the lovely Natasha, nor the narrator and his sardonic smile that held the audience spellbound, but the grandiose and enormous truth of the lurid illumination of the bombed cities and the fields of massacres.

Tolstoy had written his book before Verdun and Ypres; before Stalingrad and Hiroshima, Nagasaki, Coventry, Dresden, Hamburg, Algeria, all the ominous names that crowd upon us now. Tolstoy had taken for granted that life would go on, whatever happens. From the audience of 1955 that pleasing assurance had been removed.

Until this day I have felt the enormous gust of air that invaded the theatre. For many, politics had become a word that divided people instead of uniting them. At this moment the interaction between theatre and politics, revealing a theme that meant life and death for both, became perfection itself.

And this was truer than the assurance of success can give. Because an astounding thing had happened. Everything that Piscator had said in the past about *War and Peace*, every thing that he stated in his credo of Epic Theatre as the basis for the dramatization, even to the technical scheme, worked as precisely as clockwork, and was realized in this evening.

It was as if a gigantic blueprint, drawn by a genius, had unrolled itself for another generation to march upon and had schematized the exact results Piscator had incontestably equated. To me, that was evidence greater than any reviewer's most enlightened commentary could provide.

It did not dazzle me. It simply amazed me.

Shortly after, *War and Peace* went to Paris on the invitation of the International Theatre Festival. It was the first German production chosen after the war. Some of the critics in Paris hated the play, finding it a schematic piece. Some admired it precisely for that. Harold Clurman wrote on this occasion:

> *I have no quarrel with them on this account, yet I admired it. I admired it even though it isn't "my kind" of theatre, which I might define as reality through poetry or poetry through reality. The theatre, I believe, should not confine itself to any single type of entertainment. The theatre of emotion is fine, but there must also be a place for the "intellectual" theatre. Nor am I averse to propaganda— and do not consider that propaganda must necessarily fail to be art. The theatre can be creatively frivolous—and I do not often object when it is just frivolous. It can also be valuably "cold," "mental," "bad," or "mad"; it is a domain of many mansions.*
>
> *Piscator's War and Peace, in which a great battle scene is projected (or demonstrated) by the use of toy soldiers placed on a geographical plane and in which an interlocutor explains, informs, argues, even addresses the play's characters and is answered by them, is a diagram of the novel. But it is handsomely and sometimes ingeniously drawn with a distinguished sense of the possibilities of the stage. That it is not conventionally stirring, that is, it is more lesson than epic, that it has little "flesh and blood," that it contains a*

minimum of (Russian) color or (Tolstoyan) humanity does not invalidate it for me as theatre.

I have heard it said by one of Piscator's detractors that he is more engineer than director, but that is only a left-handed way of indicating that he has technical genius. His mechanical inventions, however, always serve an artistic end. This is evident not only in his production of Buechner's Danton's Death but in his production of Faulkner's Requiem for a Nun.

When I read Faulkner's play I was certain that it would be unworkable. Most of the play is an exposition through interminably long speeches, describing highly complex situations which have occurred off-stage. With the help of an excellent company, Piscator has made it absorbing. I am not sure I believe the story or trust either its psychology or its morality, but I cannot deny that the play interested me. There is a concentration, a driving intensity—very much abetted by the stylized and yet surprisingly unobtrusive geometrical black-and-silver sets—which capture attention.

Piscator's craft has a certain intellectual and aristocratic elegance—like a highly civilized prose put to the uses of an ultrarational twentieth-century mind; radical, refined, aware of what may still be useful in the traditions of the past.

It was London that brought to War and Peace the long-awaited consecration. It was a solid triumph without reservation.

When we read the London papers this time, after we had heard of the success at the Old Vic (we were in Italy for a short reprieve), we giggled with tears in our throat. Seven American producers had been battling during the first night for the option to take the play to New York. This seemed terribly funny to us, as funny as a Marx Brothers tragedy and again we laughed and we cried.

But the farce was not really at an end. The seven producers, all substantial names, vanished one by one. The final option was taken up by T. Edward Hambleton and Norris

Houghton with the Association of Producing Artists. They presented *War and Peace* with the company of APA at the Phoenix Theatre under the direction of Ellis Rabb in 1964. The play fared extremely well with the audience as well as the press and has remained in the APA repertory.

I have often thought that the biography of this play is quite a commentary on the general history of the theatre, the history of good luck (or shall we say sheer luck?), like Napoleon winning the battle of Austerlitz, not because he was the greatest soldier of all time, but because the sun began to shine at the critical moment. And almost losing Borodino, not because his talent was declining, but because some of his army happened to be looking in the wrong direction.

Tolstoy tells us that this is the same with private life. The shot with which the ham-fisted Pierre wounded the confident Dolokhov in the preposterous duel was an accident. Chance rules everything.

Can we—dare we—leave the theatre at that?

Replies have been given already.

The "New Berlin Dramaturgy" (Die Neue Berliner Dramaturgie) had until Piscator's return, attributed Epic Theatre solely to Brecht. With Hochhuth's *The Deputy*, Kiepphardt's *The Case of J. Robert Oppenheimer*, and Peter Weiss' *The Investigation*, the tide changed. "Epic Theatre is a phrase," Kenneth Tynan wrote recently, "that Brecht borrowed from Piscator in the 'twenties and went on defining until the end of his life."

Piscator gave a highly distinctive style, with considerable potency, to these new plays, which became world successes. Since Buechner's *Danton's Death*, which Piscator had produced almost immediately after his arrival in Europe, he had elaborated on his Berlin Dramaturgy. It is again Kenneth Tynan who makes the important point of Piscator's different approach to Epic Theatre:

In Buechner's masterpiece, the disillusioned Danton
("We have not made the revolution; the revolution has
made us") and the doctrinaire Robespierre are both drawn
with equal sympathy. Piscator slants his production against
both of them. Danton is played as a bombastic sensualist
and Robespierre as a frigid fanatic; the play becomes an
attack upon the principle of revolution, rather than a sad
dissection of revolutionary practice. Still, this production is
a gauntlet flung down by Piscator to Brecht.

Back in Europe, Erwin Piscator's "Epic I" (as the critic
Peter Szondi called it), his truly monumental political profile,
which held all the parts of his life work together, offered to
the audience once more the grand gestus of the Theatrical
Feast.

After more years of traveling through Europe as "a salesman of theatre," as he called himself jokingly, he finally ob-
tained the position which seemed to be the Alpha and
Omega of his life; he was nominated Intendant of the Volksbuehne in Berlin, where he had started his career.

He accepted the challenge.

In his lucid mind, he was quite aware what this possibility
represented. Not competition with the East Berlin Ensemble
Theatre, as has been erroneously stated many times, but the
task he had been waiting for. Yet if he insisted on creating
the theatre he had wanted to create since his return to Germany, it could mean his professional crucifixion.

What was it that Piscator wanted so badly from the theatre that he was willing to sacrifice his theatrical genius for
it?

A theatre for life.

To better life.

He knew that the habits of evil grow easily in the heart and
that, if he wanted a better life, the first thing he had to do
was to fight these habits.

A theatre of facts? But more . . .
A theatre of repentance
Of public confession
Of Atonement
Of Redemption.

A theatre for which he was going to bargain with stupidity, with indifference, with violence and provincialism; a theatre into which he could pour his long experience, all his energy, the energy of his ripening belief in the sanctity of life and the progressive road.

America was far away, like a dream. She no longer stole the spotlight from the many new opportunities and oppositions, which have become important.

The most confusing image was in Germany today.

He was no longer the traveler from sweet Corinth, as he had felt himself in the first says of his arrival after twelve years of absence in a distant land. He was now Orestes, son of the slain Agamemnon, the Orestes of conscious intelligence, who is bound to seek the truth—"I see in every Greek 'the Greek';" as Gerhardt Hauptmann put it: "the brother-murderer, and I hate him for this."

In a large measure, Piscator, the hard-boiled realist, had remained a Romantic. And it is Romanticism that sensitized him now to the fact that he would not be able to avoid tragedy.

Every play he touched turned in his hand, almost against his will, to anti-theatre—*The Atrides, The Deputy, The Case of J. Robert Oppenheimer, The Investigation.* Anti-theatre was his way of fighting tragedy; tragic art had failed to convey the truth, and it is the truth that he was after. Soon the bourgeois press, unable to understand how he suffered under this inner command, attacked him. He was surprised, but he knew that there was no other way for him.

It was at this moment that Rolf Hochhuth wrote a profile

about him which summed up the past and explained much of
the present:

Erwin Piscator—Protestant Without God
　　*After his return to Europe, Erwin Piscator traveled for
eleven years as a guest director, until he was given, finally
and naturally only in Berlin and only at the Freie
Volksbuehne [Free People's Stage], his own theatre again.
"Piscator is out of step with the times," said all his critics,
such as Eugene Ionesco. But even his friends say that,
because within the stagnating conformism of our society,
nothing more honorable could be said about the aggressive
man of seventy with the Hohenzollern profile. He is the
last surviving champion of the truly clean, sermon-on-the-
mount type of socialism of the 'twenties; a grateful guest
of America who has sharp words for all who question
America's pure motives during World War II or in the
area of current political affairs. He is the enormously gifted
experimenter with the theatre, who never ceased to hope
after 1916 that the way to an understanding of all peoples
would lead via socialism. After all, "100 million dead line
the road of my generation." Erwin Piscator is indeed as
remote from the spirit of the times as civil courage, or his
strong social conscience, or the Christian program that the
CDU [Christian Democratic Union] adopted in Ahlen
sixteen years ago, only to throw it out again quickly when
success made it no longer necessary. As a result, Piscator
became as suspect with the "left" (are we still permitted
to say that today?) as, for example, Otto Brenner. Piscator
shares Brenner's solitary demand that workers and clerks
should participate in the means of production of the nation,
just as he denied the government's official claim, in the face
of half a million retired people with less than 200 marks a
month, that there are no longer any proletarians.
　　Like his famous forebear, the Bible translator, Johannes
Piscator, in 1600, he is a theologian, a man of Christian
nature—but as his God, like the God of many others, died
in Flanders or before Verdun, his stirring Ethos is firmly
grounded in this earth. He knows that at best politics, and*

> *no longer theology, can lead a step forward toward*
> *humanism, which is the aim. For this reason he insists on*
> *his social-critical theatre, without ever forgetting, of course,*
> *that art and party loyalty are mutually exclusive. But, like*
> *the authors at the time of the Enlightenment, in another*
> *day, Piscator sees the stage as a moral institution, as a*
> *platform from which to call upon man to honor man.*
> *"Most people," he says, "have not even enough imagination*
> *to visualize their own lives, let alone those of others." Thus*
> *he lives, and lives only to help our imagination, and to stage*
> *plays, with such an intensity as to remind us of the word of*
> *the mystic: "Whoever comes too close to me, comes too*
> *close to the fire."*

He became more and more impersonal in life. Even with his friends. Even with me. But, in spite of it, he never forgot the goals he had set for himself. Germany must not forget so soon.

There was an aura about his appearance which was like lightning. The homecoming Greek, the optimistic post-Pascalian with the heritage of his mother's French mind, became the German Protestant, born in Ulm and brought up in Marburg. And as a German, he took up his part of tradition; as a Protestant, his part of revolt:—"Here I stand."—And as an artist, he was part of the people, an artist who made lifelong theatre—for a better life.

"Bettering life," writes René Drommert (*Die Zeit*, Hamburg, No. 48, 1965), "I think Piscator has, particularly during the later years, directed all his efforts against the worsening of mankind." Drommert sums up brilliantly in a single sentence the preoccupation of Piscator. "Theatre once before was a sterile, neutral and esthetic art form, unable to stop the advance of barbarism—this must not happen again."

This is what could be considered Piscator's mission. He never expected to be heard by all men, yet he stood to the very end at the barricades of the rebels, against barbarism, together with Brecht, Toller, Refrisch, Hasek, Plivier, Paquet and others. Theatre, yes, but theatre for a purpose—to put into effect ideas that could serve mankind. He had not changed since his time of reckoning, which began on August 4, 1914 in the trenches of Ypres.

Did he repeat himself?

He did so on purpose when he saw that the lesson had not been learned. And he did it successfully. Germany's theatre was put back on the world map through him. "Can this be held against him?" asked René Drommert once more:

> At the age of 69, when most officials have been pensioned off, Erwin Piscator once again came forward as the great "Lion of the Theatre." Once again he set forth his artistic, and at the same time political, programme. Now he has a shrewder, cooler and more realistic outlook, advocated tenaciously and with vigor a number of humanitarian ideas (such as pacifism) in plays like Hochhuth's Deputy or Kipphardt's The Case of J. Robert Oppenheimer or The Investigation by Peter Weiss, plays which aroused the greatest interest not only in Berlin but also abroad. Can this success be held against him?
>
> The political theatre of Piscator, bound up with this pure, moral and courageous personality, cannot perhaps be repeated. It was, however, a high peak in the landscape of German theatre, which cannot be leveled out, and which should be carried forward in its richness of variety.

And Drommert refers to a letter he had received from Piscator from the hospital in Starenberg where he had gone for a checkup. It was a letter full of optimism. "Already thirty years ago eyewitnesses thought that they had seen him shot in the prisons of the Kremlin . . . but no, despite his many enemies, he was again 'soon on the way to recovery.'

"On the 30th of March he died in the Starenberg hospital following an operation. He was a grand and admirable person, with nothing in his life with which to reproach himself;

he stood faithfully by the standards which he set for himself."

• • •

Even with his death, the Piscator experiment was not over. The Berliner Ensemble paid a tribute to Piscator and quoted Brecht:

> Piscator is the greatest theatre man of all time. There was always protest with this man, always fight. His love for experimentation, his great scenic innovations, never existed for themselves. They served one goal—to transform man through all the existing artistic, as well as technical means of the theatre. . . . Even the contrasts in Piscator's lifework; his mistakes and his detours, cannot diminish the grandeur of this fighting Humanist. He will leave a legacy which we should use.

• • •

Tributes were paid all over Europe to "the uncomfortable Piscator."

Profound changes have taken place in the American theatre since Piscator's "experiment" in New York. The debate on Epic Theatre will continue. But its existence cannot be denied. More than any other man in the theatre Piscator had shown us the greatness of a profession, which unlike many others will have its part in the future of man; a part, perhaps rendered more urgent by the knowledge that, for the first time, man has the power to control his future.

There are many who are going to participate in the future dialogue of guardian and rebel. There are some who believe, like Piscator, that the artist is consummately able to direct evolution and that, if man is no longer looked upon as the center of the universe, he is perhaps able to become something finer and more important, "the arrow," as Teilhard de Chardin says, "pointing the way to the final unification of the world in terms of life."

Life and art, reshaping each other, probing our modern existence, will take control of the future as one. Therein, in this response to each other, rises the phoenix of the Piscator experiment.

. . .

All I can remember at this hour is a small room; a décor with three leading actors in it: the room in which we first met with Alvin Johnson. It could have been the setting for World Theatre.

I can still see the Aphrodite of Cyrene.

Now that I look at her from this great distance in time, I know that her empty eyes, the blind eyes of all stone creatures, cannot hold any emotion nor radiate any vision. It is the stone pitted against life, untouchable and untouched even by the dynamic powers of this great city—even the flow of light coming toward her through, alas, a too narrow window.

Was it this window that narrowed the vision, that decided the fate of "The School That Came to Stay"?

Who can answer for life and death?

For our coming and going?

The Rebel or the Guardian?

Who is the final Answerer?

Perhaps it was the fear of hubris that did not allow Aphrodite's beauty to be touched by the influence of love. The fear of hubris that broke the bond with religion, and with it the bond with art.

In my memory Aphrodite remains beauty absolute, simple and everlasting. She will be with me without diminution or any change, because she is part of the past I shared with him. Now, I am left alone to share the memory with the reader.

APPENDIX

The following biography of Erwin Piscator was supplied by Walter Rigdon, editor of *The Biographical Encyclopaedia & Who's Who of the American Theatre*, © James H. Heineman, Inc.

PISCATOR, ERWIN Producer, director, play-adapter. b. Erwin Friedrich Max Piscator, Dec. 17, 1893, Ulm, Kreis Werzlar, Ger., to Carl Piscator and Antonia (Laparose) Piscator. Father, merchant. Grad. high school, Marburg, Ger., Arbitur 1913; attended Univ. of Munich, 1913-14; Professor Artur Ktuscher Seminar, Munich, 1913-14. Member of P.E.N. Club, Dramaturgische Gesellschaft. Married Apr. 17, 1937, to Frederike V. Czada, known as Maria Ley, teacher-director. Served German Army, 1915-18, director of Front Th. Address: (home) 17 E. 76th St., New York, N.Y. 10021, tel. RE 7-4202; (bus.) c/o Freie Volks-buehne, Berlin, Ger.

THEATRE Mr. Piscator began in 1913 as an apprentice, playing minor roles at the Hoftheatre (Munich, Ger.). He founded Das Tri-

bunal, an avant-garde theatre, and directed plays by Strindberg, Wede-
kind, Sternheim, and the works of Ernst Toller and Georg Kaiser in
progress (Koenigsbert, 1919-20); founded Das Proletarissche Th. (Proletarian Th.), which performed plays in workers' halls in Berlin suburbs,
including Maxim Gorki's *Enemies*, Franz Jung's *Die Kanaker* and *Wie
lange noch, du Hure Buergerliche Gerechtigkeit*, K.A. Wittfogel's *Der
Krüeppel*; Upton Sinclair's *Prince Hagen*, and *Russia's Day*, which was
written collectively; took over the Central Th. (Berlin, 1923-24), where
he produced Gorki's *The Barbarians*, Rolland's *Le Temps Viendra*, and
Tolstoy's *The Power of Darkness*; directed R.R.R. (*Revue of Red Up-
roars*) in various halls and assembly rooms (Nov. 1924); became direc-
tor of Volkstheatre (Berlin, 1924-27), where he directed *Fahnen* and
Sturmflut by Paquet, O'Neill's *The Moon of the Carribbees*, Rehfisch's
Wer Weint um Juckenanck?, Leonhardt's *Segel in Horinzont*, Zech's
Das Trunkene Schiff, Gorki's *A Night's Lodging*, and Welk's *Gewitter
ueber Gottland*. He directed an historical and political revue entitled
Trotz Alledem (Grosse Schauspielhaus, Berlin, July 12, 1925); Schiller's
Die Raeuber (*The Robbers*) (State Th., Sept. 11, 1926); and Paquet's
Sturmflut (Chamber Th., Hamburg, Ger., 1927).

Mr. Piscator founded the Piscator Th. on Nollendorfplatz, Berlin,
which opened Sept. 3, 1927, with his production of Toller's *Hoppla,
wir Leben*. He also directed Tolstoy's *Rasputin, the Romanoffs, the war,
and the people who rose against them* (Nov. 12, 1927); Max Brod and
Hans Reinmann adaptation of Hasek's novel, *The Adventures of the
Good Soldier Schweik* (Jan. 23, 1928); Lania's *Konjunktur* (Apr. 8,
1928); produced Bloch's *Le Dernier Empereur*, with Karl-Heinz Mar-
tin as guest director (Apr. 14, 1929); and directed Mehring's *Der
Kaufmann von Berlin* (Sept. 6, 1929). Also, at the studio of the Piscator
Th., the following plays were presented (1927-28): Jung's *Heimweh*,
Sinclair's *Singing Jailbirds*, Rombach's *Der Heilige Krieg*, and Muehsam's
Judas.

He directed *What Price Glory?* (Th. in der Koeniggraetzer Strass,
Mar. 1929); staged a touring production of Crede's *218* (1929); directed
Plivier's *Des Kaiser Kuli* (Lessing Th., Berlin, 1930).

In 1936, Mr. Piscator emigrated to Paris, where he began the dramatic adaptation of Leo Tolstoy's *War and Peace* with Alfred Neumann; and emigrated to the U.S. in 1938.

He founded and directed (1939-51) the Dramatic Workshop at the
New Sch. for Social Research, N.Y.C., where he presented many productions, as well as at the President Th., Rooftop Th., and other N.Y.C.
theatres. Among his productions were *King Lear* (Dec. 1940), *The
Chalk Circle* (Mar. 1941), *Any Day Now* (May 1941), *The Criminals*
(Dec. 1941), *The Coward, He Who Gets Slapped*, Bruckner's adaptation of Lessing's *Nathan the Wise* (Mar. 11, 1942), *War and Peace*
(Apr. 1942), *The Aristocrats* (Apr. 1946), *A Marriage Proposal* (Dec.
1946), *Mourning Becomes Electra* (Dec. 1946), *Tonight We Improvise* (Apr. 1947), *The Flies* (Apr. 1947), *Lysistrata* (May 1947), *The*

Good Hope (May 1947), All the King's Men (Jan. 14, 1948), The Millionairess (Apr. 1948), The Burning Bush (Dec. 16, 1949), and Matthews' adaptation of Kafka's The Trial (Apr. 1950).

Also presented during the same period were Outside the Door, Chaff, Winter Soldiers, Emil and the Detectives, There Is No End, Nights of Wrath, The House in Berlin, Shaw's Village Wooing, What Price Glory, The Devil and Daniel, Alice in Wonderland, Prologue to Glory, Private Lives, Escape, The Inspector General, Turandot, Hannele, A Dream Play, The Little Foxes, Arsenic and Old Lace, Ghosts, The World We Live In, Home of the Brave, Aria da Capo, Private Hicks, All My Sons, The Imaginary Invalid, Juno and the Paycock, Waiting for Lefty, The Hasty Heart, The Time of Your Life, Romeo and Juliet, The Taming of the Shrew, Androcles and the Lion, The Devil's Disciple, The Man of Destiny, The Petrified Forest, Of Mice and Men, Machinal. The Male Animal, The Great Theatre of the World, Spring Source, The Shadow of a Gunman, As You Like It, The Sea Serpent, A Midsummer Night's Dream, 18 experimental plays, and six musicals. In summer stock theatres he presented The Women, Blithe Spirit, Claudia, Three Men on a Horse, Dark Eyes, The Countess of Arcis, and The Corn Is Green.

In Oct. 1951, Mr. Piscator returned to Germany, and has since directed productions in West Germany, Holland, Sweden, Switzerland, Italy and France.

He directed Hochwaelder's Virginia (Grosses Schauspielhaus, Hamburg, Ger., Nov. 30, 1951); Nathan der Weise (Nathan the Wise) (Marburg Th., Ger., May 14, 1952); Buechner's Leonce und Lena (Marburg Th., Oct. 27, 1952); Buechner's Dantons Tod (Danton's Death) (Marburg Th., Nov. 1, 1952); Love of Four Colonels (Zurich Th., Switz.) Androcles and the Lion (Haag Comedy Th., Holland, Jan. 1, 1953); Hochwaelder's Das Heilige Experiment (The Holy Experiment) (Haag Comedy Th., Holland, Feb. 14, 1953); Macbeth (Oldenburg State Th., Ger., Sept. 1, 1953); Caesar and Cleopatra (Haag Comedy Th., Holland, May 15, 1954); Les Sequestres d'Altona (The Condemned of Altona) (City Th., Frankfurt am Main, Ger., Jan. 18, 1954); The Crucible (Natl. Th., Mannheim, Ger., Apr. 20, 1954; Volkstheatre, Gothenberg, Sweden, Feb. 8, 1955); War and Peace (Schiller Th., Berlin, Ger., Mar. 20, 1955); Requiem for a Nun (Schlosspark Th., Berlin, Ger., Nov. 10, 1955); The Crucible (Marburg Th., Ger., Apr. 20, 1955); Les Sequestres d'Altona (Tuebingen Landestheatre, Ger., June 15, 1955); War and Peace (Darmstadt Landestheatre, Ger., Sept. 19, 1955); The Case of Pinedus (Natl. Th., Mannheim, Dec. 30, 1955); Requiem for a Nun (Volkstheatre, Gothenberg, Sweden, Feb. 1956); Dantons Tod (Danton's Death) (May 4, 1956); and War and Peace (Luebingen Landestheatre, June 24, 1956; City Theatre, Krefeld/M-Glabach, Ger., Nov. 21, 1956).

Mr. Piscator directed Friedrich Schiller's Die Raeuber (The Robbers), which was the opening production of the Natl. Th. (Mannheim, Ger.,

Jan. 1, 1957); *The Dance of Death* (I and II) (Thalia Th., Hamburg, Ger., 1957); three Russian one-act plays by Tolstoy and Chekhov (Schlosspark Th., Berlin, Ger., 1957); *Mourning Becomes Electra* (Essen, Ger., 1958); Weissenborn's *Goettinger Kantata* (Stuttgart, Ger., 1958); Kaiser's *Gas I & II* (Bochum, Ger., 1958); Kaiser's *Nebereinander* (Thalia Th., Hamburg, Ger., 1959); Frisch's *Biedermann und Brandstifter* (Natl., Th., Hamburg, Ger., 1959); Schiller's *Don Carlos* (Chamber Th., Munich, Ger., 1959); *War and Peace* (Th. des Nations, Paris, Fr., 1960); *Die Raeuber* (*The Robbers*) (Essen, Ger., 1960); Jahnn's *Der Staubige Regenbogen* (Frankfurt, Ger., 1960); Blacher's *Rosamunde Floris* (German Opera, Berlin, Ger., 1960); *The Dance of Death* (I and II) (Essen, Ger., 1960); Sternheim's *1913* (Chamber Th., Munich, Ger., 1960; Frankfurt, Ger., 1961; Essen, Ger., 1961); *Requiem for a Nun* (Th. des Nations, Paris, Fr., 1961); *Becket ou 1* (*Honneur de Dieu*) (Essen, Ger., 1961); *Death of a Salesman* (Volksbuehne, Berlin, Ger., 1961); Brecht's *Fluechtlingsgespraeche* (Chamber Th., Munich, Ger., premier 1962); and *The Balcony* (Frankfurt, Ger., 1962).

He became general director of the Freie Volksbuehne, Berlin, in 1962, and has directed there the first complete performance of Hauptmann's *Astride Tetrology* (1962), also Anouilh's *La Grotte* (1962), the premiere of Hochhuth's *Der Stellvertreter* (*The Deputy*) (1963), Rolland's *Robespierre*, as the opening bill of the new Volksbuehne Th. (1963), and *The Merchant of Venice* (1963). He directed Verdi's *I Masnadieri* (Florence, It., 1963); a touring production of *Der Stellvertreter* (West Germany, 1964); *Le Diable et le Bon Dieu* (Frankfurt, Ger., 1964); and Strauss' *Salome* (Florence, It., 1964).

War and Peace, which was adapted from the novel by Tolstoy by Mr. Piscator, Alfred Neumann, and Guntrum Prufer, was presented by the Association of Producing Artists (APA) (Phoenix, N.Y.C., Jan. 11, 1965; Greek Th., Los Angeles, Calif., Aug. 31, 1966). He directed *The Case of J. Robert Oppenheimer* (Th. du Parc, Brussels, Mar. 1965) and *Die Ermittlung* (*The Investigation*) (Freie Volksbuehne, Berlin, Oct. 19, 1965). A D D E N D U M Mr. Piscator directed a production of *Saint Joan* (Washington, D.C., 1940), in which Luise Rainer made her U.S. stage debut.

F I L M S   Mr. Piscator directed *Der Aufstand der Fischer von St. Barbara* (USSR, 1932-35).

T E L E V I S I O N   A N D   R A D I O   For West German radio, he directed Else Langner's *Heimkehr* (1953); and for Hessian radio and television, he directed *Les Sequestres d'Altona* (1956).

P U B L I S H E D   W O R K S   He wrote a book of confessions and accounts entitled *Das Politische Theatre* (1929), and *Das Politische Theatre als Dokument der Zwanziger Jahre*, a new edition of the earlier work (1963).

AWARDS He received the Goethe Prize (1953); German Federal Distinguished Service Cross (1958); and was appointed President of the Academy of the Performing Arts (1961).

RECREATION Tennis, swimming.

NOTE Mr. Piscator died Mar. 30, 1966, in Starnberg, Bav., Ger., following emergency surgery for a ruptured gall bladder, at the age of 72.

BIBLIOGRAPHY

A) GENERAL BOOKS

Plays by the dramatists mentioned in this volume, and individual studies of most of them, are readily available, and listing of them here would be aside from the main purpose of the work. A few anthologies of plays are listed, because of their informative introduction or included essays.

Abalkin, N. *Das Stanislawski-System und das Sowjet Theater*. Berlin. Henschelverlag, 1953.
Abel, Lionel. *Metatheatre: A New View of Dramatic Form*. New York. Hill & Wang, 1963.
Adamov, Arthur. *Ici et Maintenant*. Paris. Gallimard, 1964.
Alquié, Ferdinand. *Philosophie du Surréalisme*. Paris. Gallimard, 1955.
Americanisches Theater. Anthology. Vorwort S. Melchinger Frankfurt am Main, 1960.
Anders, France. *Jacques Copeau et le Cartel des Quatre*. Paris. A. G. Nizet, 1959.

Antoine, André. *Memories of the Théâtre Libre.* Miami, Florida. University of Miami Press, 1964.

Arnoux, Alexandre. *Charles Dullin, Portrait Brisé.* Paris. Emile-Paul Frères, 1951.

Artaud, Antonin. *Lettres d'Antonin Artaud à Jean-Louis Barrault.* Paris. Documents de la Revue Théâtrale, 1952.

Bablet, Denis, and Jacquot, Jean. *Le lieu Théâtral dans la Société Moderne.* Paris. Editions du Centre National de la Recherche Scientifique, 1963.

Bahr, Hermann. *Expressionismus.* Munich. Delphin Verlag, 1919.

———— *Expressionism.* London. F. Henderson, 1925.

Balakian, Anna E. *Surrealism: the Road to the Absolute.* New York. Noonday Press, 1959.

Barrault, Jean-Louis. *Betrachtungen über das Theater.* Zurich. Verlage der Arche, 1962.

———— *Nouvelles Reflexions sur le théâtre.* Paris. Flammarion, 1959.

———— *Le Phénomène Théâtral.* Oxford. Clarendon Press, 1961.

———— *Reflections on the Theatre.* London. Rockliff, 1951.

———— *Reflexions sur le Théâtre.* Paris. J. Vautrain, 1949.

———— *The Theatre of J.-L. Barrault.* (Translation of *Nouvelles Reflexions sur le Théâtre*) London. Barrie & Rockliff, 1961.

Baty, Gaston. *Lettre à une jeune Comédienne.* Paris. Presses Littéraires de France, 1953.

———— *Le Masque et l'encensoir: Introduction à une Esthétique du Théâtre.* Paris. Bloud & Gay, 1926.

———— *Rideau Baissé* (Includes *Le Masque et l'encensoir*) Paris. Bordas, 1949.

———— *Théâtre Nouveau: Notes et Documents.* Paris. A la Société des Spectacles, 1927 (?)

Bedouin, Jean-Louis. *André Breton.* Paris. Editions P. Seghers, 1963.

Bentley, Eric R. *From the Modern Repertoire.* Anthologies.
 Series I 1949, 1955
 Series II 1952
 Series III 1956. Bloomington. University of Indiana Press.

———— *The Life of the Drama.* New York. Atheneum, 1964.

———— *The Playwright as Thinker.* New York. Reynal & Hitchcock, 1946. Published as *The Modern Theatre*, London. R. Hale, 1948.

Beres, Pierre. *Cubism, Futurism, Dadaism, Expressionism, and the Surrealist Movement.* Preface by Paul Eluard. New York. Pierre Beres, 1948.

Blau, Herbert. *The Impossible Theater.* New York. Macmillan, 1964.

Block, Anita. *The Changing World in Plays and Theatre.* Boston. Little, Brown, 1939.

Block, Haskell M. and Shedd, Robert G., editors. *Masters of Modern Drama.* New York. Random House, 1962.

Boury, François. *Louis Jouvet.* Bourges. Editions Gilco, 1953.

Breton, André. *Les Manifestes du Surréalisme.* Paris. Le Sagittaire, 1955.

———— *What is Surrealism?* London. Faber & Faber, 1936.

Brustein, Robert. *The Theatre of Revolt*. Boston. Little, Brown, 1964.

Carter, Huntly. *The Theatre of Max Reinhardt*. London. F. & C. Palmer, 1914.

Cezan, Claude. *Louis Jouvet et la Théâtre d'Aujourd'hui*. Paris. Editions Emile-Paul Frères, 1938.

Chekhov, Michael. *To the Actor*. New York. Harper, 1953.

———— *To the Director and Playwright*. Compiled by Charles Leonard. New York. Harper & Row, 1963.

Cheney, Sheldon. *Expressionism in Art*. New York. Tudor, 1948.

Clark, Barrett and Freedley, George. *A History of Modern Drama*. New York. Appleton-Century, 1949.

Clurman, Harold. *The Fervent Years*. The Story of the Group Theatre and the Thirties. New York. Knopf, 1945.

———— *Lies Like Truth*. New York. Macmillan, 1958.

Cocteau, Jean. *Cocteau par lui-même*. Paris. Editions du Seuil, 1957.

———— *Le cordon ombilical; souvenirs*. Paris. Plon, 1962.

———— *Essai de critique indirecte*. Paris. B. Grasset, 1932.

———— *Journals*. Edited and translated with an Introduction by Wallace Fowlie. New York. Criterion, 1956.

———— *Leben und Werk des Jean Cocteau*. Wien. K. Desch, 1961.

Coe, Richard N. *Eugene Ionesco*. New York. Grove, 1961.

Cole, Toby. *Acting, a Handbook on the Stanislavski Method*. Introduction by Lee Strasberg. New York. Lear, 1947.

———— (Editor) *Playwrights on Playwriting* (Ibsen to Ionesco). New York. Hill & Wang, 1960.

Cole, Toby, and Chinoy, Helen K., editors. *Actors on Acting*. New York. Crown, 1957.

Copeau, Jacques. *Les Amis du Vieux-Colombier*. Paris. Les Editions de la Nouvelle Revue Française, 1920.

———— *Etudes d'art Dramatique* (includes "Un essai de renovation dramatique"). Paris. Nouvelle Revue Française, 1923.

———— *Souvenirs du Vieux-Colombier*. Paris. Nouvelles editions latines, 1931.

Corrigan, Robert W. *Theatre in the 20th Century*. (Articles from the Tulane Drama Review) New York. Grove, 1963.

———— (editor) *The Modern Theatre* (40 plays with essays and letters). New York. Macmillan, 1964.

———— (editor) *The New Theatre of Europe* (5 plays with essays by the playwrights). New York. Dell, 1962.

Cruickshank, John. *Albert Camus and the Literature of Revolt*. New York. Oxford University Press, 1960.

Dali, Salvador. *Conquest of the Irrational*. New York. J. Levy, 1935.

Dane, Clemence. *Approaches to Drama* (Presidential Address). London. The English Society, 1961.

Dean, Alexander. *Fundamentals of Play Directing*. New York. Farrar & Rinehart, 1941. Holt, Rinehart & Winston, 1960.

Dickinson, Thomas, H. *The Theatre in a Changing Europe*. New York. Holt, 1939.

Dictionnaire abrégé du surréalisme. Paris. Galerie Beaux-Arts, 1938.

Diderot, Denis. *The Paradox of Acting.* Together with Archer, William, *Masks or Faces?* Introduction by Lee Strasberg. New York. Hill & Wang, 1957.

Dietrich, Margarete. *Das Moderne Drama.* Stuttgart. A. Kroner, 1961.

Doisy, Marcel. *Jacques Copeau; ou, l'absolu dans l'art.* Paris. Le Cercle du Livre, 1954.

Doubourg, Pierre. *Dramaturgie de Jean Cocteau.* Paris. B. Grasset, 1954.

Downer, Alan. *Recent American Drama.* Minneapolis. University of Minnesota Press, 1961.

Dullin, Charles. *Souvenirs et Notes de Travail d'un acteur.* Paris. O. Lieutier, 1946.

Duprey, Richard A. *Just off the Aisle.* Westminster, Md. Newman Press, 1962.

Dürrenmatt, Friedrich. *Theaterprobleme.* Zurich. Verlag der Arche, 1955. Also in *Four Plays* (*Problems of the Theater*). London. J. Cape, 1964. Also in *Tulane Drama Review,* vol. 3, No. 1, Oct. 1958.

Edmundson, James S. *Charles Dullin and the Contemporary French Theatre.* New York. (Columbia University thesis), 1958.

Eisner, Lotte H. *L'Ecran démoniaque,* Paris. A. Bonne, 1952.

Esslin, Martin. *The Theatre of the Absurd.* New York. Doubleday, 1961.

Federal Theatre Plays. Vol. 1. Prologue to Glory; One-Third of a Nation; Haiti.

———— Vol. 2. Triple-A Plowed Under; Power; Spirochete. New York. Random House, 1938.

Fergusson, Francis. *The Idea of a Theatre.* New York. Doubleday, 1949.

Flanagan, Hallie (Ferguson). *Arena* (story of the Federal Theatre). New York. Duell, Sloan & Pearce, 1940.

Fowlie, Wallace. *Age of Surrealism.* New York. Swallow Press, 1950. Bloomington. Indiana University Press, 1960.

———— *Dionysus in Paris.* New York. Meridian, 1960.

Frank, Waldo D. *The Art of the Vieux Colombier.* Paris. Nouvelle Revue Française, 1918.

Französisches Theater. Anthology. Vorwort S. Melchinger. Frankfurt am Main, 1959.

Französisches Theater der Avantgarde. Anthology. Vorwort H. Schwab. München. Felisch, 1961.

Gagey, Edmond M. *Revolution in American Drama.* New York. Columbia University Press, 1948.

Garten, H. F. *Modern German Drama.* London. Methuen, 1959, 1964.

Gascoygne, David. *A Short Survey of Surrealism.* London. Cobden-Sanderson, 1935.

Gassner, John. *Form and Idea in the Modern Theatre.* New York. Dryden Press, 1956.

———— *Ideas in Drama* (contains "Brecht and the Drama of Ideas"). New York. Columbia University Press, 1964.

—— Producing the Play (with Philip Barber's New Scene Technician's Handbook). New York. Dryden Press, 1941.

—— The Theatre in Our Times. New York. Crown, 1954.

Gassner, John and Allen, Ralph G., editors. Theatre and Drama in the Making. Boston. Houghton Mifflin, 1964.

Ghislein, Brewster, editor. The Creative Process. New York. New American Library, 1952.

Gorchakov, Nikolai Mikhailovich. Stanislavski Directs (Foreword by Norris Houghton). New York. Funk & Wagnalls, 1954.

—— Vakhtangov Metteur en Scène. Moscow. Editions en langues étrangères.

—— The Theatre in Soviet Russia. New York. Columbia University Press, 1957.

Gorelik, Mordecai. New Theatres for Old. New York. French, 1940. Dutton paperback, 1962.

Gropius, Walter, editor. The Theater of the Bauhaus. Middletown, Conn. Wesleyan University Press, 1961.

Grossvogel, David I. Four Playwrights and a Postscript. Ithaca. Cornell University Press, 1962. Also issued by Cornell in 1965 as The Blasphemers: The Theatre of Brecht, Ionesco, Beckett, Genet.

—— The Self Conscious Stage. New York. Columbia University Press, 1958.

Guicharnaud, Jacques, with Beckelman, June. Modern French Theatre (Giraudoux to Beckett). New Haven, Conn. Yale University Press, 1961.

Harvey, John. Anouilh: A Study in Theatrics. New Haven, Conn. Yale University Press, 1964.

Hauser, Arnold. Sozialgeschichte der Kunst und Literatur. 2 vols. Munchen. C.H. Beck'sche Verlags, 1953.

Hethmon, Robert H., editor. Strasberg at the Actor's Studio. New York. Viking Press, 1965.

Hill, Claude and Ley, Ralph. The Drama of German Expressionism: A German-English Bibliography. Chapel Hill. University of North Carolina Press, 1960.

Hocker, Karla. Gesprache mit Berliner Kunstlern. Berlin. Stapp Verlag, 1964.

Hort, Jean. Les Théâtre du cartel et leurs animateurs: Pitoëff, Baty, Jouvet, Dullin. Geneva. A. Skira, 1944.

Ihering, Herbert. Berliner Dramaturgie. Berlin. Aufbau Verlag, 1947.

—— Junge Schauspieler. Munich. K. Desch, 1948.

—— Schauspieler in der Entwicklung. Berlin. Aufbau Verlag, 1956.

—— Theaterstadt Berlin. Berlin. Bruno Henschel und Sohn, 1948.

—— Von Reinhardt bis Brecht. 3 vols. Berlin. Aufbau Verlag, 1958-1961.

Ionesco, Eugene. Notes and Counternotes. New York. Grove, 1964.

Jacobsen, Josephine and Mueller, William R. The Testament of Samuel Beckett. New York. Hill & Wang, 1964.

Johnson, Alvin. *Pioneer's Progress*. Lincoln. University of Nebraska Press, 1960.

Jouvet, Louis. *Le Comédien désincarné*. Paris. Flammarion, 1954.

———— *Ecoute, mon ami*. Paris. Flammarion, 1952.

———— *Reflexions du comédien*. Paris. Editions de la nouvelle revue critique, 1938. Librairie Théâtral, 1952.

———— *Témoinages sur le Théâtre*. Paris. Flammarion, 1952.

Kazin, Alfred. *Starting Out in the Thirties*. Boston. Little, Brown, 1965.

Kenner, Hugh. *Samuel Beckett*. New York. Grove, 1961.

Kernan, Alvin B., editor. *Classics of the Modern Theatre*. Anthology. New York. Harcourt, Brace & World, 1965.

Kerr, Alfred. *Gesammelte Schriften*. 2 vols. Berlin. S. Fischer, 1917-1920.

———— *Das Neue Drama*. Berlin. S. Fischer, 1909.

———— *Was wird aus Deutschlands Theater?* Berlin. S. Fischer, 1932.

Kesting, Marianne. *Panorama des zeitgenössischen Theaters*. Munich. R. Piper, 1962.

Kitto, H.D.F. *Form and Meaning in Drama*. London. Methuen, 1960.

Knapp, Bettina L. *Louis Jouvet, Man of the Theatre* (Foreword by Michael Redgrave). New York. Columbia University Press, 1958.

Krutch, Joseph Wood. *The American Drama since 1918*. New York. Random House, 1939.

Laban, Rudolf. *The Mastery of Movement on the Stage*. London. Macdonald & Evans, 1950.

Lawson, John Howard. *Theory and Technique of Playwriting*. New York. G. P. Putnam's Sons, 1936.

Lerminier, Georges. *Jacques Copeau et l'art du comédien*. Paris. Cahiers du Compagnie Rénaud-Barrault, 1955.

Le Sage, Laurence. *Jean Giraudoux, Surrealism, and the German Romantic Ideal*. Urbana. University of Illinois Press, 1952.

Lessing, Gotthold. *Laocoon*. London. J. M. Dent & Sons, 1961.

Lewis, Allan. *American Plays and Playwrights of the Contemporary Theatre*. New York. Crown, 1965.

———— *The Contemporary Theatre*. New York. Crown, 1962.

Lewis, Robert. *Method—or Madness?* New York. Samuel French, 1958.

Lumley, Frederick. *Trends in Twentieth Century Drama*. London. Barrie & Rockliff, 1956, 1960, 1961.

Malraux, André. *Psychologie de l'art*. 3 vols. Geneva. A. Skira, 1947-1950. Also published as *Les Voix du silence*. Paris. Nouvelle Revue Française, 1952.

———— *Psychologie der Kunst*. Hamburg. Rowohlt, 1958.

———— *The Psychology of Art*. 3 vols. (The Bollingen Series, 24) New York. Pantheon, 1949-1950.

———— *The Voices of Silence*. New York. Doubleday, 1953.

Marcel, Gabriel. *Théâtre et Religion*. Lyons. E. Vitte, 1958.

McMahon, Joseph H. *The Imagination of Jean Genet*. New Haven, Conn. Yale University Press, 1963.

Melchinger, Siegfried. *The Concise Encyclopedia of Modern Drama.* New York. Horizon, 1964.

———— *Drama zwischen Shaw und Brecht.* Bremen. C. Schünemann, 1957, 1959, 1961.

———— *Theater der Gegenwart.* Frankfurt am Main. Fischer, 1956.

———— *Modernes Welttheater.* Bremen. C. Schünemann, 1956.

———— *Welttheater: Bühnen, Autoren, Inszenierungen.* Braunschweig. G. Westermann, 1962.

Meyerhold, Vsevolod. *Le Théâtre Théâtral.* Paris. Gallimard, 1963.

Moore, Sonia. *An Actor's Training: The Stanislavski Method.* London. Victor Gollancz, 1960. *The Stanislavski Method.* New York. Viking, 1960.

Murdoch, Iris. *Sartre.* New Haven, Conn. Yale University Press, 1953.

Nadeau, Maurice. *Histoire du surréalisme.* Paris. Editions du Seuil, 1946.

———— *The History of Surrealism.* New York. Macmillan, 1965.

Nicoll, Allardyce. *The Theatre and Dramatic Theory.* London. Harrap, 1962. New York. Barnes & Noble, 1962.

———— *World Drama from Aeschylus to Anouilh.* London. Harrap, 1949, 1951.

Oxenhandler, Neal. *Scandal and Parade: The Theatre of Jean Cocteau.* New Brunswick, N.J. Rutgers University Press, 1957.

Popkin, Henry, editor. *The New British Drama.* Anthology. New York. Grove, 1964.

Pörtner, Paul. *Experiment Theater: Chronik und Dokumente.* Zurich. Die Arche, 1960.

Pronko, Leonard C. *Avant-Garde: The Experimental Theatre in France.* Berkeley. University of California Press, 1962.

———— *The World of Jean Anouilh.* Berkeley. University of California Press, 1961.

Queant, Gilles. *Encyclopédie du Théâtre Contemporaine.* Paris. Olivier Perrin, 1959.

Rabkin, Gerald. *Drama and Commitment.* Bloomington. Indiana University Press, 1964.

Read, Herbert. *Art Now.* London. Faber & Faber, 1948.

Reinhardt, Max. *Bildnis eines Theatermannes.* Hamburg. Rowohlt, 1953.

Rice, Elmer. *The Living Theatre.* New York. Harper & Row, 1959.

Ripellino, Angelo Maria. *Majakowskij und das Russische Theater der Avantgarde.* Koln. Kiepenheuer & Witsch, 1959.

Ruhle, Jurgen. *Das Gefesselte Theater.* Koln. Kiepenheuer & Witsch, 1957.

———— *Theater und Revolution.* Munchen. Deutscher Taschebuch Verlag, 1963.

Samuel, Richard and Thomas, R. Hinton. *Expressionism in German Life, Literature, and the Theatre.* Cambridge, England. W. Heffer & Sons, 1939.

Sarment, Jean. *Charles Dullin.* Paris. Calmann-Lévy, 1950.

Sartre, Jean-Paul. *Saint Genet.* New York. Braziller, 1963.

Sayler, Oliver M. *Max Reinhardt and his Theatre.* New York. Brentano's, 1924.

Schlemmer, Oskar. *Bild und Bühne.* Baden-Baden. Staatlichen Kunsthalle, 1965.

Schnurre, Wolfdietrich. *Berlin eine Stadt wird geteilt.* Olten. Walter Verlag, 1962.

Schulze-Vellinghausen, Albert. *Theaterkritik 1952-1960.* Hannover. E. Friedrich, 1961.

Sebag, Lucien. *Marxisme et Structuralisme.* Paris. Payot, 1964.

Shaw, Leroy R., editor. *The German Theatre Today* (a symposium). Austin. University of Texas Press, 1963.

Sievers, W. D. *Freud on Broadway.* New York. Hermitage, 1955.

Simon, Pierre Henri. *Histoire de la littérature française au XXe siecle.* Paris. A Colin, 1957.

——— *L'Homme en procès: Malraux, Sartre, Camus, Saint-Exupéry.* Neuchatel. A la Baconnière, 1950.

——— *Théâtre et Destin.* Paris. A Colin, 1959.

Sokel, Walter H. *Anthology of German Expressionist Drama.* New York. Doubleday, 1963.

——— *The Writer in Extremis: Expressionism in 20th century German Literature.* Stanford, California. Stanford University Press, 1959. New York. McGraw-Hill, 1959.

Sollers, Philippe. *Drame.* Paris. Editions du Seuil, 1965.

Stanislavski (also Stanislavsky), Konstantin Sergeyevich, originally Konstantin Sergeyevich Aleksieev. *An Actor Prepares.* New York. Theatre Arts, 1944. With Introduction by John Gielgud, 1948.

——— *An Actor's Handbook.* New York. Theatre Arts, 1963.

——— *Die Arbeit des Schauspielers an sich selbst.* Berlin. Henschel Verlag, 1961, 1963.

——— *Stanislavski on the Art of the Stage.* Introductory essay on Stanislavsky's System by David Margarshack. London. Faber & Faber, 1950. New York. Hill & Wang, 1961.

——— *Building a Character.* New York. Robert M. MacGregor, 1949.

——— *Creating a Role.* New York. Theatre Arts, 1961.

——— *Stanislavsky's Legacy.* New York. Theatre Arts, 1958.

——— *Stanislavski and the World Theatre. Stanislavski, Man and Actor. Stanislavski's letters.* (Translation of the Russian centennial collection). Moscow. Progress Publishers, 1964 (?)

Steiner, George. *The Death of Tragedy.* London. Faber & Faber, 1961.

Syjher, Wylie. *Comedy.* New York. Doubleday, 1956.

Szondi, Peter. *Theorie des modernen Dramas.* Frankfurt am Main. Suhrkamp, 1956, 1959.

——— *Versuch über das Tragische.* Frankfurt am Main. Insel Verlag, 1961.

Taubman, Howard. *The Making of the American Theatre.* New York. Coward McCann, 1965.

Taylor, John Russell. *The Angry Theatre*. New York. Hill & Wang, 1962.

———— *Anger and After*. Baltimore, Md. Penguin, 1963.

Thomas, John Gerald. *The Federal Theatre Project, 1935-1939*. A survey and evaluation. New York. (Columbia University thesis), 1958.

Tynan, Kenneth. *Curtains*. New York. Atheneum, 1961.

Valentin, Karl. *Die Masken des Komikers*. Freiburg. Verlag Herder, 1958.

Vermeil, Edmond. *Germany in the Twentieth Century*. New York. Frederick A. Praeger, 1956.

Vilar, Jean. *De la Tradition Théâtrale*. Paris. L'Arche, 1955.

Waxman, Samuel N. *Antoine and the Théâtre Libre*. Cambridge. Harvard University Press, 1926. New York. Blom, 1964.

Wellworth, George E. *The Theater of Protest and Paradox*. New York. New York University Press, 1964.

B) EPIC THEATRE: WORKS BY OR ON PISCATOR AND BRECHT

Aughtry, Charles E. *Landmarks in Modern Drama* (Anthology and essays; includes Brecht's "The Alienation Effect in Chinese Acting"). Boston. Houghton Mifflin, 1963.

Bogard, Travis and Oliver, William I., editors. *Modern Drama: Essays in Criticism*. (includes "How Epic is Bertolt Brecht's Epic Theatre?" by Heinz Politzer). New York. Oxford University Press, 1965.

Bertolt Brechts Dreigroschenbuch. (includes a record: "Brecht Sings"). Frankfurt am Main. Suhrkamp Verlag, 1960.

Brecht, Bertolt. *Brecht on Theatre: The Development of an Aesthetic*. (Translated and with Notes by John Willett). London. Methuen, 1964. New York. Hill & Wang, 1964.

———— *Early Plays*. New York. Grove, 1964.

———— *Plays*. 2 vols. London. Methuen, 1961.

———— *Schriften zum Theater. Uber eine nicht-Aristotelische Dramatik*. Berlin. Suhrkamp Verlag, 1957, 1963.

———— *Seven Plays*. (Introduction by Eric Bentley). New York. Grove, 1961.

Bronnen, Arnolt. *Tage mit Bertolt Brecht*. Wien. K. Desch, 1960.

Demetz, Peter, editor. *Brecht* (Collection of critical essays). Englewood Cliffs, N.J. Prentice-Hall, 1962.

Esslin, Martin. *Brecht: A Choice of Evils*. London. Eyre & Spottiswoode, 1959.

———— *Brecht: The Man and His Work*. New York. Doubleday, 1961.

Fromm, Erich, editor. *Der Friede: Idee und Verwirklichung*. Heidelberg. L. Schneider, 1961.

Goldhart, Gerda. *Bertholt Brecht Porträts*. Zurich. Verlag die Arche, 1964.

Gray, Ronald. *Bertolt Brecht*. New York. Grove, 1961.

Grimm, Reinhold. *Bertolt Brecht: die Struktur seines Werkes*. Nürnberg. H. Carl, 1959.

—— *Bertolt Brecht und die Weltliteratur*. Nürnberg. H. Carl, 1961.

—— *Bertolt Brecht*. Stuttgart. J.B. Metzlersche Verlag, 1961.

Grosz, George. *Hintergrund: 17 zeichnungen zur aufführung des in der Piscator-bühne*. Berlin. Malik Verlag, 1928.

Hink, Walter. *Die Dramaturgie des späten Brecht*. Göttingen. Vandenhoeck und Ruprecht, 1959.

Ihering, Herbert. *Bertolt Brecht und das Theater*. Berlin. Rembrandt Verlag, 1959.

—— *Reinhardt, Jessner, Piscator, oder Klassikertod?* Berlin. Rowohlt, 1929.

Kaufmann, Hans. *Bertolt Brecht: Geschichtsdrama und Parabelstück*. Berlin. Rutten & Loening, 1962.

Kesting, Marianne. *Das Epische Theater*. Stuttgart. W. Kohlhammer Verlag, 1959.

Klotz, Volker. *Bertold Brecht: Versuch über das Werk*. Darmstadt. H. Gentner, 1957.

Mann, Otto. *Bertolt Brecht: Mass oder Mythos*. Heidelberg. W. Rothe, 1958.

Mayer, Hans. *Bertolt Brecht und die Tradition*. Pfullingen. Gunther Neske, 1961.

Piscator, Erwin. *Outside the Door* (Borchert, Wolfgang. English by Erwin Piscator and Zoë Lund-Schiller, presented at the President Theatre, New York, March 1, 1949) Paris. 1949.

—— *Das Politische Theater*. Berlin. A Schultz, 1929. Reinbeck bei Hamburg. Rowohlt paperback, 1963.

—— *Le Théâtre Politique*. Paris. L'Arche, 1962.

—— *Krieg und Frieden*. Nach dem Roman von Leo Tolstoi . . . von Alfred Neumann, Erwin Piscator und Guntram Prufer. Hamburg. Rowohlt, 1955. (*War and Peace*. English translation by Ashley Dukes. Presented at the Studio Theatre, season of 1941-1942. Typescript at New York Public Library.)

Rinser, Luise. *Der Schwerpunkt*. Frankfurt am Main. S. Fischer Verlag, 1960.

Serreau, Genevieve. *Bertolt Brecht, dramaturge*. Paris. L'Arche, 1955.

Strelka, Josef. *Brecht, Horvath, Dürrenmatt*. Wien. Forum, 1962.

Weideli, Walter. *The Art of Bertolt Brecht*. New York. New York University Press, 1963.

Willett, John. *The Theatre of Bertolt Brecht: a Study from Eight Aspects*. London. Methuen, 1959, 1960. New York. New Directions, 1959, 1960, 1964.

C) PERIODICALS

Pertinent informative and critical material may be found in various issues of the journals here listed. Specific references to these and other periodicals are given below.

> L'Avant-Scène
> Cahiers, Compagnie Madeleine Renaud—Jean Louis Barrault
> Educational Theatre Journal
> Modern Drama
> New Theatre
> New Theatre Magazine
> Prompt
> Quarterly Journal of Speech
> La Revue Théâtrale
> Theatre Annual
> Theatre Arts
> Théâtre Populaire
> Tulane Drama Review
> Weltbühne
> World Theatre

Act. Act 2, Scene 3, Winter 1956. "In Memoriam Bertolt Brecht."

Akzente. 1954, Heft 1. Benjamin, Walter. "Was ist episches Theater?"

———— 1960, Heft 4. Völker, K. "Groteskformen des Theaters."

———— 1960, Heft 6. Hildesheimer, W. "Erlanger Rede über das absurde Theater."

Bühnentechnische Rundschau. Jahr 53, Heft 5; Okt. 1959. Piscator, Erwin. "Technik eine künstlerische Notwendigkeit des modernen Theaters."

Comoedia. 1931. Bragaglia, A. Giulio. "Il Teatro di Piscator."

Educational Theatre Journal. IV, 2; May 1951. Goodman, Henry. "Bertolt Brecht as 'traditional' Dramatist."

Encore. XI, 6; Nov. 1964. Crane, Muriel. "Brecht: Have We learned the Lesson?"

Encounter. XXXIV; 1956. Luthy, Herbert. "Of Poor Brecht."

Europe. Année 35, no. 133-134; 1957. Special issue on Brecht.

Forces Vives. No. 4; 1953. Copeau, Jacques. "Le Théâtre du Vieux Colombier: son but, son esprit, ses réalisations."

High School Thespian. May, 1944. Hewitt, Barnard. "Erwin Piscator."

Jahrering. 1960-1961. Jens, W. "Antike und moderne Tragödie."

Kenyon Review. VII. Viertel, Berthold. "Bertolt Brecht, Dramatist."

———— XI. Thompson, Lawrence. "Bert Brecht."

———— XXI. Borneman, Ernest. "Credo Quia Absurdum: An Epitaph for Bertolt Brecht."

Merkur. 1960, Heft 8. Franzen, E. "Das Drama zwischen Utopie und Wirklichkeit."

———— 1965, Heft 6.

Modern Drama. I; Dec. 1958. Kern, Edith. "Brecht's Popular Drama and its American Popularity."

———— IV; Feb. 1962. Wenty, John C. "An American Tragedy as Epic Theatre: The Piscator Dramatization."

New Theatre. Dec. 1934. Belasz, Bela. "Piscator's First Film."

———— Sept. 1934. Lee Strasberg. "The Magic of Meyerhold."

New Theatre Magazine. III, 3; Apr. 1962. Reeves, Geoffrey: "The Fate of Bertolt Brecht." Shaktman, Ben. "Brecht on Broadway."

The New Yorker. Sept. 12, 1959. Tynan, Kenneth. "The Theatre Abroad: Germany."

Partisan Review. VIII, 2; Mar. 1941. Greenberg, Clement. "Bertolt Brecht."

Prompt. No. 3; 1963. Bernard, Heinz. "The Theatre of Erwin Piscator."

———— No. 5; 1964. Piscator, Erwin. "Novel Into Play."

Quarterly Journal of Speech. Feb. 1952. Gassner, John. "A Modern Style of Theatre."

La Revue Théâtrale. Année 7, No. 19; 1952. Barrault, J.L. "Entretiens sur le théâtre."

Rocky Mountain Review. XII, 3; Spring 1948. Benjamin, Walter. "Eight Notes on Brecht's Epic Theatre."

Sinn und Form. Jahr 9, Heft 1-3; 1957. Special Brecht issue.

————Jahr 16, Heft 5; 1964.

Theatre Annual. XII; 1954. Melnitz, William W. "Max Reinhardt." XVIII; 1961. Elder, Judith. "The Cartel of Four."

Theatre Arts. Jan. 1949. Bentley, Eric. "A Traveler's Report."

Theatre Guild Magazine. VII; June 1930. Wadsworth, P. Beaumont. "Piscator the Rebel."

Théâtre Populaire. No. 2; Jan. 1955. Dort, Bernard. "Une nouvelle dramaturgie." Bertolt Brecht. "Petit organon pour le théâtre." Habart, Michel. "Vocation et Provocation."

———— No. 26; Sept. 1957. Benjamin, Walter. "Qu'est-ce que le théâtre épique?"

———— No. 32; 1958. Vinaver, Michel. "La fin et les moyens d'acteur."

Theatre Time. II, 2; 1950. Gassner, John. "What's Happened to Expressionism?"

Tomorrow. Feb. 1942. Piscator, Erwin. "The Theatre of the Future."

Tulane Drama Review. IV; Sept. 1959. Gorelik, Mordecai. "An Epic Theatre Catechism."

———— IV; May, 1960. Vesvolod Meyerhold. from "On the Theatre."

———— VI; Sept. 1961. Frisch, Max. "Recollections of Brecht." Hecht, Werner. "The Development of Brecht's theory of Epic Theatre."

Weltbühne. Jahr 25; Sept. 17, 1929. Ossietsky, Carl von. "Die Kaufleute von Berlin."

World Theatre. VII; 1958. Sartre, Jean-Paul. "Brecht et les classiques."

———— XIV; 4. Hecht, Werner. "The Berliner Ensemble and the Spirit of Brecht."

For the association of Erwin Piscator and Maria Ley Piscator with the New School for Social Research, consult the Catalogue of the Dramatic Workshop of the New School. See also the New School Bulletin from 1940 to date, especially the following issues: XVI, 1; Sept. 1958. XVII, 1; Sept. 1959. XVII, 31; April 1960. XIX, 3, Sept. 1961. XIX, 11, Jan. 1962. XIX, 20, May, 1962. XXI, 3; Sept. 1963. XXI, 11, Jan. 1964. XXII, 3; Sept. 1964. XXII, 11; Jan. 1965. XXII, 17; April, 1965. XXIII, 3; Sept. 1965.

INDEX